Spree

# Contents

# Acknowledgments

It took the skills and support of many individuals to bring *Spree* to life and I'd like to thank those people for everything – their contributions were invaluable.

Thank you to Andrew Clelland, Dean Debienne, Alan Duffy, Jeremy Hainsworth, Peter Menzies, Dave Nickolchuk, Peter Oliva, Tina Shipley, Craig Stapleton, Lana Vanzetta, and Marty Wombacher for their friendship and for allowing me to indulge in various forms of neurotic behaviour during the hectic year I spent writing and researching.

Thank you to my excellent friend and trusty legal counsel, Karen Powell, for her enduring guidance and support.

Thank you to my research assistant, Ashley Menzies, whose help and input proved priceless.

Thank you to Kirsten Bowen, Laurel Colins, Gwendolyn Gawlick, and Christina McDowell for so graciously taking the time to answer my questions.

Thank you to Rosalee Hiebert and Russ Bugera, the visual creative types who took over after the words were finished.

Thank you to Janet Eger at Holt Renfrew Canada for her enthusiasm and support and truly serendipitous experience.

Thank you to the team at Arsenal Pulp Press – Brian Lam, Blaine Kyllo, Kiran Gill Judge, and Robert Ballantyne – without whom there would be no *Spree*.

And finally, thank you to my parents, Richard and Rena Klaffke, my brother Brad, and, of course, my beloved daughter, Emma, to whom this book is dedicated.

# Author's Note

Love it or loathe it, shopping is an important part of our everyday lives. This is nothing new. For centuries, humans have engaged in some form of shopping, whether it be the early days of trade and barter or this season's search for the perfect dress at the local mall.

Originally, we shopped because we had to, but by the late 1800s, shopping – particularly at big city department stores – had become a gathering place for women, a social salon of sorts.

In the 1900s, the popularity of shopping as a leisure activity grew, and by the time mall culture emerged mid-century, shopping was already eating up a significant amount of our spare time. The relatively mundane and generally miserable tasks of shopping for food or socks or household appliances aside, a new kind of shopping had appeared and we found ourselves shopping because we *wanted* to.

Fifty years later, it's more difficult than ever to accurately characterize our complex relationship with shopping.

For some, shopping is art; for others, it's a sport. It can be a vice and it can be a cause. Some love it. Some hate it. Rarely is someone indifferent.

Over the course of thirteen months, I spent much of my time delving into the checkered past of the popular pastime, unearthing all kinds of surprises along the way. I discovered true tales of Victorian shoplifters and department store wars, rummaged around (figuratively, anyhow) for shopping skeletons in Imelda Marcos' expansive closets, and even happened upon infomercial parody pornography.

I explored the origins of home shopping parties, the image of the shopper in cinema, and the lure of discount shopping, cobbling together the nuts-and-bolts history of shopping, as well as odd and unusual trivia (who knew psychics have been used to nab shoplifter, or how superior shopping skills are revered in Southeast Asia?). I will never think of shopping in the same way ever again.

*Spree* itself is an oddity, much like some of the stranger facts in this book. It was intended as a comprehensive history lesson, but one that was designed to appeal to shopaholics, pop culture aficionados, and armchair historians alike - anyone who's curious as to how shopping grew from something we needed to do, to something we wanted to do, to the sport it resembles today.

Enjoy.

*Pamela Klaffke*

For Emma

# Shopping Gets Its Start

# Shopping 101

*The evolution of trade and currency (and* Schoolhouse Rock*)*

ithout money there would be no shopping. Whatever its form - cash, credit, services, or goods for trade - money truly is what makes the shopping world go 'round. It always has.

Before delving into the mechanics, social implications, and cultural history of shopping, it's important to take a look at the evolution of trade and currency.

The evolution of trade and currency, however, can be a little dull. Thankfully, everything a person ever needed to know about money can be learned from *Schoolhouse Rock*.

In 1973, the American television network ABC launched the educational three-minute spots, airing them between Saturday morning cartoons. The animated musical segments tackled grammar ("Conjunction Junction"), American history ("I'm Just a Bill"), multiplication ("Three is a Magic Number"), and science ("Telegraph Line"). *Schoolhouse Rock* ran until 1985, when it was quietly dumped from the ABC schedule.

A few years later, in 1992, the original spots returned to TV thanks to the wave of *Schoolhouse Rock* nostalgia among pop culture aficionados now in their twenties and thirties. ABC then commissioned a new series of *Schoolhouse Rock* songs, including eight money-related tunes.

George Newell, the former New York adman who, along with fellow creative director, Thomas Yohe, took on his boss's challenge to create *Schoolhouse Rock* in the early 1970s, penned the ditty "This for That" in 1996. True to traditional *Schoolhouse Rock* form, the lyric offers a crash course in the history of money. Here, essentially, is how it goes.

It was every man for himself in caveman times. If a man saw something he desired, he'd best grab it before someone else came along. And if, perchance, another did happen upon the same item - say, a big stick or something else suitably rugged - at the same time, a struggle would likely ensue. The situation was, well, Neanderthal, not to mention eerily similar to scenes witnessed today

## This for That

### (George Newell)

When we lived in caves
There were no shopping
  malls
And people's manners
  were Neanderthal
No bodegas, no delis, no
  corner stores
Shopping trips turned into
  tugs of war
When not having pull got
  this man mangled
He thought he'd try an
  easier angle

I'll give you this for that
That for this
We'll make a trade called
  "barter"
I'll give you this for that
That for this
We'll have it made with
  barter

at designer outlet malls on weekends during clearance season. But instead of men fighting over sticks and rocks and wild pigs, it's usually women jostling over heavily discounted high-end purses and shoes.

The full-out caveman fighting ended with the introduction of barter. (Sadly, the same cannot be said for aggressive outlet shoppers.)

Cattle and other livestock like oxen and sheep were often used as currency, to trade for goods or services. In different parts of the world, tea, fur, tobacco, rice, and even beetle legs and whale's teeth were used to barter with. The same time period (from about 9000-6000 BCE) also saw the first agricultural crops grown by the industrious people of Mesopotamia.

The people of this ancient land, which stood between the Tigris and Euphrates rivers – where Iraq is today – learned to irrigate land, which meant more food than necessary to feed their families. Grain became a commodity and was often used to trade for everything from land to wives or slaves. Whether it was cows or barley, trade flourished in Mesopotamia, but along the way became both cumbersome and complicated.

It was impossible to barter with someone who had something you wanted unless you had something they wanted as well. That was the only way the system could work. Unfortunately, as the Mesopotamians made advances, building the first cities and embracing new forms of transportation such as the wagon, the barter system turned into a mind-boggling maze.

Naturally, the more sophisticated the society, the more widespread and varied the needs for goods and services. Say, for instance, you had your eye on a sweet parcel of land near the river, but the owner would only part with it in exchange for a variety pack of primo livestock and you had only barley to trade.

What then? If you really wanted the land, you'd have to find someone willing to do an animals for grain trade, then in turn, buy the land. Depending on what you were in the market for, purchases could require several transactions. Shells changed all that. Around 1200 BCE, the Chinese started using cowrie shells as currency, though some anthropologists believe that the use of shell beads as money could date back as early as 2500 BCE. During that period, the Egyptians and Mesopotamians are

Now, barter worked well
At least in theory
But a wallet full of yaks
Could make you weary
For an "udder" disaster
Shiny shells were far more
   portable
Why not use them for
   what's affordable?

I'll give you this for that
That for this
With shiny shells, why
   barter?
I'll give you this for that
That for this
Shelling out shells is
   smarter

For farmers in ancient
   Mesopotamia
The barley they grew was
   the money mania
When hauling big sacks
   put their back in traction
They invented coins to
   lighten transactions
Now, when a man had a
   debt to settle
He'd dig out some coins
   made of precious metal

I'll give you this for that
That for this
Silver or gold or copper
That for this
With coins you're a smarter
   shopper

Then China made money
   even more desirous
Printing it on paper made
   of crushed papyrus
Take one from Column A
   and one from Column B
The Chinese paid their
   checks in paper currency

When Columbus set out
  on that famous charter
He had no paper money,
  so he had to barter
He took along some beads
  for currency
So barter played a part in
  our discovery
Balboa and Pisarro and
  Sebastian Cabot
Even Coronado had the
  trading habit

I'll give you this for that
That for this
They loaded up with gold,
  then parted
I'll give you this for that
That for this
And soon the whole world
  was charted

Today we use cash and
  spend with ardor
But that doesn't mean we
  still don't barter
When a football team
  needs a pulling guard
Or a kid like you is into
  trading cards

Take this for that
That for this
Bills and coins are smarter
But when you pay for that
Remember this
It all started out with
  barter

said to have used metal rings as currency and to have measured it in shekels (one shekel would weigh approximately the same as three modern-day pennies), the first standard weight of measure. The rings, of course, were the precursor to coins, which surfaced in Lydia in 687 BCE. Made of electrum, a natural alloy of gold and silver panned in the Turkish kingdom, the coins were crudely stamped with images of lions and other ferocious animals.

Coins caught on quickly and it wasn't long before the Greeks, Persians, Macedonians, and Romans had jumped on the bandwagon. But that didn't mean trading in grain completely ceased. Grains, along with lesser metals such as copper, lead, and tin, remained in use, especially as "small change" when purchasing inexpensive items or to make up the difference when a transaction didn't add up to an exact number of shekels.

Meanwhile, in China, another version of coinage was starting to circulate. Around 600-300 BCE (and perhaps even earlier), the country produced its first round coins made from inexpensive base metal. While the coins made buying everyday items easy, because they were so cheaply produced and held little value, it was impractical to haul around the large quantities of heavy coins necessary to make major purchases.

Coins remained the primary form of currency in many parts of the world until once again the innovative Chinese developed an alternative. The country had issued deerskin leather money in 118 BCE, but it was during the T'ang Dynasty (618-907 CE) that China produced the world's first paper money.

The notes, which appeared in 806, solved the country's cash crisis. At the time, there was a shortage of copper to make coins, so an alternative had to be found. Paper money – or "flying money" as it was known because it was so lightweight – was the answer and existed in China as currency until 1455 when it was abolished. In 1375, the Ming Dynasty issued a single-denomination currency called the Precious Note of Great Ming. But having notes with only a single value was inconvenient and was replaced by silver. Paper money didn't reappear again in China for more than 200 years.

Word of paper money had already spread to the West by the time China reverted to silver. In 1275, Marco Polo wrote of it after visiting China, though almost 400 years would pass before any Western banks issued it as currency; Sweden was the first, in 1661, followed by France in 1720, England in 1797, and Germany in 1806.

America adopted paper money in 1690, its precursor being the American Native Indian shell money, wampum. The cylindrical wampum beads made from clam shells was the currency early European explorers discovered when they landed on the shores of New England, and had been used by the Native Americans for an unspecified number of years before the settlers arrived. What is known is that during the sixteenth and seventeenth centuries, there is a record of the currency having been used to pay for everything from taxes to Harvard tuition. Wampum survived well into the twentieth century; until the mid-1900s, wampum could still be used to ride the Brooklyn ferry.

Across the Atlantic in England, there was no wampum trading in the seventeenth century. The Brits had paper money, but had opted, in 1816, to set their currency standard to gold.

The gold standard went unchanged in Britain until 1930, by which time the developed world had settled on cash as currency. Barter, it would be easy to think, was just a quaint, old-fashioned trading habit only used in ancient cultures where people simply didn't know any better. That would an easy thing to think, but it would be wrong.

Like the *Schoolhouse Rock* song says: "Today we use cash and spend with ardor. But that doesn't mean we still don't barter." Barter is no longer the preferred method for most transactions, but it has quietly survived even as checks, credit cards, ATMs, and debit cards have infiltrated modern society. Since the 1960s, barter clubs – or trading exchanges – have existed with the purpose of aiding individuals and corporations looking to barter goods and services.

Just like the barter system of ancient Mesopotamia, modern barter is not exactly simple. Trading exchanges are not the same as swap clubs, where members trade one item or service directly for another. Rather, the exchanges assign a value to whatever a member might be offering, and will even issue credit so participants don't have to wait until another member "purchases" their services to

Precious Note of Great Ming.

Wampum.

# Biggest, Largest, Richest

## World records of shopping

Since 1955, the *Guinness Book of World Records* has been the authoritative source for all things big. From the world's tallest living man (7 feet, 8.9 inches) to the world's fastest jet (Lockheed SR-71A Blackbird), the *Guinness Book* folk scrupulously keep track and document records set in both mundane and unusual categories. Shopping is no exception. Here's a look at the title holders.

Biggest Fashion Retail Chain: Gap Inc, with 3,676 stores and $13.67 billion sales worldwide

Largest Retail Firm: Wal-Mart Stores Inc, with revenues of $191,329 million in the fiscal year ending January 31, 2001

Largest Shopping Center: West Edmonton Mall, Edmonton, Alberta, Canada, covering 49 acres

Largest Underground Shopping Complex: PATH Walkway, Toronto, Ontario, Canada, spanning 4 million feet

Largest Department Store: Macy's Herald Square, New York City, at 2.15 million square feet

get what they're looking for. For instance, a commercial artist looking for free or discounted office space may offer corporate logo design services to the members of a small business trading exchange.

Barter is, in fact, one of the best kept secrets in Western business. Over 400,000 businesses in the U.S. alone belong to trading exchanges. As of 1998, the International Reciprocal Trade Association (IRTA) estimated that commercial bartering was growing at a rate of more than 10 percent per year. This is due largely to the growth of trading exchanges on the Internet.

For a membership fee of about $100–500 and a commission of five to 12 percent on each transaction, sites such as *9barter.com*, *bartertrust.com*, and *vbarter.com* allow businesses to trade services, unload overstock, and potentially score new sales, all without laying cash on the line. Sometimes, it seems, something old truly can become new again.

Macy's Herald Square, 1942. *Photo by Marjory Collins, courtesy Library of Congress (LC-USW3-007681-D).*

# Shopping Made Easy

*Key consumer innovations and inventions*

## THE CASH REGISTER

It was 1878 and Dayton, Ohio saloon owner James Ritty was not a happy man. He suspected that members of his staff were stealing from his business by taking customers' cash and pocketing it. Unfortunately, Ritty had no way of proving that pilfering was a problem. The next year he did. With the help of his brother, Ritty invented and patented the first mechanical cash register named "Ritty's Incorruptible Cashier."

While his invention may have helped put a stop to employee dishonesty, the stress of running both his bar business and his fledgling cash register company proved too much and prompted Ritty to sell the latter to Jacob H. Eckert of Cincinnati. Two years later, Eckert turned the business over to John H. Patterson, who added the paper roll to record sales. The cash register was a hit with business owners and the distinctive ring that marked the completion of every sale was referred to in early cash register ads as "the bell heard around the world."

Replica of the Ritty Model 1 Cash Register, created for the St. Louis World Fair (1904).

## THE SHOPPING CART

It was Oklahoma City grocer Sylvan Goldman who, in 1936, began work on what would become the first shopping cart. Goldman's original contraption consisted of two wire shopping baskets attached to a folding chair on wheels. It was crude, but it worked, and after refining the design somewhat, he patented his invention in 1940.

Then in 1946, competition arose. Orla E. Watson of

Largest Menswear Store: Slater Menswear, Glasgow, Scotland at 28,000 square feet

Most Expensive Shopping Street: Fifth Avenue, New York City, where retail space costs an average of $580 per square foot to rent

Oldest Shopping Mall: Galleria Vittorio Emannuele, Milan, Italy, built in 1877

Most People in a Department Store in a Day: approximately 1.07 million people flocked to Nextage Shanghai in China on December 20, 1995

Shortest Escalator: Okadaya More's Shopping Mall, Kawasaki-shi, Japan, at 2 feet, 8 inches

## You Can Say That Again

Kansas City, Missouri applied to patent *his* version of the shopping cart - one that required no assembly and could be conveniently stored by pushing one cart into another, much like the carts of today.

Goldman contested Watson's patent application. The situation was not resolved until 1949 when Goldman decided to hand over his patent to Watson in exchange for licensing rights.

### THE BAR CODE

It took two grad students at the Drexel Institute of Technology in Philadelphia to come up with the first bar code in 1948. Bernard Silver and Norman Joseph Woodland took on the challenge after Silver happened to overhear the president of a local food store chain chatting with a Drexel dean about developing a system that could read product information and speed things up at the checkout counter.

The patent for Silver and Woodland's invention, which coded product identity using a series of white lines on a dark background, was issued on October 7, 1952. The bar code wasn't put to commercial use via scanning until 1967, when a Kroger grocery store in Cincinnati adopted the technology, albeit using labels that had to be manually affixed to products and were presented in a bull's eye pattern instead of a bar.

The bar code revolutionized the shopping process, but Bernard Silver didn't have a chance to revel in that success; he died in 1962 at the age of 38. His inventing partner Woodland, on the other hand, was honored in 1992 when U.S. president George Bush awarded him the National Medal of Technology in recognition of the duo's achievement.

## Next Up

Just when you thought shopping had gotten about as high-tech as it could get, along came innovations to make shopping life even easier. Look for retailers to encourage a do-it-yourself attitude amongst their customers. Self-checkouts that enable shoppers to scan products, fork over cash, then stuff their purchases in a bag themselves, all under the watchful eye of a video camera, are already fixtures in some North American big-box and grocery stores.

And those who are predisposed to bouts of laziness will be happy to hear that the Philips Home Shopping Device is inching its way towards the mass market. Just use the remote control-like gadget to scan the UPC codes of your favorite food and household products, send that info electronically to a local supermarket on the system, and sit back and wait – the goods will be delivered right to your door.

"They came, they saw, they did a little shopping."
– anonymous graffiti on the Berlin Wall after East Berliners were allowed into West Berlin (as reported in *Newsweek*, December 4, 1989)

"Americans are fascinated by their own love of shopping. This does not make them unique. It's just that they have more to buy than most other people on the planet. And it's also an affirmation of faith in their country, its prosperity, and limitless bounty. They have shops the way that lesser countries have statues."
– British journalist Simon Hoggart, in his book, *America: A User's Guide* (1990)

"We used to build civilizations. Now we build shopping malls."
– American travel writer Bill Bryson, in his book, *Neither Here Nor There* (1991)

# Charge It!

*Consumers go crazy for cashless society*

**T**hings could have been very different had Frank McNamara not left his wallet in another suit that night in 1949. McNamara was having a business dinner at Major's Cabin Grill in New York City one night when he found himself in an embarrassing situation. The mishap got him thinking – thinking of a way consumers could tap into a line of credit with a restaurant instead of having to worry about carrying cash. The idea stuck and in February 1950, McNamara was back at Major's Cabin Grill presenting the first universal credit card when the check came.

That dinner, referred to in the industry as "The First Supper," launched McNamara's Diners Club credit card. In 1951, he distributed 200 cards, having arranged for 27 New York restaurants to accept the cardboard cards, not knowing what a remarkable influence the credit card would have in decades to come.

Credit, which is derived from the Latin root *credo*, meaning "to trust," had existed long before Frank McNamara came along. It can be traced back more than 3,000 years, to Assyria, Egypt. The credit *card*, on the other hand, is primarily a twentieth-century invention, although literary references to credit cards can be found in two short stories (by Pauline Curtis and Elton Smith) written in 1890.

Western Union issued a metal card to preferred customers in 1914 that allowed them to operate on a credit system. The cards were dubbed "metal money" and soon set off a trend – particularly among petroleum companies and hotels.

In 1924, the General Petroleum Corporation introduced metal money to its preferred customers and employees;

Frank McNamara, founder of Diners Club.
*Courtesy Diners Club.*

American Telephone and Telegraph (AT&T) issued the Bell System Credit Card in the late 1930s.

The use of credit was scaled back during the Second World War, but in 1946, Brooklyn banker John Biggins introduced Charge-It, the first credit card system to be issued by a bank and used at area shops. Three years later, Frank McNamara's Diners Club pushed the burgeoning credit card industry further, opening up a new (cashless) world for merchants, banks, and consumers. And during the next decade, the credit card business flourished.

The first Diners Club card. *Courtesy Diners Club.*

In 1958, the Bank of America debuted its Bank-Americard in California; it became Visa in 1976. The same year, the first American Express purple cardboard charge cards were issued, although technically the AMEX cards were not credit cards since customers could not carry a balance and were required to pay each bill in full. The next year the company became the first to unveil plastic cards.

By the time MasterCharge – which would be re-christened MasterCard in 1979 – surfaced on the American west coast in 1967, credit card fever had already resulted in distribution of more than five million cards in the U.S.

That was nothing. Thirty years later there would be approximately 1.4 billion cards in circulation – and that was only in the United States. Worldwide, Visa estimated charges totaling more than $2 trillion in 2002.

But with such staggering credit card spending came staggering credit card debt, a situation that could be the source of serious stress and anxiety, not to mention that it could bankrupt individuals and ruin families.

In dealing with credit card debt, some consumers

have been more inventive than others. Take, for example, the case of the Brooklyn-based television producer responsible for the website *SaveKaryn.com*.

In June 2002, bogged down with $20,221.40 of credit card debt amassed by gorging on designer shoes, handbags, and clothes, Karyn Bosnak created a website for the sole purpose of raising the cash to pay off her debt. Her online begging prompted a range of reactions. Sympathetic strangers sent money, others were outraged (including "Bob" and "Ben," the founders of *DontSaveKaryn.com*) and the media stepped in to cover the story.

It's unlikely that the future of credit card usage will be inspired by Bosnak's if-I-mess-up-someone-else-will-bail-me-out attitude or, conversely, that many will heed her cautionary tale. Instead, we're almost certain to enjoy a future of more cards, more debt and, of course, less cash.

# Consumers and Consumerism

chapter

**ii**

# World of Wares

*Learning to shop at the Crystal Palace*

s tempting as it may be to label twentieth-century Americans the first true-blue shopaholics, that would be wrong. Shopping as sport, as a phenomenon, was evidenced much earlier. The moniker *shopaholic* had yet to be coined, but shoppers in Victorian England were among the first to embrace hobby shopping – browsing, strolling, gabbing socially with friends.

A critical shift in shopping practice and attitude evolved during Queen Victoria's long reign – from 1837 to 1901 – and many scholars point to the Great Exhibition of 1851 as a significant turning point.

By all accounts, the exhibition was huge and overwhelming in its scope. The Queen's husband Albert is often credited with the idea of erecting a spectacular exhibition hall to house the event and after considering many designs, settled on a gleaming glass-and-iron building conceived by a royal gardener, Sir Joseph Paxton.

Grand entrance to the Crystal Palace.
*Courtesy Mary Evans Picture Library.*

The Crystal Palace was built on 14 acres in London's Hyde Park and featured nearly one million square feet of glass. With its distinctive domed glass ceiling and 772,784 square feet of floor space, it was the perfect arena to showcase a world of goods.

From May 1 to October 15, the Crystal Palace was home to exhibitors from 32 nations, although half of the building was devoted exclusively to British wares. (In fact, many historians have noted that the British side of the exhibition was purposefully more posh than the half to which the rest of the world's displays were relegated, even labeling the second half as inferior and shabby.) More than six million people walked through the doors of the Crystal Palace during the exhibition – officially named the Great Exhibition of the Works of Industry of All Nations – taking in more than 13,000 exhibits.

The exhibition's displays were designed to highlight the best goods and industrial advances each country had to offer: was German porcelain, rubber from India, Egyptian carpets, Russian furs, and Roman mosaics; in fact, there was so much to see that the catalog that accompanied the exhibition spanned four volumes.

That the Great Exhibition of 1851 was a consumer paradise in many ways foreshadowed changes in shopping habits and consumer behavior. Although an exhibition and not a marketplace, the event introduced visitors to the concept of browsing and exposed them to a plethora of merchandise, carefully grouped, displayed, and free to touch – much like the experience everyday shoppers would soon have in local stores.

From kitchen appliances and Jacquard looms to tools and textiles, the exhibition offered a sneak peak at the heady days of consumerism that lay ahead. The concept was clever and most successful, selling the notion of shopping to the English middle class who, up to that point, were reluctant to part with their money and rarely spent much on items not deemed necessities.

The Crystal Palace exhibition did the trick. Never before had the public been aware that there were so many *things* to need or want or maybe even buy. The Great Exhibition filled the minds of the masses with images of cultural wares, practical goods which incorporated new technologies, and – most importantly – frivolous things they didn't previously know they craved.

Opening of the Great Exhibition, Crystal Palace, May 1, 1851.
*Engraved by George Cruikshank, courtesy Library of Congress*
*(LS-US262-93899)..*

# Born to Shop
*The rise of kid consumers*

I magine a world with no toys. No Barbies, no action figures, and definitely no Disney. Maybe the occasional rich kid would have a primitive-looking folk doll, but up until the 1830s, childhood was very serious business.

Children made do without the simplest of toys – no brand-name gizmos and no cool clothes. Kids in pre-Victorian England were groomed for the workforce from an early age, since they were expected to pull their own weight in the household (or at least contribute) as soon as they were able. Let's just say there wasn't much opportunity for a 10-year-old to play after he'd spent a long, grueling day down in the mines.

Child laborers eventually got a break. Laws were enacted in England that effectively curbed the use of child labor and challenged the notion that a child was simply the property of his parents, who were free to exploit him as they saw fit. Children of the time were, in many ways, little adults. Even their clothing was often of a grown-up style, crafted in miniature, a fact which the casual observer of fashion could note, has ironically come full-circle 200 years later (though with a decidedly slutty edge).

Less work meant more time, and for many, more time translated into better education, especially during the reign of Queen Victoria, starting in 1837. But still . . . no toys.

It would take another significant historic marker to light the spark of kids' consumerism. As the Industrial Revolution took hold and mass manufacturing became commonplace, so did the concept of toys for regular kids.

Up until the late 1800s, toys (and even books) were the exclusive domain of the wealthy. Mass manufacturing and the Industrial Revolution transformed society and by the turn of the century, middle-class children were introduced to the wonders of toyland.

It didn't take long for savvy manufacturers and advertisers of the time to recognize the potential of this burgeoning market. For the first time, products – whether toys, clothes, or furniture for the nursery – were designed specifically for children, with a child's style in mind. It was brand new territory and the "little adults" were at last viewed as a distinct market, with needs, wants, and characteristics different from those of their parents.

But it was the parents who those savvy manufacturers and advertisers were trying to reach. The typical advertising style of the time bears an uncanny resemblance to what we call "advertorial" today.

Heavy on text and mimicking the style of editorial content, the advertorials regularly featured testimonials singing the praises of a particular product. The ads were conceived to appeal to the household breadwinner, Mr Dad, whom it was assumed made the majority of purchasing decisions.

This image changed early in the twentieth century when marketers recognized the influence of women. Although Mrs Mom may not have been the one to bring home the bacon, she was the one who fried it up.

By the end of the Second World War, the now-familiar image of the picture-perfect, storybook family began to emerge – most notably in North America. Mom, Dad, two kids, a dog, and the house with the white picket fence was the postcard image of the suburban dream more than two decades before the suburbs existed on any mass scale.

These two factors resulted in a whole new breed of advertising and marketing strategy: one that enticed the homemaker to buy. The marketing of children's  products was accomplished primarily through print advertising, catalogs, and via radio.

Few marketers bothered to address children directly. Most media was not intended for kids, but for whole families, and because as a group they didn't have any spending power or perceived influence, it was their mothers who were considered the desirable target.

• *Window shopping* sounds like a civilized way to spend an afternoon, but once you uncover its origins, it may be a different story. The English term, which has been around since 1922, is a translation of the French term *faire du léche-vitrine*, which when literally translated, means window licking. Yum.

French window shoppers, circa 1850.

• Since *flea market* is extremely close to the direct translation of *Marché aux Puces* (meaning "market of the fleas") the most widely accepted theory of the English term's origin is simply that it's based on the French. The dubious quality – and rumored bug infestation – of the second-hand goods sold at outdoor markets in Paris, gave English speaking bargain hunters what would become a favorite term starting in 1922.

• The *mall* wasn't always the mall. The enclosed shopping complexes we call malls today weren't so named until 1961. But the term "mall"

Then came television.

TV infiltrated post-war homes and the simultaneous Baby Boom - starting in 1945 and reaching its peak in 1957 - meant a new generation was raised soaking up television advertising. In the 1950s it would have been impossible to predict the full extent of its impact on children, but to this day, TV advertising remains the most potent form of reaching an audience.

The first TV toy ad was for Mr Potato Head and aired in 1952. The groundbreaking commercial didn't trigger the wave of marketing to kids one might assume. In fact, it wasn't until three years later, when

Mr Potato Head.

Disney's *Mickey Mouse Club* hit the airwaves, that marketers took serious notice of children as consumers. And even then, it was a hard sell.

As author Stephen Kline details in his 1993 book, *Out of the Garden: Toys and Children's Culture in the Age of TV Marketing*, the *Mickey Mouse Club* was responsible for two important firsts: it was the first television program aimed specifically and exclusively at kids, and it was the first to encourage advertisers to directly address children through buying commercial time on the show.

While many advertisers were initially weary of the radical concept, toy giant Mattel wasn't, and the company led the pack in reaching the growing kids' market. In 1954, author Kline notes, advertising dollars spent targeting kids totaled approximately $1 million. Two years and one very successful season of the *Mickey Mouse Club* later, spending in the category had jumped to about $25 million.

Disney and Mattel became powerful allies and the companies forged a relationship that remains intact today. (Care to guess who produces Disney's *Toy Story* playthings?)

Eager to follow in the footsteps of the *Mickey Mouse Club*, children's advertisers and entertainment producers alike flooded the market with new shows and new ads. Forward-thinking market researchers began probing the minds of kids in an effort to determine what they wanted in a toy, and by the 1960s, the children's market was booming. At last, the little ones had cachet, consumer influence, and a demographic to call their own.

The marriage between toy manufacturers and entertainment companies proved enormously lucrative for both sides over the next 50 years. Perhaps the best evidence of such cozy and profitable relationships is in the rise of "promotional toys."

You know the ones, the toys inspired by, based on, and marketed in conjunction with another form of media, most often a feature film or television show.

Early examples of such cross-promotion strategies had appeared back in the 1890s with the Brownies, dolls based on Palmer Cox's series of children's books. Toys based on kids' comics like *Foxy Grandpa*, *Little Nemo*, and *Mutt and Jeff* also hit the market within a few years of the Brownies.

A handful of movie stars, too, received the toy treatment. A Charlie Chaplin doll – believed to be the first celebrity doll – was introduced in 1911, followed by the *Our Gang* characters, and dolls of child stars Mickey Rooney and Mary Pickford in the 1920s.

The grand poohbah of promotional toys waded into the arena in 1930. Having found success with his animated films, Walt Disney released the first Mickey Mouse doll in 1930 and soon his big-eared mug was plastered on everything from alarm clocks to watches. Not long after his debut, Mickey was joined by other Disney friends the Three Little Pigs and Donald Duck, while rivals over at Warner Bros jumped on the bandwagon with Bugs Bunny and Daffy Duck merchandise.

Promotional toys proved an effective marketing tool in the first half of the twentieth century, but character or personality toys were played with alongside wooden building blocks, generic plush animals, and rat-a-tat-tat gun sets. Toys with licensed images were, for the most part, deemed harmless. Parents didn't give the playthings

relating to actual malls – as in tree-lined, outdoor promenades – has been around since at least 1737, deriving its name from The Mall, a promenade in London's St James Park.

• The teens of the 1980s inspired a slew of shopping words. The unprecedented amount of time this generation of Valley Girls and their guys spent at the mall resulted in terms *mall rat*, *mallie*, and *shopaholic* in the early '80s. The verb *malling* (as in: to hang out at the mall as a social activity) wasn't far behind, entering the lexicon late in the decade.

• The language of shopping keeps evolving. No matter how ridiculous or silly freshly-minted shopping words such as *magalog* (a hybrid catalog-magazine like those published by Abercrombie & Fitch) or *retail leakage* (the practice of urban dwellers fleeing to suburban malls and big-box stores to do their shopping) sound, such terms may well be absorbed into our collective shopping vocabulary. Other terms to keep an ear out for include *mallternative* (to describe the innocuous and virtually interchangeable pop music played in retail stores) and *shoppertainment* (a heightened shopping experience that incorporates entertainment-style gimmicks like in-store fishing or rock climbing).

much thought until the mid-1980s. In 1980, about 10 percent of the toys sold in the U.S. were promotional toys; seven years later the figure hovered at around 60 percent.

It was a new era of kids' consumerism.

A decade earlier, the growing number of hours children were spending in front of the television barely elicited a shrug. Even less concern was expressed regarding the spin-off toys that went hand-in-hand with their new viewing habits. So what if a kid wanted to play with a doll made in the likeness of her favorite TV character? Who cared if a little boy set out on a mission to collect the entire series of *Star Wars* action figures?

There were a few dissenting voices in the crowd, but not many. The only high-profile children's television producer that professed to market its promotional toys only to adults – not to the kids themselves – was the Children's Television Workshop, the company behind *Sesame Street.* That assertion, however, inspired skeptical eye-rolling, for it's not as though CTW exactly held back on releasing toys featuring Big Bird, Cookie Monster, and later Elmo. Especially Elmo.

The promotional toy boom that began in the 1980s was a boon for advertisers and manufacturers, but an increasing burden for parents. With more latchkey kids than ever before, the criticism of TV-as-babysitter evolved. Both parents worked outside the home and many felt guilty about the time spent away from their children. Allowances increased, more gifts were bought, and all of a sudden, kids found themselves the primary object of advertisers' attention.

The children of the 1980s, as opposed to their counterparts a century before, had spending power of their own as well as plenty of influence on that of their parents'.

The slacking and snacking revolution among kids spread into the 1990s and spilled into the new century, sparking the mobilization of consumer watchdog groups and a rash of special studies and media reports addressing the evils of kids' consumerism.

The average four to 12-year-old makes 15 requests per shopping trip, according to James U. McNeal, author of *The Kids Market: Myths and Realities.* The not-for-profit group, The Center for a New American Dream, provides facts for concerned parents and has concluded that the average American child watches TV for almost five hours per day and is exposed to about 55 commercials in that period. Children's spending tripled in the 1990s, with four to 12-year-olds dropping more than $40 billion of their *own* cash in 2000. Twenty percent of U.S. children are requesting toys by brand name by age three, and by 2000, experts estimated that children had influence over $200 billion of their parents' purchases.

It's not a pretty picture - unless you happen to be in the children's toy business. Which, by the way, is doing quite well. According to Toy Industry of America data, sales of traditional toys (the definition excludes video games) in the United States were $23 billion in 2000, more than eight percent higher than 1996. Sales of  action figures, the ultimate promotional toy, jumped a staggering 36 percent in 2001 versus the year before.

Advertisers are also shelling out more to buy that precious TV time. Toy industry advertising on cable and network television grew almost 18 percent between 1997 and 2001, with the total for 2001 ringing in at $617,167,900.

The basic concern parents and watchdog groups have about raising such shopping savvy and promotional-toy-loving kids, is that the children are abandoning imaginative play in favor of shiny, flashy, Hollywood-style pizzazz. Promotional toys, therefore, should be avoided at all costs - unless, of course, a child nags a parent the national average of nine times and they give in to the request for a new action figure, TV-inspired doll, or game.

# Barbie and Board Games

*Toys for the young shopping set*

I t happens every so often. A child – an *innocent* child – is born with a defect that sets the little one apart from his or her peers. The child, the target of ridicule and schoolyard taunting, appears normal physically, but he or she is missing one crucial instinct: the intuitive urge to shop.

The situation is particularly heart-breaking when it is a young girl who is afflicted. Think of the hours she could have spent eating chocolate malts while shopping for shoes at the local mall. Think of the missed girly-girl bonding opportunities while window shopping and talking about boys. And think of the sad, empty experience of flipping through a fashion magazine and not even fanaticizing about standing in a swanky dressing room of an equally swanky Paris shop, barking orders at the salesgirl to bring more dresses! More skirts! More *pantalons*!

It's a sad, sad story.

The widespread empathy and fear for children suffering this horrible defect has been addressed by concerned members of the toy and book industries. (If these poor children were not born to shop, we will teach them. Damnit.)

And teach they do. Dolls, games, books – toy manufacturers have been churning out shopping-related merchandise since the Victorian game, *Shopping: Or the Art of Buying and Selling.*

While Smurfette pushed a shopping cart around in the 1980s and Enid Blyton's Noddy character sang the praises of consumerism on a record distributed with Kellogg's cereals in 1966 England, board games,

Barbies, and books account for much of the shopping-themed merchandise.

The initial thinking behind shopping board games was about money – not just the toy companies' making it, but teaching children about it as well. Whitman's *The Game of Shopping at the Supermarket* and the imaginatively titled *Shopping Center Game*, were typical '50s: clean-cut and cute.

In the 1960s, Milton Bradley introduced *Cut Up Shopping Spree Game* while fashion dolls Velvet and Crissy went to town in the *Velvet and Crissy Shopping Spree Game*. The English Mr Men characters (based on the books by Roger Hargreaves) did the same in the 1978 board game, *Mr Men Shopping Spree Game*.

The 1980s and '90s brought kids such classic games as *Bargain Hunter*, *Meet Me at the Mall*, *Let's Go Shopping*, *It's Only Money*, *Monopoly: QVC Edition*, the *West Edmonton Mall Game*, and the batteries-not-included *Electronic Mall Madness*.

Cool Shoppin' Barbie.

The technological developments that made it possible for *Electronic Mall Madness* to "talk" was also responsible for *Cool Shoppin' Barbie*. Introduced in 1997, the doll was a joint venture between Mattel and credit card giant MasterCard. Each Barbie came complete with a MasterCard, unlimited play "credit," and a register that prompted Barbie to say "thank you" and "credit approved" when the card is swiped.

To its credit (no pun intended), Barbie manufacturer Mattel has taken steps to ensure that the doll has reflected the varied opportunities for and ambitions of modern girls. She's been a doctor, a dentist, an astronaut, and President of the United States. But whatever she does for a living, you can almost guarantee she's going to be spending up a storm come payday.

And Barbie gets around. She's shopped at Bloomingdale's (Savvy Shopper Barbie), FAO Schwarz (FAO Shopping Spree Barbie), Meijer (Meijer Shopping

*Buy Nothing Day calls for a 24-hour shopping moratorium*

Not everyone is impressed with the way so many North Americans have embraced consumerism and shopping. Kalle Lasn, the Estonian Canadian behind the slick and often poignant anti-consumerism magazine, *Adbusters*, and the not-for-profit organization, the Media Foundation, has spearheaded the annual Buy Nothing Day event since 1992.

Although the major American networks have always refused to air advertisements promoting Buy Nothing Day (this may have something to do with the spots likening consumers to pigs), Lasn and his supporters find other ways to get their message out.

Vicki Robin, co-author of the best-selling anti-consumerism bible, *Your Money or Your Life*, and a revered big-wig in the Voluntary Simplicity Movement, suggested Lasn move Buy Nothing Day from its original September date to the Friday following American Thanksgiving in November. It's the biggest shopping day of the year in the biggest shopping country on earth, a fact that increases the relevancy of Buy Nothing Day and draws considerable media attention.

Activity on Buy Nothing Day is most notable in left-leaning, activist-friendly cities like Seattle, Washington and Burlington, Vermont. The action in Seattle has included demonstrations outside shopping malls where Buy Nothing Day supporters cut up credit cards while others distribute questionnaires to shoppers posing questions like "Do I need it?", "How long will it last?", and "How much will I use it?" to encourage consumers to think before they buy.

A little thought never hurt any purchase and it's hard to argue with much of the reasoning behind Buy Nothing Day, particularly when that animated pig starts rattling off statistics pertaining to North American consumerism. Perhaps for one day, as the pig suggests, shoppers should "give it a rest."

Fun Barbie), Spiegel (Shopping Chic Barbie), and Wal-Mart (Wal-Mart Shopping Time Barbie). When she hit Benetton (Benetton Shopping Fun Barbie) in 1991, she was accompanied by two other Benetton shoppers, pal Kira and boyfriend Ken.

The shopping-education experience doesn't stop at games and dolls. Hundreds of children's shopping books have been published through the years, from the highly collectible 1948 Little Golden Book, *Let's Go Shopping with Peter and Penny* to the '60s book, *Elizabeth's Shopping Spree* by David O. White. Well-known children's characters like Caillou, Arthur, Mickey Mouse, Paddington Bear, Scooby Doo, and – you guessed it – Barbie all have at least one shopping book title to their name.

But perhaps the best lessons about consumerism and shopping can be taken from Ted Dewan's *Crispin: The Pig Who Had it All*. In the story, Crispin is inundated with more and more toys which are often cheaply made and easily broken. All is well and good in Crispin's world as the toys keep coming. That is, until he gets bored and Santa leaves him a big, mysterious box as a present. The pig is justifiably perplexed, wondering what amazing toy it could possibly contain. When all is revealed it turns out Crispin's gift is the best toy of all to play with, and the one thing he didn't have: a big box.

BUY NOTHING DAY

# Teen Power

*Doing whatever it takes for a piece of the lucrative youth market pie*

**P**ity the pre-1950s teenager. In addition to the requisite angst, gangly awkwardness, and spotty complexion, the pre-postwar adolescent suffered unfortunate neglect. But not at the hands of their parents, mind you.

No, it was the manufacturers, the advertisers, and the so-called consumer experts who shunned the pimply set in favor of attracting the attention of older, wage-earning adults. Teens, the marketplace largely dictated, were no more useful than small children, and not nearly half as cute.

The prosperity of postwar America vaulted the perception of the lowly teen. On December 20, 1948, *Life* magazine devoted its cover story to teenagers, pointing out that for the first time teens had spending power and were the latest, greatest untapped market. Armed with allowances and income from part-time or summer jobs, teen cash hit stores in a hurry and soon advertisers were vying for the dollars of this emerging demographic powerhouse.

The youth, it was believed, would remain loyal to the products and brands they were introduced to in their teenage years and advertisers invested heavily in the theory that they were cultivating customers for life.

The teens of the 1960s blew that idea to shreds, as the infamous Baby Boomers took over Teen Town. The sheer numbers of these freshly minted teens made even the most jaded and old-fashioned marketers take notice. But what was particularly notable was the Boomers' attitude.

As a group, they were the first teenagers to recognize their influence. The Baby Boomers didn't hesitate to use (and some would assert, abuse) their position as consumers. The "customers for life" concept didn't fly with these brazen shoppers who - unlike their parents' generation - would switch brands on a whim, often favoring convenience and current brand status over anything else. Conversely, the burgeoning anti-consumerism movement taught the youth of the 1960s to be wary of marketing messages, eager advertising and, of course, The Man.

But The Man and his evil-doing disciples did not stop teen spending from rising. Nor did they prevent the Baby Boomers from morphing into a collective spending machine and giving birth to the most consumer-oriented generation ever to walk the Earth.

In 1962, American teenagers spent about $10 billion. Forty years later there are 32.6 million teens roaming the malls of the United States, spending in excess of $155 billion annually. Call them what you will - Echo Boomers, Millennials, the Baby Boomlet, Generation Y, Generation Next - the offspring of spendaholic Baby Boomers are worthy contenders for the grand crown of Consumerism their parents have held for over 30 years.

Between 1997 and 2001, teen spending grew exponentially, jumping from $64 billion to the aforementioned figure of $155 billion. Such rich numbers are enough to bring marketers and manufacturers to the brink of orgasm - or at the very least, be a wet dream. But getting the attention of teens is no easy task.

Consumer behavior studies have shown that the current crop is a generation used to getting what they want. In 2002, the consumer watchdog agency, The Center for a New American Dream, published statistics stating that 55 percent of young people will keep on asking for what they desire, even if their parents' initial answer is no.

But having the means and knowing the tricks to get what they want is only half the equation. Modern teens are also very confident and specific in regards to *what* they want. Be it a style, a brand, or an experience, they know what they like when they see it.

The situation has caused headaches for marketers around the globe and has forced the people behind teen-targeted products to rethink traditional marketing and research strategies.

Number one rule: focus groups are out. Having grown up privy to the how-to's behind the conventional collection of consumer views and attitudes, many of today's teens think nothing of messing with marketers' minds – and results. (Q: "So, tell me honestly, what do you think of this new band, Dixie Doom?" A: "Oh, yes. Goth/country music is going to be the biggest thing ever.") So, with the usual research practices widely believed to be unreliable when it comes to teens, marketing and advertising types have been forced to turn to the teenagers themselves for help.

Advisory councils comprised of desirable members of the demographic have become the big trend in excavating information from youth. The key difference between focus groups and advisory councils is that the teens involved with advisory councils are often dealing directly with the source as opposed to an agency representative. The teens see first-hand the impact their opinions make and, as some have pointed out in media interviews, advisory councils are a great place to make useful professional connections.

They don't earn money for their valuable contributions, but free test swag such as clothes and music have been known to find their way into the eager hands of teen "advisors."

If a company does it right, the advisory council shtick works. Following the lead of success stories *CosmoGirl!* and *Teen People*, nearly all of the teen magazines now use advisors. At *Teen People,* two full-time staff are employed to oversee the magazine's teen council.

Teen clothing giant Delia's also taps the brains of their teenage girl clientele, formally soliciting the opinions of 30 trend-setting teens as well as inviting feedback online through the company's virtual "affiliate program."

Even shopping malls, like the Hudson Mall in Jersey City, New Jersey, seek advice from its teen advisory council, sometimes in exchange for classes on job interview techniques and assistance with college applications.

While there is no magic formula for success in the crowded and competitive youth market, there is one sure thing: teens today are all too aware of their worth in the marketplace and they're too smart to give anything up for free.

# Inside the Retail World

chapter

iii

---

## 'Tis the Season

### Macy's windows on the (retail) world

It's a Christmas tradition. Since 1874, Macy's department store in Manhattan has been a holiday draw. The flagship store, which has occupied its Herald Square location since 1902, spans an entire city block and has 50 display windows, all of which are put to use during the festive season.

Fancy, tricked-out windows are a mainstay of department stores and boutiques alike, but what makes the Macy's windows special is the fact that North Americans may never have seen Christmas evolve into a commercial spectacle if not for the department store and its seasonal windows.

It wasn't until the 1860s that America got all Christmas crazy. In 1867, Macy's became the first department store to stay open late on Christmas Eve – until midnight – in an effort to encourage and promote last-minute holiday shopping. Seven years

 istory, at times, can be a little sketchy. Records may be vague, recollections may vary, and historians will bicker.

Such is the case regarding the murky past of the department store.

Some historians contend the blueprint for the modern department store was English and others insist that the American model was the real thing. But the store that gets the most votes as the world's first true-blue department store is the Bon Marché in Paris.

Originally a dry goods store, the Bon Marché was bought in 1852 by Aristide Boucicaut. Along with his wife, Boucicaut ran the Alexandre Gustave Eiffel-designed store and carried outerwear, linens, and assorted housewares. While the store's roster of goods would incite nothing more than a disinterested shrug today, in the mid-nineteenth century, it was unusual for a shop to carry such a variety of merchandise.

Boucicaut quickly broke tradition in other areas of retailing as well. He instituted a fixed price system that did away with the haggling that was typical and expected in most Paris shops. He permitted shoppers entrance to the store free of charge, encouraging browsing, a habit that had, until then, not been allowed; prior to the advent of the department store, whenever a customer entered a shop, they were required to make a purchase. Shopping was a thought-out, practical activity that resulted almost exclusively in the purchase of life's essentials.

Boucicaut also introduced a cash returns policy, provided daily delivery to customers' homes, and held the occasional sale. As a result, the Bon Marché and its newfangled ways of retailing caught on with Paris shoppers and is considered a great influence on early American department stores and even on important writers of the day – most famously, Emile Zola. Zola was said to have spent considerable time wandering the aisles of the Bon Marché when researching his 1881 book, *Au Bonheur*

*Des Dames* (*The Ladies' Paradise*), and the character of Octave Mouret is believed by scholars to be based on Aristide Boucicaut.

By the time Zola's book was published, the department store was a fixture in Paris. Its early success had enabled Boucicaut to expand the store's size, and its selection. In 1872, the Bon Marché was stocking foodstuffs, toys, children's wear, sporting goods, and furniture; by 1877 it was the biggest department store in the world.

Bon Marché, 1910. *Courtesy Mary Evans Picture Library.*

The impact of Boucicaut's Bon Marché cannot be ignored, but as historian Alison Adburgham states in her book, *Shops and Shopping: 1800-1914*, years before the spotlight fell on Boucicaut and his store, establishments in England were holding sales, setting fixed prices, and selling a variety of goods. Adburgham specifically points to Bainbridge's in Newcastle and Kendal Milne & Faulkner in Manchester.

The former, she asserts, introduced fixed prices in 1841 and was carrying fabric and accessories in addition to clothing and furs by 1845. The latter held its first sale in 1837.

In the U.S., A.T. Stewart moved and expanded his Manhattan dry goods shop founded in the 1820s, to a four-storey location near City Hall in 1846. Called the Marble Dry Goods Palace, it is widely acknowledged as the first American department store.

The simultaneous flurry of activity on both sides of the Atlantic is at the crux of the confusion. Because most department stores were originally basic dry goods shops that morphed into bigger establishments with diverse stock, pin-pointing the exact moment an individual store ceased being a dry goods shop and was christened a department store is difficult, if not impossible, to determine.

It is clear, however, that the department store represented the natural evolution of the dry goods shop and that the innovations put into practice by Boucicaut and

later, Christmas gifting had permeated the culture and Macy's launched another innovative concept: Christmas theme windows.

The first windows, at the store's original "Ladies Mile" location on 14th Street, are said to have showcased dolls. The windows in 2000 were a showy Disney-theme spectacular, featuring 64 animatronic characters. More than a century apart, both sets of windows served the same purpose – to sell merchandise.

It is estimated that up to 70 percent of a store's annual sales revenue is generated during the holidays, so it's little wonder that Macy's takes its sales windows very seriously.

According to writer Bruce Horowitz's exclusive report in *USA Today*, "Sales Windows to Macy's Soul" (November 27, 1998), approximately 8,000 shoppers walk by Macy's Christmas windows every hour, every day during the month leading up to Christmas, resulting in a whole lot of exposure.

Of the 50 windows, the most stunning and anxiously anticipated are always the six facing Broadway. Each of the Broadway windows can cost up to $25,000 to design; many of the others average out around $5,000 apiece.

A bona fide tourist

attraction and significant investment, Macy's takes care in choosing the year's theme, a process which begins in late spring. Other than any theme with religious overtones, all ideas are game as long as it's more commerce than art.

Some stores take a more arty or esoteric approach to window display, but Macy's is all about the bottom line. Merchandise is put in the window to sell.

Visual designers and merchandisers take on the challenge when sketching out the look of each window. Then, after employing a team of prop makers (whose primary material in window design is Styrofoam), the Macy's team starts to assemble the windows in late October, a month before the full 50 are revealed.

The expense and extravagance of Macy's Christmas windows has come under scrutiny in recent years. With department store sales slipping and more consumers taking to hassle-free online shopping, the relevance of Macy's block-square advertisement seems to defy logic (and good business reasoning). But then again, tradition doesn't have to make sense, does it?

his contemporaries were as much a sign of the times as anything.

Squabbling over who did what first seems pointless on another front. Defining a department store was – and is – subjective. The *American Heritage Dictionary of the English Language* may tell us that a department store is "a large retail store offering a variety of merchandise and services and organized in separate departments," but historians' definitions are often far more specific.

Some insist the term department store only be used to describe merchants that have a minimum number of departments. Those departments, then, may have to include certain categories like women's clothing or children's wear. Sometimes it's the number of employees that count (a popular number bandied about in the old days was 25) or the store's accounting system (some experts say detailed and separate books must be kept for each department in a real department store).

The only point everyone can agree on is that a department store must, by its very name, have a variety of departments.

By the late 1800s there were plenty of stores with lots of departments. Americans, in particular, embraced these one-stop-shopping emporiums. In the 1860s, brothers Lyman and Joseph Bloomingdale were in business selling the fashion fad of the day – hoop skirts – out of their Ladies' Notion Shop in New York City. When they opened the Bloomingdale Brothers Great East Side Bazaar in 1872, the store was well on its way to becoming a full-fledged department store. But Bloomingdale's was hardly the only game in town.

A shopping hub was emerging in lower Manhattan. Dubbed the Ladies' Mile, the shopping strip stretched from 14th to 23rd Streets on Sixth Avenue and included retailers Siegel-Cooper & Company Dry Goods Store (founded 1896), Stern Brothers Department Store (founded 1878), B. Altman Dry Goods Store (founded 1877), Lord & Taylor (founded 1867), and R.H. Macy's Dry Goods Company (founded 1861).

Business boomed at Macy's, which in 1877 already had 24 departments. The store, founded by Rowland H. Macy and sold to Bavarian immigrants Isidor and Nathan Straus in the 1896, was doing over $1 million in sales at the time of Macy's death in 1878. The Straus

44

brothers were largely responsible for building the store's impressive reputation and had the foresight to capitalize on key trends, the most significant being the 1902 expansion and move uptown to the Herald Square location Macy's has occupied for more than century.

Macy's was already well-established and raking in the cash when high-end Siegel-Cooper opened its opulent doors in 1896. The store was a stand-out on the Ladies' Mile and was noted for its European flavor and extravagant interiors. It was not just a store, as it housed an art gallery, a theater, and even a dentist's office. Siegel-Cooper was also known as being the first department store to have an air conditioned environment, and pioneered the concept of free samples and product demonstrations for its customers.

In its heyday, New York City's Ladies' Mile had some of the biggest and the best department store shopping in the world. But there were pockets of important department store retailers popping up elsewhere as well.

John Wanamaker opened his Grand Depot store in the renovated Pennsylvania Freight Station in Philadelphia in 1876; the city's Strawbridge & Clothier opened the next year. Marshall Field – the man who famously quipped, "Give the lady what she wants" – set up shop in Chicago in 1881.

In Canada, Timothy Eaton opened his first Eaton's store in downtown Toronto in 1869, and the renowned trading post, the Hudson's Bay Company, which was founded in 1670, had become a department store too. Of the long list of splashy North American department stores, the international reputation of a lone English enterprise eclipsed them all. No other department store has quite the colorful history of Harrods.

When merchant Charles Henry Harrod assumed a small London grocery shop in 1849, it's unlikely he could have imagined the shopping legend he was sparking. Harrod ran his unassuming grocery business, eventually passing the reigns to his son, Charles Digby Harrod. It was Charles Jr who is credited with putting the store on the path to great success by expanding and diversifying the company.

In 1874, the Knightsbridge store introduced the name "Harrod's Stores" and over the next few decades Charles Jr (and later, subsequent owners, the Burbridge

## From Athens to Orange County

### Influential malls that changed the shopping experience

Would someone *please* tell the historians at the back of the room to stop quibbling.

Like the early history of the department store, the roots of the shopping mall are debatable. Markets, arcades, and shopping centers in Athens, Istanbul, Brussels, and Milan have each been singled out as the first shopping mall by various experts.

But let's forget the conjecture and just consider the facts: the who, what, when, where, and even the occasional why behind the most historically significant shopping hubs.

150 BCE:
STOA OF ATTALOS
(AKA STOA OF ATTALUS),
ATHENS, GREECE

The Ancient Greek arcade was once the center of shopping excitement in Athens. It is believed that 21 merchants occupied each floor of the two-storey, colonnaded structure that lies at the base of the Acropolis. Today, the restored building functions not as a shopping center, but a museum.

Known locally as the *Kapalicarsi* (meaning "covered bazaar"), Istanbul's Grand Bazaar has been *the* place to score spices, crafts, jewelry, and exquisite carpets for more than five centuries. The marketplace in the center of the old city is also frequently cited as the original shopping mall. Built during the reign of Mehmet the Conqueror, the Grand Bazaar had humble beginnings, starting with just two wooden warehouse structures. These were later rebuilt in stone due to the risk of fire. Expansion continued through the years and the Bazaar is now home to approximately 4,400 shops.

Galleria Vittorio Emanuele.

1877:
GALLERIA VITTORIO
EMANUELE,
MILAN, ITALY

The covered, open-air shopping center still stands today and is recognized by the *Guinness Book of World Records* as the world's oldest shopping mall. Named after Italy's first king and a favorite destination of

family) would buy up the property surrounding the original store to facilitate Harrods' growth. The move made Harrods a premier shopping destination and by 1884, the store boasted 80 departments.

It was an amazing feat, especially considering that the previous year the store had been destroyed by fire less than three weeks before Christmas and had to be rebuilt. The 1883 fire was only the first Harrods' disaster; two more would follow: a bomb explosion in 1974 that caused chaos, but injured no one, and in 1983, another bomb – planted by the Irish Republican Army – that exploded in the store, killing six and injuring 93.

Not all of Harrods' storied past involves fire and tragedy. It has long been recognized for its popularity with the Royal Family and was once quite publicly known for its eccentric whimsy. Not only could customers pick up typical department store fare like food, clothing, housewares, and gifts, but shoppers – particularly famous ones – could get their hands on pretty much anything (and everything) they could think of.

Noel Coward

The best examples of Harrods' over-the-top service involve animals. Comic actress Beatrice Lillie once purchased an alligator from Harrods as a Christmas gift for her pal, playwright Noel Coward. In 1967, the self-proclaimed king of Albania, known as Leka, bought an elephant as a gift for then California governor Ronald Reagan; Reagan promptly named the elephant GOP and bequeathed it to the public zoo in Sacramento.

Ronald Reagan

Non-celebrities, too, reaped the benefits of Harrods' animal-friendly nature for years, taking advantage of the now-defunct kennel service that was offered to customers who couldn't bear to be far from their pets.

The early years of department stores marked the first signs of mass consumer culture among the upper-classes targeted by many of the shops. Stores in Europe and North America introduced shoppers to the concept of leisure shopping for the first time. No longer did consumers need something specific in mind when stepping into a department store. And since they weren't obligated to spend a single cent, shopping emerged as a hobby, something stores were happy to encourage, as it often resulted in shoppers shelling out for unnecessary items bought on impulse.

By the turn of the century, department stores were thriving. But, as with other retail enterprises, the two World Wars had a devastating impact on business. Stores closed - some temporarily, some forever - as shoppers had more serious concerns than cruising the aisles for the latest luxuries or fashion styles. The bargain basements that first opened in the late 1800s became massively popular as people pinched pennies, and soon there was a department store to suit almost every budget.

Following the end of the Second World War, consumers were back in action, itching to shop. Department store owners were understandably ecstatic and those canny enough to recognize the rise of the new middle-class shoppers were especially prosperous.

Many department stores had previously catered to an exclusively wealthy clientele or sold bargain necessities to those much further down the wage scale, but by the 1950s, a new middle-income consumer was eager to spend as sport.

They bought into the new suburban dream, fanning out from the city core. Shopping shifted from downtown to suburbs peppered with shopping centers and malls. Department stores expanded to meet new consumer demands, opening satellite stores in suburban communities.

Some stores recognized the trend more quickly than others and had set up suburban shops as far back as the early 1930s. In the United States, the first to make the leap were Marshall Field's (to Evanston, Lake Forest, and Oak Park, Illinois) and B. Altman (to White Plains, New York). But the 1950s was the defining decade for department store growth, and the suburban expansion did not slow for more than 30 years.

Store after store was built in mall after mall, causing business in many flagship downtown locations to wane. Rapid suburban growth coupled with increased competition and the conglomerization of department store

opera composer Giacomo Puccini and writer Mark Twain (who once said he could happily live there), the Galleria was built between 1865 and 1877 and designed by Giuseppe Mengoni. Its distinctive architecture – which features a four-storey domed-glass roof – is said to have been inspired by London's extravagant exhibition hall, the Crystal Palace.

1896:
ROLAND PARK
SHOPPING CENTER,
BALTIMORE, MARYLAND

Euro-style malls (or, more aptly, arcades) were never truly embraced in North America. The first hints of the shopping mall we know today came courtesy of Baltimore businessman Edward H. Bouton. His Roland Park Shopping Center may have hosted only six tenants, but it was arguably the first strip mall, with a set of shops set back from the street and parking spaces in front.

1916:
MARKET SQUARE,
LAKE FOREST, ILLINOIS

The National Register of Historical Places acknowledges Market Square, in an affluent suburb of Chicago, as the first planned shopping center, a title also claimed by Highland Park Shopping Center in Dallas 15 years later. The project was originally conceived in 1911 by Arthur T. Aldis and Howard Van Doren Shaw; when it was completed four years later, the first business to open was Charlie Paulsen's barber shop.

### 1922:
### COUNTRY CLUB PLAZA,
### KANSAS CITY, MISSOURI

Designed with a Spanish flair and financed by developer J.C. Nichols, Country Club Plaza was the first shopping center built in conjunction with a new suburban community specifically to cater to local residents.

### 1931:
### HIGHLAND PARK
### SHOPPING VILLAGE,
### DALLAS, TEXAS

Duking it out with Lake Forest's Market Square as the first planned shopping center, the sprawling 10-acre Highland Park Shopping Village (built by Hugh Prather Sr) was unique in that it stood on a single parcel of land that was not disrupted by intersections and streets the way earlier shopping centers had been.

### 1949:
### TOWN & COUNTRY
### SHOPPING CENTER,
### COLUMBUS, OHIO

Town & Country was the first shopping center to introduce nighttime shopping. Developer Don

chains – which not so many years before were almost all family-owned and operated businesses – resulted in an ugly financial scenario for several big name stores starting in the late 1980s.

In the decade spanning 1989 to 1999, Macy's, Bloomingdale's, and Barneys New York all filed for Chapter 11 bankruptcy protection (although all managed to survive). In Canada, the venerable Eaton's department store went out of business twice. In 1999, the struggling chain declared bankruptcy. It was bought by Sears Canada, downsized, and reopened only to see the name disappear from the retail scene for good in 2002 when Sears closed most of Eaton's locations and converted the few remaining stores to the Sears name.

Some analysts have called into question the validity of department stores in the twenty-first century, labeling them retail dinosaurs. While discount merchants like Wal-Mart thrive, traditional department stores struggle to find new ways to lure customers. Many have reduced or eliminated "hard goods" departments, which sold household appliances and electronics, in favor of expanding their fashion floors, and others have promoted a commitment to exemplary customer service.

The years ahead are undeniably uncertain, but the impact department stores had on shoppers and how they shop is not. The department store, as antiquated an idea as it may seem today, set off the wave of avid consumerism that forever changed the way we shop: browsing over bargaining, want over need, and shopping as sport.

# From Paper Cone to Portable Art

*The evolution of the shopping bag*

**J**ust imagine: a long, long time ago shoppers buying from markets, street vendors, and stores would pick and choose their purchases, pony up the required payment, and that would be that. No pomp, no circumstance, and – more importantly – no shopping bag.

In fact, until the sixteenth century, there was no packaging to speak of and customers were expected to bring their own shopping paraphernalia like baskets and bowls. If a shopper wanted more than he could stuff into such carry-alls – tough. The system was cash and whatever-you-can-carry.

Packaging didn't become commonplace until the early 1800s. Until then, paper was hand-made, making it too expensive to justify wrapping shoppers' purchases in. But with the manufacturing advances of the Industrial Revolution came machines to economically produce sheets of low-grade wrapping paper, which in turn became the materials for the first shopping bags.

The first bags were funny, cone-shaped things – paper twisted into a triangle, then folded at the bottom. The flat bags begat new shapes: square and oblong, and sometimes a merchant would stamp the name of the business on its front, foreshadowing the shopping-bag-as-advertising explosion that occurred more than a century later.

Whatever its shape, the flat bag had limitations, particularly regarding the amount of merchandise that could be carried and its awkward lack of handles. The flat-bottomed, three-dimensional gusset bag (complete with handles) served to alleviate the dilemmas of the flat bag and was the precursor to the block-shaped carrier bag we know today.

The carrier bag of the early twentieth century has a shady history. The U.S. patent for a durable, brown paper bag with string handles was awarded in 1912 to St Paul grocer Walter H. Deubener, who was said to have

Town & Country at night.

Casto attempted to draw after dark crowds by hiring a woman whose act was diving into a small, fiery pool from 90 feet above. She performed in the Town & Country parking lot and curious spectators flocked to the scene, stayed to peruse the stores, and kicked off a shopping trend.

### 1950:
### NORTHGATE SHOPPING CENTER, SEATTLE, WASHINGTON

At the end of the Second World War in 1945, there were less than a dozen shopping malls in the United States. Most featured a basic, strip-style design, but Northgate dared to be different. The Seattle shopping center was the first open-air pedestrian mall laid out with two strips of shops facing each other and a pedestrian promenade running down the middle.

1951:
SHOPPERS WORLD,
FRAMINGHAM,
MASSACHUSETTS

A short drive from Boston, Shoppers World's claim to fame was its unusual circular design (built by the Jordan Marsh Co). It also has one important first to its name: it was the first shopping center with two levels.

1956:
SOUTHDALE SHOPPING
CENTER,
EDINA, MINNESOTA

Often referred to as the first modern mall, Southdale was also the first fully enclosed, two-level, climate-controlled shopping environment that included two department stores (or, as they would become known in the industry, "anchor stores"). Minneapolis department store owner Donald Dayton built the mall in part to provide a comfortable refuge for shoppers during the harsh Minnesota winters. The mall's advertisements enthused that "Everyday will be a perfect shopping day!" at Southdale.

Its design was inspired by early pedestrian malls such as Milan's Galleria Vittorio Emanuele.

invented the bag. The Interstate Bag company of Walden, New York (now known as Amko Packaging Corp) claimed the paper carrier bag (with cord handles) as its invention in 1907.

It is Deubener, however, who is credited as the inventor of the shopping bag we know and love. He came  up with the idea in hopes of solving a problem he noticed among his customers: they would only buy what they could carry. After four years of experimentation, Deubener unveiled his modestly named "Deubener Shopping Bag." Selling for five cents, the bag could hold up to 75 pounds of merchandise and made its inventor a very rich man – by 1915, he was selling more than one million bags per year.

Prolific inventor Margaret Knight then devised and patented the first machine to efficiently manufacture square-bottomed, grocery store-type bags, making shopping bags more accessible to retailers and common to the shopping public.

In 1939, Interstate Bag was back on the scene with a significant advance in manufacturing technology that pushed the shopping bag into the future. Until that time, handles had to be attached in a process separate from producing the bag itself. Interstate solved the problem by introducing a machine that would automatically attach the handles to the bags, bringing the cost of manufacturing down enough that retailers could afford to give bags away with purchases instead of charging for them.

With every shopper leaving a merchant's store with her purchases in a bag, the paper shopping tote became an ideal advertising forum, although the concept wasn't fully exploited until the late 1950s and early '60s. Printed, logo signature bags were the domain of the big department stores, but it is New York City's Bloomingdale's which made the most widely recognized impact with early ad bags.

In 1961, Bloomingdale's introduced a special edition shopping bag with a French tarot card design. Touted as the first designer shopping bag, Bloomingdales' success inspired other stores to follow suit, starting what would become a long tradition in commissioning graphic artists, painters, photographers, and architects to design shopping bags.

The worlds of art and shopping bags collided quite literally in 1964 when Pop Artists Andy Warhol and Roy Lichtenstein designed bags for "The American Supermarket," a New York art exhibit. Each bag – Warhol's featuring his famous rendition of the Campbell's soup can and Lichtenstein's a turkey – was produced in a limited edition of 300 and have since become much sought-after collectors' pieces. At Sotheby's Contemporary Prints auction in 1998, a Warhol bag that was initialed and dated fetched $4,312 even though it was in less-than-pristine condition.

The design branch of the Smithsonian Institution, the Cooper-Hewitt National Design Museum in New York City, premiered its touring exhibit of shopping bags, "Portable Graphic Art," in 1978, and today has more than 900 examples in its archives. Both private and museum collections of "portable art" have been exhibited from Spokane to Chicago. The Newark Public Library's Special Collections Division has one of the largest shopping bag collections in the world with more than 1,400, and the Benz Gallery of Floral Art at Texas A&M University has more than 1,200.

Shopping bags featuring the work of artists like David Hockney and Keith Haring, photographers Annie Leibowitz and Richard Avedon, and architects such as Michael Graves, have meant both a windfall and a challenge for shopping bag collectors. No one can collect them all, so many collectors zero in on a specific area of interest. For some, it's souvenir travel bags, for others it's special edition, seasonal bags only available around Christmas or Valentine's Day. And for many, it's department store bags.

Since its early credit as the birth mother of the designer shopping bag, Bloomingdale's has been a leader

Viennese architect Victor Gruen designed Southdale and believed malls would become the new town centers, even insisting on referring to them as "shopping towns."

But not everyone was excited by the idea of Gruen's "shopping towns" or impressed by the proliferation of shopping centers. The year Southdale opened, *Business Week* magazine published a piece entitled, "Too Many Shopping Centers." At the time there were 2,000 in the United States.

1981:
WEST EDMONTON MALL,
EDMONTON,
ALBERTA, CANADA

Advertised as the "Eighth Wonder of the World," the world's biggest shopping mall was built in four phases and was finally completed in 1998. With 800 stores eating up 5.5 million square feet, West Edmonton Mall was the first shopping-mall-as-tourist-attraction. Inside, visitors were overwhelmed by the Fantasyland Hotel and the Galaxyland Amusement Park, the Ice Palace featuring an NHL-sized skating rink, and two theme shopping "streets": Europa Boulevard and New Orleans-flavored Bourbon Street.

The Canadian mall also houses the world's largest wave pool, indoor lake (complete with a submarine and dolphins), and indoor miniature golf course. And it may not stop there. A new phase of the mall is pending and will include a concert and sports arena, an office tower, and perhaps even an apartment building.

1985:
OLD HYDE PARK VILLAGE,
TAMPA, FLORIDA

Old Hyde Park was one of the first shopping malls slapped with the moniker "lifestyle center." According to the International Council of Shopping Centers, a lifestyle center is usually built in an open-air configuration and serves as a "multi-purpose leisure-time destination" not just devoted to retail, but to dining and entertainment (i.e., movie cinemas) as well.

Centers like Old Hyde Park and The Arboretum at Great Hills in Austin,

in shopping bag design. Most notably, the store is known for its instantly recognizable Big Brown Bag. Originally designed to hold large purchases from the linen department, the bag debuted in 1973 and was soon followed by its sisters, the Little Brown Bag and later, the Medium Brown Bag. The Big Brown Bag may not have "Bloomingdale's" printed in bold on its face, but shoppers worldwide know exactly where it's from.

And those same shoppers know the value of a good bag.

The modern shopping bag has evolved into a status symbol. Toting one around makes a statement about where you've been and where you shop. Many shoppers, although not die-hard collectors, can't bear to part with a bag from a big-label store or one that's particularly unique.

Carefully folded, stored in closets, or slid into drawers, status shopping bags are rolled out for all kinds of occasions. Baked extra cookies for the neighbors? The tin will fit perfectly into that red glossy tote from Saks Fifth Avenue. Trekking downtown to return those overdue library books? Only sturdy Neiman Marcus from last Christmas will do. Bringing a tiny box of gourmet chocolates to that dinner party at your particularly pretentious friend's place? It must be Tiffany & Co's signature blue bag. No one needs to know you only bought a key ring.

Aerial view of West Edmonton Mall.

## Out With the Old

*From high tech to homey, modern retail environments forge new ground*

 t isn't enough to simply paint the walls, stock the shelves, and open the doors. Today's retail stores are not just about shopping, but about individuality and entertainment.

As cookie-cutter chains that sell cookie-cutter clothes have fallen from grace, a new kind of retailer has emerged, or rather, returned: smaller-scale, boutique-style shops that often focus on the experience of shopping itself.

Whether it's stark minimalism or cluttered kitsch, cutting-edge retailers around the globe have seized an adventurous design spirit that often translates into full-blown "event shopping" for consumers.

Arguably the most hyped shop opening in recent years was Prada's 30,000 square foot flagship store in Manhattan's SoHo district. Designed by Dutch journalist-and-screenwriter-turned-architect, Rem Koolhaas, the expansive store cost between $30 and $50 million to build (Merrill Lynch put the estimated cost at $41 million) and opened in December 2001.

Working in collaboration with the Italian brand's designer, Miuccia Prada, and her husband, Patrizio Bertelli, Koolhaas created an experimental space at once designed to sell fashion as well as to screen films, produce plays, and exhibit art. The bleacher-style stairs, for example, may display shoes by day and offer seating for a public arts event at night.

Even the store's dressing rooms have design aficionados flocking to see the space. With the touch of a button, the dressing room doors go from opaque to transparent, catering to – one can only assume – the exhibitionist shopper. Touch-screen technology allows the upmarket clientele to explore the

Texas pioneered the concept that has now been taken a step further by the "lifestyle villages" sprouting up in Charlotte, North Carolina and San Jose, California. The developments feature high-end shops in an open-air layout with stylish studio and loft living spaces for rent above.

1992:
MALL OF AMERICA,
BLOOMINGTON, MINNESOTA

By the end of the 1980s there were some 35,000 malls in the U.S. – California with the most and Wyoming with the least. So, what did America need next? Another mall, of course. A really, really big one: 4.2 million square feet, to be exact.

Second in size only to West Edmonton Mall, the Mall of America was built on the former Met Stadium site, which once played host to Major League Baseball's

Minnesota Twins and the NFL's Minnesota Vikings. The mall itself sits on 45 acres of land (the total property takes up 78 acres) and draws 42.5 million customers every year. Like its big brother to the north, the mall is a tourist attraction and has two indoor amusement parks, including Camp Snoopy.

1993:
THE LAB,
COSTA MESA, CALIFORNIA

At the height of the alternative fever that blazed through youth culture in the early 1990s came the world's first self-described "anti-mall." The brainchild of former Quicksilver surf wear president, Shaheen Sadeghi, The Lab was conceived as a multi-function space for trend-conscious California youth who weren't satisfied with the typical mall experience.

The converted Orange County canning factory has tenants like Tower Alternative and Urban Outfitters. Nightlife and entertainment have also been incorporated into the space – there's a playhouse for live theater events, and The Lab often hosts spoken word and music happenings with a live DJ spinning discs in its common areas.

origins and manufacturing of garments and also get an all-important rear-view visual of themselves in the outfit they just tried on.

While Koolhaas and fellow architects Frank Gehry (who designed Issey Miyake's latest New York space that also opened in 2001) and Philippe Starck (of Jean Paul Gaultier's Madison Avenue flagship store) may reign as the darlings of retail design, event environments are nothing new to the Japanese.

Fashion designer Rei Kawabuko of Comme des Garçons has been designing – in conjunction with firms like London's KRD and Future Systems – her minimalist shops since 1975. The first Comme des Garçons store, in the Aoyama district of Tokyo, included elements such as frosted glass and sterile white tiles long before the look became popular more than 15 years later. Kawabuko also made it a priority in her retail spaces to incorporate art exhibitions and installations.

Another Japanese retail innovator is Issey Miyake. Not only did the designer choose esteemed modern architect Frank Gehry to design his flagship Manhattan store in Tribeca, he enlisted the services of Tokyo's Curiosity Inc for his Me Issey Miyake  shop. The store is a sales forum for Miyake's one-sized Me stretch shirts and features vending machines as the exclusive form of stocking and selling. Each shirt is rolled into a sealed plastic tube similar to that of a poster and, just like a Coke machine, drops the product into an accessible slot once the customer has selected the desired color and texture.

Slick, high-tech surroundings are only rivaled by retail environments with a decidedly personal twist. Bookshops like Barnes & Noble have built-in coffee bars and lounging areas designed strictly for that purpose. Williams-Sonoma offers cooking classes and demonstrations, while sporting goods retailers such as Sports Authority let customers try their luck in batting cages and chat with golf pros. And at Diesel shops, the label's young, fashion-forward clientele are frequently treated to a live DJ spinning discs in-store.

That is personalization on a grand, mass market scale. The most personal of personalization can only be found at the growing number of by-appointment boutiques and salons.

"Shopping isn't just about fashion anymore. It's about an experience," New York retailer Ellen Carey told writer Jane Keltner in the July 2002 story, "House of Style," published in the U.S. edition of *Elle*. Carey is the proprietor of Seedhouse, a Manhattan by-appointment salon that sells furniture, art, clothing, and accessories from a Chelsea townhouse.

Private shopping in a cozy townhouse is also the idea behind Decollage, a "fashion gallery" in New York's West Village that features four theme rooms, including The Pink Penthouse and The Jade Room.

Across the Atlantic in London, designer Matthew Williamson hired his mother to oversee his private, one-off, appointment-only boutique, taking the personal touch to a whole new (and familial) level.

Private luxury shopping and large-scale event environments can be interpreted as a backlash – or, as some have aptly dubbed it, a "Gaplash" – to the monotony of mall culture and shoddy customer service. Something had to change.

Bring on the tea and champagne.

1999:
BLUEWATER,
KENT, ENGLAND

The Brits and Europeans have never been as eager to jump on the shopping mall bandwagon as their North American cousins. But the bigger-is-better, more-more-more attitude finally started to break through in the late 1990s. Nestled in the English countryside 40 minutes from London, shoppers will find Bluewater, Europe's largest shopping mall to date.

Comprised of three distinct malls and "leisure villages," the Bluewater shopping experience was designed with more than spending in mind. Fifty acres of landscaped parkland surround the three mall buildings, providing the perfect settling for a relaxing post-shopping nature stroll.

2002:
THE CAMP,
COSTA MESA, CALIFORNIA

Riding on the success of his "anti-mall," The Lab, developer Shaheen Sadeghi was at it again in 2002, this time with an innovative shopping experience aimed at outdoors enthusiasts. The Camp, which consists of five separate buildings joined by landscaped grounds designed to evoke a desert, a meadow, and even a

## Music to Shop By
### The big business of retail music

**R**iding an elevator must have been a pretty scary thing in the 1930s. If it hadn't, who's to say whether consumers today would be able to walk into stores like Pottery Barn or chain cafés like Starbucks and purchase compilation CDs of music hand-picked to enhance the company's image.

Perhaps I should explain.

In 1922, General George Squier developed a new technology that allowed music played on phonographs to be transmitted over electrical lines. He called his invention Muzak, a hybrid of "music" and one of his favorite companies, "Kodak." In 1934, Squier took Muzak to market, founding Muzak Corp, and carved out a niche for his company selling calming, soothing music that was piped into elevators to put nervous riders at ease.

Muzak was the first elevator music and became the granddaddy of the "business music" industry that now generates over half a billion dollars per year in the United States. Call it what you will: there's business music, retail music, foreground music, and background music, but it all translates into big bucks.

Muzak is classic background music – easy-listening sounds programmed in 15-minute intervals so cleverly that shoppers, clients, and elevator riders don't really notice it's there. Background music is designed to subconsciously set a mood, provoke a feeling, or encourage spending. According to Jane and Michael Stern's *Encyclopedia of Bad Taste*, one study

forest, is an experiment in extreme retailing.

The Billabong store features a full-scale skate ramp and wading pool for testing surfboards, while Liburdi's Scuba Center has a scuba training pool in-store. Shoppers can gather around The Camp's fire pit or take a yoga class. Called a "shopping playground" by New York trend-spotting agency, Youth Intelligence, The Camp represents a new chapter in mall history.

Ted Nugent.

showed that supermarket shoppers bought nearly 40 percent more when subjected to the subconscious shopping sounds of Muzak.

(Some, however, found Muzak more annoying than relaxing, including rocker Ted Nugent. In 1989, he offered to buy the company for $10 million for the expressed purpose of erasing the tapes and eradicating Muzak forever. His offer was not accepted.)

But back in the 1950s, background music was too new to annoy, and certain FM radio stations adopted a background music format specifically to be played in retail stores and homes. Muzak, too, had identified this market and had already expanded beyond elevators and into shops and homes as well, offering a three-channel subscription service that started in Cleveland and cost $1.50 each month.

Background music remained the sounds of choice for retailers until 1971 when AEI Music Network started selling the idea of foreground music. Instead of the music in retail outlets playing softly and going unnoticed, companies like AEI brought it out of the background and more overtly to the shopper's attention. This was no subliminal sell – the music made a statement.

Foreground music became a highly effective tool in building an image or brand. But building that brand took more than simply tuning the radio to the station the store's customers most likely listened to. AEI (which merged with competitor DMX Music in May 2001), PlayNetwork, and other foreground music content providers made it their business to program the right songs for the right business to project the right image - and get the shoppers shopping.

Subscription services enabled retailers to maintain consistency throughout their stores (so you could walk into any Gap anywhere and hear a similar four-hour loop), and eliminated the hassle of dealing with CDs and paying all the appropriate royalty fees (which were included in the subscription rate). Music content providers have something for everyone, offering hundreds of styles and sub-genres of music for very specific target markets. Consequently, subscription music has become the norm amongst retail powerhouses like the Gap, J. Crew, the Limited, and Bloomingdale's.

## Walk This Way

### *Fitness craze invades America's malls*

Imagine, if you will, that instead of working up a sweat at the gym you could get your heart going at your local shopping mall. Cashmere and shoes have had heart-racing effects on shoppers for decades, but shopping as actual exercise is relatively new.

Mall walking is simple: groups of walkers gather at the local mall early in the morning for a brisk walk – usually about 30 minutes – past the shops shortly before they open for the day. Most popular

Mall walkers.

with seniors and those who live in either very hot or very cold climates, mall walking is often promoted by community associations and by the malls themselves (which tend to offer walkers discounts at various retailers and food establishments to keep them in the mall after their walk).

Mall walking first registered on the pop culture radar around 1992, the same year WalkSport America founder, Sara Donovan, began partnering with malls across the U.S. to launch mall walking programs. Donovan is arguably mall walking's biggest champion and in fall 2002, her how-to fitness/lifestyle book, *Mall Walking Madness: Everything You Need to Know to Lose Weight and Have Fun at the Same Time*, was published.

That a person needs to shell out $16.95 for a book that teaches them how to walk around a mall may seem absurd to some. But the perception of absurdity is nothing new in the mall walking world. Since its first big splash in the early 1990s, mall walking and

Programmed foreground music had such an impressive impact on brand-building that by the late 1980s, retailers were starting to capitalize on the music-image connection in a whole new way: they started selling branded compilation CDs.

Lingerie chain Victoria's Secret was the first big name to issue custom CDs; *Classics by Request* by the London Symphony Orchestra was released in 1988. Soon the company best known for sexy models in sexy lingerie in sexy catalogs had also made a name for itself selling classical music. Since 1998 only 10 classical music CDs have sold more than one million copies in the United States and half were Victoria's Secret compilations.

Eddie Bauer, Old Navy, Banana Republic, Lane Bryant, Neiman Marcus, Pottery Barn, and Restoration Hardware have all issued custom compilations. But not one of those companies has taken its commitment to music as seriously as Starbucks.

The company, which has been selling its own CDs since 1995, has an in-house division – Hear Music – dedicated to selecting the songs you'll find on the next Starbucks release. The coffee company's CDs sell exceedingly well and have even earned the praises of at least one of the artists whose music has been featured. Singer-songwriter Shawn Colvin thanked the company in her Grammy acceptance speech in 1998, two years after one of her tunes appeared on Starbucks' *Songs of the Siren.*

It's impossible to know just how many retail-brand compilation CDs are sold each year, since there's no industry sales tracking system currently in place. But to say *lots* would be a gross understatement.

The appeal of the CDs may be attributed to factors other than the music. Jeff Daniel, executive vice-president of Rock River Communications, a New York company that specializes in putting together retail music compilations, has a couple of theories. Daniel suggested to *Business 2.0*'s Andy Raskin in the June 2002 issue that consumers like the CDs because it's an accessible and affordable way to get a piece of the lifestyle the store is selling.

He also noted that many shoppers are overwhelmed by mega-record stores and find it easier to pick up a disc at the checkout of Pottery Barn than to take on the daunting task of music shopping in a 10,000-square-foot store with endless choices.

The future of retail music looks rosy. In addition to compilation CDs, background music, and foreground music, stores are also starting to take things to the next – visual – level. Monitors playing music videos and short MTV News-style interview segments with the musical flavors of the month will further the music/retail image connection, particularly in shops catering to the youth market. It's a magic formula retailers have come to believe in: the right music and the right image just may equal big sales.

mall walkers have been the subject of much ridicule.

This is especially true in Europe and the U.K., where the very American idea of mall walking is baffling. To this point, BBCi's *Keeping an Eye on Oxford* website included mall walking as one of its top 10 American sayings Brits are confused by in its July 4, 2002 posting, "Independence Day Celebrated English Style." Finding its place alongside corn dogs, grits, and use of the word "shorts" to refer to male underwear, it seems mall walking is not the fitness fad destined to unite the world.

# Shopping at Home

*chapter*
**iv**

## MONTGOMERY WARD

The great-grandfather of the modern, general merchandise catalog, Aaron Montgomery Ward launched his mail-order business in Chicago in 1872. Prior to Ward's entry into the new world of shop-by-mail, catalogs had existed only as specialty publications, zeroing in on a particular type of goods. The tradition dates back as far as the sixteenth century when books were purchased via catalog in Venice. Two hundred years later, in the 1700s, the English adopted the practice of catalog shopping by ordering china through the mail. But neither the Italians nor the English attempted to broaden the scope of catalog shopping the way Ward did.

After a successful stint working for and learning from Chicago retailer Marshall Field, Ward struck out on his own. Drawing on his expertise as a store sales clerk, manager, and especially his experience as a traveling salesman, Ward sought to bring the shops to a rural population who, at that time, accounted for the majority of Americans.

A page from a Montgomery Ward catalog.

Farming was a big deal and farmers were potentially big customers. In 1860, there were two million farms in the United States; by 1900, that number had grown to 5.7 million. In 1880, 71.8 percent of the U.S. population lived in rural areas and by then many farm families were already shopping by mail thanks to Ward's catalog. The publication, which began as a simple one-sheet price list, was dubbed the "farmer's bible" and grew to a mammoth four-pound book by 1904.

Ward was practically guaranteed success from the get-go when he struck a deal with the agricultural organization, the National Grange (AKA the Order of Patrons of Husbandry). His affiliation with the Grange gave

Ward access to an eager clientele. The members of the fraternal order were, by many historical accounts, being gouged by shady salesmen taking advantage of the fact that farmers had limited access to a limited variety of merchandise and could not afford the time away from their land to take a horse and buggy into the nearest town to shop.

The potential of Ward's business became even greater as railway tracks connected the country. Built between 1860 and 1910, the railroad system enabled catalog companies to deliver merchandise promptly. The free rural delivery of mail, which began in 1896, also served to benefit Ward and his growing list of competitors.

The initial years of the general merchandise catalog were busy and profitable. At the turn of the century, Montgomery Ward and Co was posting $8.7 million in sales annually and Ward was labeled the first consumerist for his commitment to quality and customer satisfaction. In fact, he was the first to offer "satisfaction guaranteed": if you didn't like what you got, you could send it back for a refund.

But the times, as they say, were a-changing.

After Ward's death in 1913 (he was 69), the business soldiered on, but was slow to recognize and respond to cultural change. The advent of the automobile meant shoppers in pursuit of goods were able to travel longer distances in less time. It was also an era when the population base was shifting from the country to the city, and by 1920, for the first time, more Americans lived in urban settings than rural environments.

And with urban life came shopping - real, live, in-person-style shopping. James Cash Penney's J.C. Penney department stores were horning in on the catalog shopping business and in order to survive, Montgomery Ward and Co opened its first retail outlet in 1926.

But it was too little, too late, and Ward's would never recapture the glory it experienced in the early days of mail-order shopping. There was a brief glimmer of excitement when, in 1939, a Montgomery Ward copywriter created the Christmas character Rudolph the

Red-Nosed Reindeer for a seasonal promotion. But even a beloved children's character wasn't enough to restore magic to the brand.

The company's mail-order division, however, existed in tandem with its retail operation until 1985, when it was finally shut down. Fifteen years later, the company built by Aaron Montgomery Ward more than 100 years before was shuttered, and all 250 Ward's department stores were closed after a failed attempt to resuscitate the brand and the business.

## SEARS

There is one word used to describe Richard Warren Sears that pops up consistently: huckster. Not known for his business acumen or deft dealings, Sears was more of a showman, at times prone to exaggeration if it would help sell a product.

R.W. Sears

But the railroad agent and part-time watch seller knew a good thing when he saw it, and the mail-order model pioneered by Montgomery Ward piqued his interest. In 1886, Sears jumped into the business, selling watches by mail from his North Redwood, Minnesota base. Along the way he hired a watch repairman who would become an integral part of his next venture.

In 1888, Alvah C. Roebuck partnered with Sears to form a new company selling both jewelry and watches by catalog. By 1894, the partners had relocated to Chicago – a hub of American retail and mail-order – and expanded the selection of mail-order merchandise. Sears launched its first full-fledged general merchandise catalog à la Montgomery Ward and Co in 1896. It had 753 pages.

Although his name remained front and center, Alvah Roebuck had left the company (in 1895). It is Sears' new partner, clothing manufacturer Julius Rosenwald, who is often credited with having the business savvy to take Sears – and catalog shopping – to a whole new level.

Incorporated as Sears, Roebuck and Co, the Sears catalog – or the "Big Book" as it was nicknamed – grew big and grew fast, with Sears himself writing much of the catalogue's copy.

It was clear early on that Montgomery Ward had some serious competition in Sears and Rosenwald. While Ward was earnest in his offerings of quality wares, Sears was most concerned with price point and convenience, not to mention giving Ward a run for his money. Sears notoriously competed with Ward, assuming the slogan "The Cheapest Supply House of Earth" in 1894 when Ward's was already "The Cheapest Cash Supply House in America." Sears also imitated Ward's style with the 1896 slogan, "Satisfaction Guaranteed or Your Money Back."

Customers responded. The rural folk whose dollars drove the catalog shopping industry shelled out $1.273 million for Sears' catalog merchandise during the first year of the "Big Book" in 1896. Four years later, annual sales had jumped to $10.6 million, surpassing Ward's sales by nearly $2 million.

Sears, Roebuck and Co continued to grow by leaps and bounds, and wasn't even slowed by Richard Sears' retirement in 1908. By that time, customers could buy almost anything under the sun from the Sears catalog, including houses.

Sears' mail-order house business boomed in the 1920s, after the First World War. The kit homes, which included all building materials and, for an extra charge, a consultation with an interior designer, ranged in price from a mere $629 for the Selby model to almost $5,000 for the more deluxe Glen Falls house. Sears offered more than 80 home styles and by 1926 had sold more than 34,000 in the United States. Over 100,000 dotted the American landscape by 1934, the year Sears got out of the housing business as a result of the Great Depression.

Knowing when to get in and when to get out helped Sears, Roebuck and Co enormously in its early years. In 1925, Sears expanded its operations to include retail "catalog centers." The first, located on Chicago's west side, represented a new direction for the company. That year, Sears recorded sales of $243 million, 95 percent of which was done through catalog sales. Five years later, that figure had dropped dramatically, to 54 percent, the balance coming from its more than 300 stores. Retail, it was clear, was the wave of the future.

Sears' future still included its "Big Book" and seasonal catalogs like the *Christmas Wish Book*. But general merchandise catalog sales continued to decline as each decade passed, with customers favoring either shopping in person or ordering from specialty catalogs.

In 1993, a year when both the regular catalog and the *Christmas Wish Book* clocked in at over 1,600 pages, Sears closed its in-house catalog division, choosing instead to license its name to specialty catalogs. Sears did, however, bring back the *Wish Book* two years later.

But the saga of Sears and catalogs was not over yet. In 2002, Sears acquired the mail-order company, Lands' End, for $1.9 billion. Lands' End issued its first catalog, selling sailing equipment, in 1964; in 1975, the catalog first featured clothing, which is what it would later become known for.

Sears' plan for the catalog company includes bringing the preppy, sporty line to a retail customer. There's no word on whether, or for how long, the catalog will survive.

## NEIMAN MARCUS

Inspired by the response to the company's corporate Christmas card one year earlier, the first Neiman Marcus catalog made its debut in 1927. The high-end, Dallas-based retailer of ready-to-wear apparel, was no stranger to success.

The store, the brainchild of Herbert Marcus, his sister Carrie Marcus Neiman, and her husband Al, opened its doors in 1907. Business at Neiman Marcus was solid from day one and turned a profit in its first year. And the introduction of the catalog (or "The Book," as it was called) served to enhance the store's exclusive image.

The Neiman Marcus image was overseen for nearly 50 years by Herbert's son, Stanley, beginning in the 1920s. Known as "Mr Stanley" to employees, the younger Marcus was responsible for turning the release of the holiday catalog into a much-anticipated media event.

The Neiman Marcus catalog featured more upscale goods than many of its competitors, but there was nothing that made "The Book" stand out until, in 1960, Stanley Marcus introduced pricey, gimmicky His & Hers gifts as the centerpiece of the seasonal catalog. Marcus himself is said to have searched the world over for just the right outrageous feature gifts for the catalog until his retirement in 1975.

Through the years, the catalog has offered His & Hers camels, His & Hers jogging outfits, and His & Hers Thunderbirds. Other unique gifts have included a 100-year subscription to *The Wall Street Journal* for $6,000 in 1986, and the auction of a year of unlimited world travel for two and your name painted prominently on the nose of a brand-new United Airlines Boeing 777 in 1995 (the bidding began at $100,000). In 1969, the Honeywell H316 "Kitchen Computer" that is commonly believed to be the world's first home computer was sold through the Neiman Marcus catalog for $10,600.

But perhaps of all the oddities sold through the catalog, the 1971 purchase of two Egyptian mummy coffins ranks as oddest. The two coffins were sold for $5,000 to the Ancient and Mystical Order Rosae Crucis. The coffins were then authenticated and, along the way, opened. Much to everyone's surprise, one of the coffins still contained a mummy, a priest called Usermontu. Today, the coffins (and the only mummy ever bought by catalog) reside at the Rosicrucian Egyptian Museum in San Jose, California.

This sub was in the 1963 Neiman Marcus Christmas Book. It was pitched as "The Ultimate in Togetherness." The copy read: "Designed to carry two people, it cruises at a speed of 3 to 7.3 miles per hour. The slightly buoyant Mini Sub has a hull of plastic impregnated laminated glass cloth. 14 feet long, 46 inches high, 90 inches wide. It weighs 975 pounds. Battery operated. One horsepower motor. $18,700 f.o.b., Dallas."
*(From Stanley Marcus, His & Hers: The Fantasy World of the Neiman Marcus Catalogue, NY: Viking Press, 1982.)*

# Pink Cars, Plastic Bowls, and Friends for Life

*A history of home shopping parties*

**I**t's an attractive idea: set your own hours, work at home, and make some cash selling products to family and friends. Since the 1930s, direct sales gatherings – or home parties – have been the forum for selling jewelry, clothing, books, housewares, and more.

But it wasn't until 1948, when a little-known American household plastics line that was gathering dust on retail shelves adopted home parties as its primary selling strategy, that the concept truly took off.

Tupperware, the modern plastics brand with the patented air-tight seal, had been introduced by former DuPont employee Earl Silas Tupper in 1946, but sales at hardware and department stores were dismal. The newfangled, durable plastic containers (made of synthetic polymer polyethylene) with the sealing lids confused customers.

Not everyone was confused by Tupper's invention, however. Direct sellers of Stanley Home Products discovered Tupperware and recognized its potential, but envisioned a different selling approach. The keenest of the Stanley sellers was a divorced single mother from Detroit who sold Stanley to supplement her income as a secretary. Brownie Wise knew Tupperware would take off, if only women had a friendly face to guide them through the line, and the chance to check out the pastel-colored bathroom tumblers and Poly-T Wonder Bowls up close.

Wise and her Tupperware Parties were a huge hit. In 1951, she was appointed the company's vice-president of sales and distribution after her concept had generated more than $25 million in sales in just three years. She also became the first woman to grace the cover of *Business Week* magazine.

The secret of Wise's success wasn't exclusively the product itself. Women loved the handy practicality and colorful design of Tupperware, but by selling through home parties, she also helped the brand infiltrate a new American frontier: the suburbs.

The typical suburb of the 1950s was sold as a friendly, family-oriented utopia, all new and shiny and squeaky clean. The suburbs were the new American Dream. But day-to-day life in these vast new developments could be isolating – even boring – for many of the housewives who cooked, cleaned, and raised their small children inside the houses with the perfect white picket fences. Selling Tupperware, hosting parties, or merely attending one as a guest, was a welcome diversion from the hum-drum monotony of suburban reality.

Tupperware's direct selling home parties created a model for home party companies to come and the format remains virtually unchanged since its early years.

Most home parties work something like this: a local representative, consultant, or distributor (take your pick; they're all the same) finds someone interested in hosting a party in their home. The host – or, most likely, the *hostess* – supplies the coffee, the snacks, and the most significant contribution, the guests. At the party, it's the rep's job to do the demos, answer questions, and take orders. For her trouble, the hostess will usually receive a discount on any purchases she chooses to make and might be given a small gift. And the guests? All they need is a checkbook.

It looks simple. It sounds simple. But making real money as a home party rep can be difficult. Many of the companies operate on multi-level compensation structure – more than three-quarters of all direct sellers are multi-level, according to the Direct Selling Association (DSA). With home parties accounting for 27.7 percent of all direct sales in the U.S. as of 2000, that's a whole lot of multiple levels.

Popularly known as "pyramids," people can be skeptical of getting involved with multi-level direct sales. New multi-level sellers don't get much of a paycheck since they're working solely on commission and the rates are typically low. To move up, the newbie needs to recruit more reps for the company and work up to regional director status to receive a cut of every sale made by those under her. The process repeats itself with the higher levels, but just like a pyramid, there's only room for a few select achievers at the top.

Even when a home party company doesn't operate on a multi-level system, it may require its representatives to purchase a minimum inventory at regular intervals, pay for training or upgrading, or buy her own samples. Add up the required ongoing investment and a seller may end up *losing* money.

Not all of the six percent of Americans currently working as direct sellers will fall prey to these common traps. Few representatives make six figures a year, but then, many of the sellers aren't in it for the money. The sense of camaraderie created by direct sellers is an equally important draw. Between local meetings, regional, national, and global conventions, representatives are constantly encouraged by the appeal of the community the company creates. Bottom line: it's all about belonging.

Belonging can mean bonding with colleagues at motivational seminars and awards ceremonies honoring the achievements of top representatives. It can mean cheers and chants and belting out the company song on cue. Just consider the lyric for the official Tupperware song:

"I've got that Tupper feeling deep in my heart
Deep in my heart
Deep in my heart
I've got that Tupper feeling deep in my heart
Deep in my heart to stay."

The concepts of community, bonding, and belonging extend beyond the reps to the home party hosts and guests, but the experience isn't always positive. The host may have been approached by a friend or family member representing a home party company and feels obliged to open her home. The guests, in turn, may feel obliged to the host and end up shelling out for items they don't really need or want.

Certainly not all of the billions generated each year through home parties are made out of a sense of obligation. There are plenty of home party hosts who agree to host a party (or perhaps seek one out) as a result of genuine interest in and enthusiasm for a product line. Or she might simply think a home party will be fun and a great excuse to get together with friends.

However you look at it, home parties are a social experience. And some direct selling companies take the togetherness aspect of the parties business to remarkable levels.

Mary Kay Cosmetics, the direct selling company founded by the late Mary Kay Ash in 1963, emphasizes the importance of a selling sisterhood in its literature. The company holds weekly unit-sales meetings for its 850,000 "sales force members" to bond with and offer support to their colleagues. To promote the key Mary Kay sales principle that representatives not be isolated from each other, a nugget of Ash's core business philosophy is evoked. "In business for yourself but not by yourself," company literature states.

Mary Kay is famous for its home parties and its social business structure, but it's infamous for something else. Pink - or, more specifically, the exact shade of bubble gum pink every Mary Kay product comes packaged in - represents the ultimate achievement in the Mary Kay world, the highest echelon of the home party makeup and skincare corporate ladder. Once a sales force member has been awarded the Diamond Bee Pin, has earned dangling gold rung upon rung on her Golden Ladder Pin, and slips into her complementary (pink) designer suit signifying her status in the company, there's only one big step remaining.

"Pink," as it's plainly known, means pink alright - a Mary Kay pink signature Cadillac. Since 1969, when Ash had her own car dyed the same color as her corporate packaging, over 10,000 pink Cadillacs have been bestowed on the cream of the Mary Kay sales crop.

It's hard to compete with pink Caddies and diamond

pins, but even without extravagant incentives, repping home party lines is as popular as ever.

There is also a wide range of product lines to choose from. If it's linen you like, you may want to sign on at Linen World. There's Discovery Toys, DK Books, the rapidly growing Pampered Chef, and the scrapbooking home party brand, Creative Memories.

Kids' toys, household wares, and crafts make up a significant portion of the home party market, but there's no shortage of options for sellers, hosts, and buyers who are looking for something a little more naughty than nice.

Lingerie home parties surfaced in the 1980s. A group of women would gather, drink white wine spritzers, giggle, try items on, giggle, peruse catalogs chock full of sexy stuff, then whip out their wallets (and giggle again). This girls-night-out theme was taken a step further in the early 1990s when party brands began to add sex toys, games, and accessories to their repertoire. The companies – sporting names like Sensations, LoveWorks, and PassionPlus – also began actively marketing parties to couples.

Regardless of clever marketing ploys and campaigns aimed at couples and at men, it always has been – and still is – women who are the driving force behind the success of home party companies, and the Direct Selling Association estimates that 72.5 percent of all direct sellers are female.

And you'd better make that *global* females. Contrary to popular perception, home parties are not an exclusively North American phenomenon. Mary Kay has reps in more than 30 countries and territories. Creative Memories consultants can be found worldwide, in countries like Germany, Japan, Australia, and Taiwan. Tupperware does $1.2 billion in sales every year and has representatives in more than 100 countries around the world; more than 85 percent of its total sales are made outside the U.S.

The global growth of home parties is just one of the factors contributing to an image shift in the business. Instead of threatening business and pulling away customers, the Internet has proven a useful resource for company reps, potential hosts, and customers alike. Companies have had to carefully think out their online strategy (will the Internet simply be a product showcase and an advertisement for the parties, or will customers be able to purchase products as well?). Like many established direct sellers, Tupperware has found a place for itself on the Internet and has created a way for web users to throw online parties.

That doesn't mean your friendly neighborhood Tupperware lady is a thing of the past. But the face of today's Tupperware Lady may not be who you'd expect. Take the face of Phranc, for instance.

Phranc with Tupperware.

One of Tupperware's leading American representatives, Phranc made a career for herself in the 1980s as a modestly successful, self-proclaimed, "all American Jewish folk singer" who just happened to be a butch lesbian who sang songs like "Do the Bull Dagger Swagger." Today Phranc has settled into a life of selling Tupperware in Los Angeles, and her selling success and passion for Tupperware was captured on film in Lisa Udelson's 2002 documentary, *Lifetime Guarantee: Phranc's Adventure in Plastic.*

Another face not traditionally associated with home parties has also surfaced. The upscale, society glamorpuss was the last woman you'd expect to be hostessing a home party, but believe it or not, she is. It's not Tupperware, Mary Kay, or The Pampered Chef she's into, though.

Well-to-do ladies in the U.S. have taken to throwing home party parties for exclusive kids' clothing lines like Petit Patapon, Emma T., and Kule. The society-set women may prefer to label their home parties as *trunk shows*, but they're direct selling home parties nonetheless.

Home parties featuring high-end kids' clothes is a burgeoning business, but it's unlikely to be the next Tupperware. That title, as anyone who's read a women's magazine in the twenty-first century, knows, is reserved for Botox.

Home parties during which women (and sometimes men) have wrinkle-smoothing Botulinum Toxin Type A injected into their face first came to attention in England in late 2000. One year later, the trend had hit North

American cities like New York, Palm Beach, and Beverly Hills. And by mid-2002, when the Federal Drug Administration (FDA) approved the use of Botox for wrinkle treatment, Botox parties had become a much buzzed-about topic in the press.

In an effort to turn-that-frown-upside-down (or at least smooth it out a little), women (and men) pay between $300–1000 to have the 15-minute procedure done en masse in the company of friends. But research conducted by the American Society of Plastic Surgeons (ASPS) in the summer of 2002 suggests that Botox parties are more hype than reality. An online survey by the ASPS found that only three percent of potential Botox users were comfortable with the idea of receiving injections in a home party setting; 93 percent felt safer having it done privately, in a doctor's office.

Tupperware, it seems, will continue to reign as the king (or rather, queen) of home party products for years to come.

# Clash of the Home Shopping Titans

*QVC squares off against HSN live – in your living room*

───────────────── ▢ ─────────────────

**T**he 1980s gave shoppers lots of things: over-sized shoulder pads and unflattering spandex among them. But the greed-is-good decade also introduced super-size shopping centers, outlet malls, and a glut of American mall movies, and brought the retail store into private homes, via home shopping cable networks. Just pick up the telephone, call in, have your credit card ready, and – presto! – you could be the proud owner of a cat-shaped crystal figurine, a decorative pair of clown dolls (one happy, one sad), or a gaudy cubic zirconia ring.

In its infancy, TV home shopping was considered trashy and low-brow. The products – and, quite often, the hosts – were tacky and kitschy. But its reputation didn't stop the format from becoming a smashing success. Viewers watched and shopped, dropping millions of dollars on clothing, jewelry, housewares, and assorted trinkets. And while they were spending, competition was brewing between the original home shopping channel, the Home Shopping Network (HSN), and its upstart, more upscale rival, QVC (which stands for Quality Value Convenience).

For nearly 20 years, the two networks have gone toe-to-toe and head-to-head in an effort to woo new shoppers and keep the old ones coming back for more. So, which is biggest? Which is best? Which nabs the title of Most-Shopped TV Network in the World? Read on.

## FOUNDING FATHERS

HSN: When radio station owner Lowell "Bud" Paxson and real estate developer Roy Speer founded the Home Shopping Network in 1981, no one could have known what different paths the two men's lives would take. Paxson would find God, while Speer would find himself dealing with an angry IRS.

A former radio announcer, Paxson was "born again"

in – where else? – Las Vegas in 1986, and has never been shy about expressing his beliefs publicly. In 1991, after selling his stake in HSN and the infomercial production company, Silver King Communications, Paxson embarked on a new media venture: the PAX TV network, which airs programming promoting family values and spirituality.

He takes his commitment to both TV and to God very seriously. As he told *USA Today* in 1998, "We've seen the Lord's hand in blessing this business, and have tried to honor that. When it came time to choose our programming, we said, 'How can we put on programs that He might not want to watch?'"

Paxson's former partner Speer, on the other hand, left the business in December 1992 with $160 million. He retained the position of chairman at HSN until the next year, when he cashed in his remaining stock for about $100 million and stepped down – but not before being accused of taking kickbacks from HSN suppliers. A few years later his personal finances were also in question as the Internal Revenue Service audited the multi-millionaire businessman, eventually taking him to court. In the end there was little doubt that Speer was a master of manipulating the American tax system, but a judge ruled that his dealings were legit and that ended the matter.

QVC: At age 63, when most of his peers were making a graceful segue into retirement, Franklin Mint founder Joseph Segel was busy launching QVC. Not many analysts had high hopes for the fledgling channel, which entered the market after 17 other shopping channels, including giants HSN and the Cable Value Network (CVN). Early numbers were bleak, but Segel stuck to it and in 1989 had bought out CVN, even though the company was twice QVC's size.

Skeptics were wrong to doubt the savvy of Joseph Segel, a man who started his first business – a printing company – at age 13 and began his studies at the prestigious Wharton School of Business just three years later. He founded The Franklin Mint, a mail-order business specializing in collectibles like decorative plates and porcelain dolls, in 1964 and was with the company until 1973. He spent seven years building QVC into a home shopping powerhouse, then retired in 1993. In 2000, he emerged again, this time backing an online stop-smoking program called *smokestoppers.com*. He also owns the swanky Le Mirador Resort and Spa on Lake Geneva, Switzerland.

## EARLY DAYS

HSN: After a successful year on Tampa Bay, Florida cable access in 1981, the world's first home shopping channel (then called just that – the Home Shopping Channel) jumped to regular cable in the Tampa area in 1982. The new concept really made waves in July 1985, when the newly-named Home Shopping Club went live nationwide. Viewers quickly embraced the format – no matter how down-market the merchandise – and made pseudo-celebrities of the channel's hosts, including Carmella Richards, whose signature was squeezing a bicycle horn when she got worked up over whatever she happened to be hawking.

QVC: Following in the footsteps of HSN and the Minnesota-based shopping channel, CVN, QVC went to air November 24, 1986, pledging a higher standard of quality than the competition. Based in West Chester, Pennsylvania, the channel promoted its "classy" image by hiring hosts who were more polished than their counterparts at HSN. The network took on the daunting task of fighting the stigmas associated with TV shopping by refusing to adopt the hard sell approach to sales and by not imposing shopping time limits on merchandise.

## BIG NUMBERS

HSN: The network did $1.93 billion in sales worldwide in 2001, employs approximately 4,400 people, and receives over 80 million calls per year. HSN ships 47 million packages annually and sells about 22,000 different products.

QVC: The stats are staggering over at QVC, which surpassed rival HSN in sales back in 1993. The network does more than $3.9 billion in sales every year, employs about 14,000 people, and received more than 133 million calls in 2001. That same year, QVC shipped over 92 million units and featured an average total of 1,680 products on air per week.

# Big Brands

HSN: It's all the usual home, beauty, and entertainment labels at HSN. The network sells goods from big brands such as Sony, Hewlett Packard, Panasonic, and Hoover. Sports-branded merchandise is also popular, with products emblazoned with Major League Baseball, NBA, NASCAR, and NFL logos. On the fashion front, designer Randolph Duke launched an exclusive clothing line on HSN in 2001, and the network sells both the Lauren Hutton Beauty line and Jacqueline Kennedy brand jewelry.

QVC: There's T-Fal and Kitchen Aid and Spalding. There's Kodak, Sega, Nintendo, and Sony. There's the exclusive deal with Warner Brothers stores to deliver Bugs Bunny and Daffy Duck merchandise direct to the homes of QVC shoppers. And fitting with QVC's upscale image, there's goods by Coach Fine Leathers, Kenneth Cole, Esprit, Dooney & Burke, and Smashbox cosmetics.

## Global Reach

HSN: The Home Shopping Network can be seen in six countries across the globe. In addition to its U.S. operation, viewers in Germany, Japan, China, France, and Belgium can shop from home.

QVC: While the number of households with QVC outside of the U.S. account for just a smidgen less than one-third of the total 125.6 million homes which receive the channel worldwide, international versions of the network are growing. Currently, QVC can be seen in Ireland, the United Kingdom, Germany, and Japan.

## Celebrity Factor:

HSN: So many B-list celebrities, so much stuff to sell. HSN pioneered the concept of celebrity sales and has played host to everyone from Suzanne Somers and Susan Lucci to chef Wolfgang Puck, socialite Ivana Trump, and interiors expert Christopher Lowell.

QVC: The queen of celebrity home shopping, Joan Rivers, calls QVC home. But Rivers is certainly not the only star to turn up on the channel. In 1997, on the network's late-night "variety show," *First Friday: Extreme Shopping*, singer Engelbert Humperdinck put his $3.95 million L.A. pad on the block. Diet and exercise motivator

Richard Simmons has sold his products on QVC, and where-are-they-now types like Britt Ekland and Catherine Bach have also been known to talk up the goods.

## SEX AND SCANDAL

HSN: After riding high as king of TV shopping for years, HSN's reputation (and bottom line) was tarnished in 1993 when co-founder and chairman Roy Speer and other top execs were accused of shady business dealings. The accusations resulted in several lawsuits and a federal grand jury investigation into the alleged financial improprieties. The investigation ended in April 1994 with no criminal charges being filed, although damage to the company's name had already been done.

QVC: Who's hot? Who's hottest? QVC host Jill Bauer, apparently. According to the 125 (presumably male) respondents to an online poll at *ezboard.com*, the former Orange County Junior Miss is the number one answer to the question: Which QVC host makes you want to masturbate? The host, who has been with the network since December 1993, captured 38.4 percent of the total votes. That must make her – and her employer – very proud.

# But Wait! Call Now!

*All about infomercials*

**B**lame it on Ronald Reagan. When the former U.S. president approved the Federal Communications Commission's deregulation of the number of commercial minutes per hour on American television in June 1984, he sparked the growth of a new advertising medium: the infomercial.

Infomercials as corporate films or videos dates back to 1936 when *Night Mail*, a 24-minute film commissioned by Britain's Travelling Post Office, was made. But the consumer-targeted, modern television infomercial didn't make its mark until the mid-1980s.

Often produced on shoestring budgets and aired in late-night time slots when advertising minutes are relatively inexpensive, the long-format, shop-at-home commercials soon became the domain of quirky miracle products, hokey demonstrations, and over-enthusiastic testimonials.

The paid programming advertisements which, by definition, run from 30 to 60 minutes each, became a showcase for the likes of veteran TV marketer Ron Popeil of Ronco, motivational speaker Tony Robbins, and the ever-Sweatin'-To-the-Oldies Richard Simmons, as well as a haven for Hollywood actresses whose careers had seen better

Richard Simmons

days. The spokesperson as celebrity or, transversely, the celebrity as spokesperson, quickly became a trademark of infomercial production.

Fitness guru Billy Blanks became a household name in 1999 thanks to his high-energy TaeBo infomercials (which, in turn, featured testimonials by B-grade celebrities such as Shannon Tweed, Carmen Electra, and

Sinbad). Television actresses of a certain age like Victoria Principal (*Dallas*), Connie Selleca (*Hotel*), and Judith Light (*Who's the Boss*) found a new audience thanks to their spokesperson gigs for skin care lines Principal Secret, Selleca Solution, and ProActiv. And who could ignore

Suzanne Somers with a ThighMaster.

the success of *Three's Company*'s Suzanne Somers, whose infomercial pitch work for the ThighMaster resulted in product sales of more than $110 million?

Sports stars are also highly sought after spokespeople for infomercials. Quick-fix exercise programs and equipment are a mainstay of infomercials, and a testimonial from a famous athlete lends an air of legitimacy to the product. That is, if you don't take a moment to think about the chubby paycheck the athlete receives for his effort.

Basketball player Shaquille O'Neal thinks Billy Blanks' TaeBo is the best. Former champion figure skater Tai Babilonia can't get enough of the Balance Bracelet. And along with his wife Kris, 1976 Olympic gold medallist Bruce Jenner launched SuperFit, his own infomercial series.

Athletes and TV stars aren't the only ones who have dabbled in the world of infomercials. Politicians, too, have been known to get in on the act.

In 1992, presidential candidate Ross Perot became the first politician to produce an infomercial to present his views and attempt to win votes. Perot, of course, failed in his bid for the White House. Instead, he was labeled a nutter, with many political pundits agreeing that his infomercial experiment did more damage than good.

But Perot's failure did not stop subsequent political candidates from snapping up airtime for their own infomercials – that is, if the broadcasters chose to accept their money. Perot himself had trouble getting his second infomercial on television in 1996, with many broadcasters simply refusing to air it. And during the 2000 federal election, broadcasters snubbed an infomercial effort by the Natural Law Party, which had recruited award-winning film director David Lynch to produce the largely unseen spot promoting presidential candidate John Hagelin.

## Who *Are* These People?

### *The average television shopper unveiled*

Ever wonder who calls in, credit card in hand, as soon as that toll-free number pops up during an infomercial? Well, according to a survey of the 2001 market conducted by The AfterMarket Co and *Response* magazine, the typical as-seen-on-TV shopper isn't necessarily who you'd think.

She's probably a Caucasian who's married, owns a home, and has a household income of $56,000 or more. She's most likely to order exercise-related products (which accounts for 43 percent of products sold) or diet/health/weight items (33 percent), and order from television two to four times per year. She's between 45 and 55 years old and it's often the on-air product demonstrations that seals the deal.

But the best news – at least for the industry – is that she's happy with the product when it arrives about two-thirds of the time, and two of every three buyers would buy from TV again.

From politicians angling for a vote to the latest kitchen or fitness revelation, within a decade of the Reagan era the infomercial business had grown into an industry of its own. And like many industries, the direct-response television (or DRTV as it's known in the business) community began to celebrate its own with awards for infomercial excellence.

Every fall in Las Vegas the Electronic Retailing Association (formerly known as the National Infomercial Marketing Association) bestows best-of awards on writers, products, producers, and hosts. In 2000, the Infomercial of the Year Award went to ProActiv 5; the next year the folks behind the Ab Doer took home the prize for Best Infomercial Product.

If the idea of official infomercial awards gives you a bit of a giggle, you're not alone. Infomercial makers are no strangers to snickers and - particularly - to being at the wrong end of countless jokes.

Infomercials have always been ripe for parody. The late comic Chris Farley played fictional cosmetics queen Lori Davis on *Saturday Night Live*, while Jim Carrey garnered laughs as the character Jimmy Tango of "Jimmy Tango's Fat Buster" when hosting *SNL*. Other sketch comedy shows like *MadTV* and *Mr Show* took on infomercials as well.

There are plenty of short film infomercial parodies to be found online, as well as sites that celebrate infomercial absurdity (try Ridiculous Infomercial Review at *Infomercial@TVHaven.com*). Canadian music group Barenaked Ladies got in on the act as well by producing an infomercial spoof for their "Too Little Too Late" DVD single. But perhaps the most unusual of all infomercial parodies is the 1998 adult video, *The Best Butt in the West 2*, which is a pornographic mock-infomercial for "The Buttalizer."

However amusing, it's unlikely that the future of infomercials lies in porn. In fact, the next big thing may just be as far from pornography as you can get. In recent years, established, big-brand businesses like America Online (partnered with another biggie, Phillips Electronics), *Monster.com*, and high-end car maker, Mercedes-Benz have ventured into infomercials, possibly signaling a shift from crass to class.

But don't look for the infomercial to lose its comedy value anytime soon. Or, for that matter, its appeal for millions of shoppers. According to the Direct Marketing Association (DMA), infomercial sales are well over $100 billion annually and are growing; by 2005 the DMA predicts sales will be about $180 billion, which means there's still all kinds of kitchen inventions, miracle skin creams, and exercise programs to be sold – and maybe even a few luxury cars too.

## Click, Click, Send

*The evolution of cybershopping*

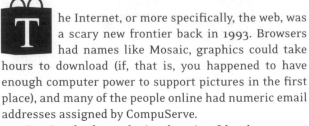

**T**he Internet, or more specifically, the web, was a scary new frontier back in 1993. Browsers had names like Mosaic, graphics could take hours to download (if, that is, you happened to have enough computer power to support pictures in the first place), and many of the people online had numeric email addresses assigned by CompuServe.

Previously the exclusive domain of hard core computer geeks, the web was starting to attract the attention of ordinary home computer users, and subsequently, the attention of enterprising companies exploring its potential for sales and marketing.

Individuals had used the Internet to buy, sell, and swap goods via email or text-based bulletin boards before the web came along. But the World Wide Web (media outlets seemed compelled to use the name in its entirety and offer a long-winded definition with every mention) was different. The use of graphics and photos on the web opened up a new world of possibilities for businesses – if only they could figure out how to best harness the promising new tool.

Approximately $200 million worth of goods were sold online in 1993, but someone had yet to sell anything on any significant scale.

Enter Randy Adams and Bill Rollinson. Adams, a MIT grad and former director of engineering for Adobe Systems, teamed up with marketing man Rollinson, who had worked at companies like Macromedia, to found the Internet Shopping Network (ISN) in June 1993. Capitalized with $250,000, ISN was up and running market trials in April of the next year. By September 1994, the California company had caught the eye of the mammoth Home Shopping Network and was gobbled up for an undisclosed sum.

At the outset, ISN dealt mainly in computer hardware and software, as many web users were computer junkies and out-and-proud geeks. But as use of the web spread, so did the variety of merchandise carried by ISN, and soon shoppers could send flowers by FTD and purchase products featured in the Hammacher-Schlemmer catalog.

It was all very exciting – except for those pesky security issues that kept popping up.

Customers were leery of shopping online, fearing their credit card information might be stolen in transit or that the unfamiliar shopping environment was somehow a sham. Such uncertainty created headaches for the growing number of online shops.

Buying from ISN or its contemporaries typically involved several key steps. At ISN, shoppers would register free of charge as a "member" and would provide personal information like their address and credit card number over the phone. They would then be assigned a "membership code" to shop with so personal data was kept entirely offline, and therefore, protected.

Other online retailers employed even more elaborate systems. The first department store company to try their hand at online selling was Seattle, Washington-based Nordstrom, Inc.

During the holiday season of 1994, Nordstrom experimented with a shop-by-email service that circumvented funds transfer issues by having shoppers place an order by email, then call a toll-free number to pay by credit card. Shopping exclusively via email meant, however, that a customer had to be very familiar with (and very sure of) exactly what they wished to buy. To do that they would likely have had to visit a store or perused a catalog. Shopping online by email was primarily a novelty, as it was probably faster and more convenient to simply walk into a store to buy or order by catalog.

The Internet Shopping Network was not so much a novelty. The site was bringing in over $1 million per month two years after its launch in the fall of 1996, and the potential of e-commerce, e-tailing, e-everything was about to explode.

Investors began throwing piles of money at web-based businesses and, for a time, the future of retail, of shopping, of shoppers, seemed to be online.

Web shopping of the late 1990s was full of promise. Retailers from the bricks-and-mortar "real world" turned out in droves, often introducing complicated websites that confused and frustrated users. Much of the time, online shopping was more trouble than it was worth.

The boom of online shopping sites was impressive, but not as spectacular as its bust. In the late '90s, consumers were still hesitant about buying online, even though many of the security issues that surfaced in the early days of web shopping had been eliminated. And the dot-com crash certainly didn't serve to boost confidence. After all, why would anyone in their right mind buy something from a company that could very well have its assets (and its stock) seized the very next day?

Still, online retailers persisted. Every big "real world" brand and store had a web presence. Turning a profit online was next to impossible, but those with deep enough pockets dug in their heels, determined to wait it out, always improving and tweaking their concepts and learning from others' mistakes.

Miss Boo from *Boo.com*.

Web-exclusive shops had a tougher time. Shades of Darwinism crept over the World Wide Web as big-name category killers like *Amazon.com* hung on while the lesser of the online shopping species were killed off and forced into bankruptcy.

Perhaps the splashiest of all online shopping disasters was *Boo.com*. The Swedish apparel site was designed to be the be-all, end-all of global web shopping and targeted the influential and fashion-forward youth market. But the *Boo.com* experience, which launched at the tail end of 1999, was plagued with problems from the start. The biggest issue was that many users' browsers didn't support the sophisticated 3D graphics the site employed, rendering shopping difficult, if not impossible.

The media outlets that had bought into the inflated hype of *Boo.com* months earlier reveled in its fall from grace. The press documented its estimated expenditures of more than $200 million in its short, six-month life and heckled the computer-generated fashion advice doled out by the site's "personal shopper," Miss Boo.

*Boo.com*'s assets were eventually bought out by *Fashionmall.com* and a much more modest site relaunched on October 30, 2000. But the situation had many experts thinking about just how much and how fast consumers were willing to spend online. It also raised important questions regarding exactly *what* shoppers were inclined to spend their hard-earned dollars on.

Only one thing was certain – it wasn't clothing.

While beauty products sites such as *Sephora.com* and *Gloss.com* flourished, moving mass market clothing over the web was difficult. No matter how accurate online fitting rooms (that virtually dressed customers in a chosen ensemble after they'd keyed in their body measurements) had become, the fear of improper fit and misrepresentation of merchandise caused many shoppers to shy away from buying clothes online.

There were a few exceptions. Selling beauty products over the web worked because customers often purchased known products and brands. They shopped online for convenience, price point, or due to geographical location (contrary to popular belief there is not a giant, real-world Sephora store in every small town in America). The same theory could be applied to apparel. In other words, if a customer knew the exact style, exact label, and exact size of a particular garment, ordering online would be just fine, but that was not the reality.

Customers were, to some extent, willing to take a risk buying clothing online if an item scored high points in one of two categories: uniqueness or price.

Rare vintage clothing sellers quickly found a home online, while access to hard-to-get designer goods through sites such as *eLuxury.com* proved handy for shoppers with a serious credit limit and not enough time. Conversely, the inexpensive, trendy teen togs sold at *Delias.com* caught on with the adolescent girl set and designer outlet sites like *Bluefly.com* catered to shoppers trolling for a bargain.

The unspoken rule about online clothes shopping went something like this: if you couldn't get that piece for that price in the real world, well then, *maybe* you'd consider buying online.

Clothing sales may have proved slow and disappointing, but adventurous shoppers were happy to try ordering hard goods like books, CDS, DVDS, and video games online. The web also proved a place for shoppers to get advice about "real world" purchases, gather consumer reports, and compare prices. At sites such as *eopinions.com*, shoppers can read reviews of products written by consumers; at *mySimon.com*, a search engine compares prices from sites all across the web to help shoppers get the best price for what they want.

And if what they want makes them blush with embarrassment, shoppers can always turn to the likes of *PrivateBuy.com* and *ShopInPrivate.com* to shop online anonymously. From birth control to pornography to hemorrhoid treatments, shy types have single-handedly fuelled the payment-for-privacy industry.

Hard-to-find items, sexual paraphernalia, discount shopping, and consumer advice – take one or more of these factors, add a simple, easy-to-use website, and an online shopping hit may not be far behind. Better yet, roll all five factors into one dazzling website.

A discounted, discontinued, explicit sexual instructional video about male masturbation with an impeccable customer satisfaction rating, anyone? On second thought, maybe not.

# Never Pay Retail: Shopping for Bargains

chapter

v

# From Five-and-Dimes to Dollar Stores

*Discount retailers give shoppers more bang for their buck*

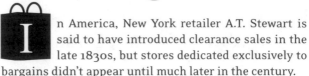

n America, New York retailer A.T. Stewart is said to have introduced clearance sales in the late 1830s, but stores dedicated exclusively to bargains didn't appear until much later in the century.

Arguably the most influential and copied early discount store model was that conceived by farmer-turned-merchant Frank Winfield Woolworth. Inspired by the clearance tables favored by shop owners of the time, Woolworth believed there was a market for stores that sold only discount merchandise. Items sold on retail clearance tables were typically priced at five cents apiece, and Woolworth's first store mimicked this pricing scheme.

But the five-cent bargain stores Woolworth pioneered were not an immediate success.

On February 22, 1879, Woolworth opened what he called the "Great Five-Cent Store" in Utica, New York. Two weeks of consumer excitement and curiosity followed, but died down quickly, forcing Woolworth to close his shop. He did not, however, abandon his vision – he simply relocated it.

His next venture was an unqualified success. Expanding his range of stock to include 10-cent items, Woolworth opened The Great Five-and-Ten-Cent Store in Lancaster, Pennsylvania on June 21, 1879. The clunky-sounding name was later changed to bear its founder's name: F.W. Woolworth & Co.

Red Woolworth's store fronts spread throughout North America and along the way, made its namesake family very, very rich. In fact, when F.W.'s granddaughter, the infamous Barbara Hutton, was born, the press nicknamed her "the million dollar baby."

Hutton did indeed come into millions when she turned 21 in 1933. Her mother had committed suicide, so Barbara inherited her share of the Woolworth fortune.

The young heiress lived an extravagant lifestyle and found herself repeatedly vulnerable to the unscrupulous intentions of gold-digging men. In all, she had seven husbands, including three princes, one count, one baron, one playboy cad, and one movie star – Cary Grant. The "million dollar baby" died in 1979, having lived out her later years at the Beverly Hills Hotel, with just $3,500 in her bank account. Eight years later, the story of her life was made into a top-rated TV movie called *Poor Little Rich Girl* and starring original Charlie's Angel Farrah Fawcett.

The Barbara Hutton saga isn't the only colorful tale in Woolworth's long history. In addition to the salacious gossip and tragedies that dogged the family, Woolworth's also made the papers after a segregation protest in Greensboro, North Carolina.

On February 1, 1960, four black college students took seats at Woolworths' "whites only" lunch counter. The foursome were refused service, but retaliated with some refusing of their own when they would not leave the premises. The story attracted national attention and that day at the Woolworth's lunch counter resulted in the abolishment of the "whites only" policy at the store's eatery in July of that year.

So significant was the Woothworth's protest that when the Greensboro store closed in 1993, the Smithsonian Institution swooped in and bought the famous lunch counter for its archives.

All Woolworth's stores were sold off when the company restructured in 1998 due to financial difficulties, and the business was renamed Venator Group Specialty Inc.

Another early discount retailer to suffer financial hardships in the late (twentieth) century was Kmart. But 100 years earlier company founder Sebastian Spering Kresge was – along with his contemporary F.W. Woolworth – at the top of the bargain shopping game.

In 1899, Kresge opened his first five-and-dime store in downtown Detroit, Michigan. By 1912, S.S. Kresge Company had 85 stores and yearly sales topping $10 million. The company saw beyond the five- and ten-cent items and soon grew to include a new family member: the dollar-or-less store.

A Kresge "5 and 10."

The two types of Kresge stores were distinguished by color. The five-and-ten stores featured red signage, while those of the higher-priced stores were green. Moving

# Cheapskates, Misers, Tightwads, and Bargain Hunters

*When fame and frugality mix*

It was deposed Christian TV matriarch Tammy Faye Bakker who said, "I take Him shopping with me. I say, okay, Jesus, help me find a bargain."

Whether or not the Lord ever deigned to smile on Bakker and bring her the discounts she prayed for, her bargain-hunting ways represent the thoughts of many shoppers – even those with celebrity status.

Tammy Faye Bakker.

Long-gone multi-millionaires like oil tycoon John Paul Getty and eccentric businessman Howard Hughes were said to be first class cheapskates. Getty, it was rumored, had a pay phone installed in his home for guests to use, while Hughes allegedly liked to use his fame and influence to score a

into a less restrictive price category also foreshadowed the company's eventual move into the lucrative discount department store business in the early 1960s.

The first Kmart store opened in Garden City, Michigan in 1962. In 1966 (the same year Sebastian Kresge died at the age of 99), the company had 162 Kmarts, 753 Kresge stores, and sales of more than $1 billion per year. A decade later, the company expanded at an unprecedented rate, opening 271 Kmart stores in just one year.

Kmart, with its notorious Blue Light Specials and accompanying overhead announcements blaring "Attention Kmart shoppers. . . ." was the epitome of discount retail in the 1960s and '70s. This is emphasized by the S.S. Kresge Company sales data of 1977. That year, almost 95 percent of the company's sales were from Kmart. All of Kresge's original five-and-dime stores were sold by 1987.

But Kmart's tenure as king of the discounters was short-lived.

The company moved into the burgeoning "super store" business in 1991 with the opening of the first Kmart Supercenter in Medina, Ohio, and worked to attract customers with exclusive lines bearing celebrity names like Jaclyn Smith, Kathy Ireland, and Martha Stewart. But Kmart lagged behind other high-profile discounters such as Wal-Mart and Target. Somewhere along the way, Kmart's identity was lost and its image became outdated.

Wal-Mart took a well-crafted, down-home, pep-squad approach to lure shoppers. Target aggressively repositioned itself as a youthful, design-conscious alternative for suburban hipsters. Kmart languished.

Newly branded Big Kmart stores opened starting in 1996. The Blue Light Special – which had disappeared a decade earlier – was brought back in 2001. Stores were renovated and the company logo redesigned. But nothing worked and in January 2002, Kmart filed for Chapter 11 bankruptcy protection. Carrying an approximately $10.2 billion debt load, the troubled company became the largest retail bankruptcy in U.S. history. They're still around, but don't have the market clout they once did.

Stock market analysts, retail experts, and disappointed Kmart staff and shoppers recognized the failings of the company's management to successfully assert the brand in an increasingly competitive discount retail sector. And many assessing the Kmart situation were fond of blaming Wal-Mart for Kmart's woes.

More than any other chain, the evolution of modern discount shopping was shaped by Sam Walton's Wal-Mart stores.

A former JC Penney management trainee, it took Sam Walton 28 years to build his chain of Wal-Mart discount stores into the number one American retailer.

Along with his brother J.L. "Bud" Walton, Sam owned franchises of Ben Franklin variety stores in Arkansas and Missouri. Drawing inspiration from early discounters such as Ann & Hope, Mammoth Mart, and Zayre, Walton became convinced his Wal-Mart store concept would work.

While most discounters concentrated their considerable efforts on cities with populations of 50,000 or more, Walton wanted to bring large-scale discount stores into smaller communities with a population range of 5,000 to 25,000.

His first order of business en route to Wal-Mart success was to approach the owners of the Ben Franklin brand to form a partnership.

A Wal-Mart greeter.

Walton's idea was rejected, so the brothers decided to go it alone, raising the necessary funds themselves.

The first Wal-Mart store opened in Rogers, Arkansas in 1962. By 1969, the Waltons had 18 Wal-Mart stores, 14 Ben Franklin shops, and were generating more than $12 in sales annually. Sam Walton took the company public the next year.

What set Wal-Mart apart from its competitors was threefold. First, it built its customer base in locations often overlooked by the likes of Kmart and Target. Second, the company went to great lengths to undercut the local competition's prices. This was achieved by making notoriously shrewd deals with suppliers and assigning pricing power to local managers who could react instantly to price fluctuations in their market. But at the heart

deal even though his bank account was bulging.

Late trashy book writer Harold Robbins amused himself (and journalists) before his death in 1997 by sharing tales of actor Cary Grant's frugal ways and took special delight in the knowledge that he had screwed Grant over in a Hollywood film deal.

Cary Grant.

Grant, along with Hughes and pop tart Britney Spears, were skewered in 2002 by *Us Weekly* magazine in its salacious cover story, "Celebrity Cheapskates Revealed!" Singer Spears, according to *Us* sources in Las Vegas and London, is a notoriously bad restaurant tipper despite her wealth.

Newspaper and Internet gossip pages have, at various times, accused Rod Stewart, Mick Jagger, Johnny Depp, Howard Stern, and Meryl Streep of being a tad on the tight-fisted side.

But the woman with the most widely talked about

thriftiness is *Today* show host Katie Couric. While Couric has admitted to liking a bargain, the tabloids have taken her to task over such violations of the Extravagant Celebrity Code as taking home a ham cooked by Martha Stewart on the *Today* show and waiting at the counter of a New York department store for 61 cents change.

Katie Couric.

The *National Enquirer* and *The Globe* may balk at Couric's shunning of stereotypical celebrity spending habits, but there is one famous miser who would almost certainly applaud her money sense.

Clark Howard, though not a movie or rock star, is a very famous man in cheapskate circles. In fact, he may be the best-known cheapskate in history – and he's said he doesn't mind if you call him that to his face. The Atlanta based syndicated radio host, newspaper columnist, and author of the book *Get Clark Smart: The Ultimate Guide to Getting Rich from*

of Wal-Mart's rise to the top was the "rah-rah" image it cultivated among its employees and customers.

Since the 1960s, all Wal-Mart employees, regardless of wage or position, were referred to as "associates," undoubtedly to emphasize the impression that at Wal-Mart, everyone is important and equal. To further boost the patriotic spirit among Wal-Mart employees, in 1975 a customized cheer was introduced to help the staff get off to a great day, every day. ("Gimme a W! Gimme an A! Gimme an L! Gimme an M! Gimme an A! Gimme an R! Gimme a T! Who's number one? The customer – always!") A new level of customer service was introduced in 1983, when Wal-Mart stores began hiring "people greeters" to do just that: greet the people as they entered the store.

But for all its success, Wal-Mart was virtually unknown outside small centers in the U.S. until its rapid expansion into the suburbs of big cities in the 1980s and 1990s. The average square footage of a typical Wal-Mart store grew to 66,400 by 1990, and it wasn't long before the company set its eye on international markets.

Sam Walton didn't live to see Wal-Mart's expansion into Canada, South America, Germany, China, Korea, and the U.K.; he died of bone cancer in 1992.

But the Wal-Marting of the world was not without obstacles and criticism. The company, which is the largest private employer in existence, has been accused of selling clothing manufactured in Honduran sweatshops and has met with less than an enthusiastic response in central Europe. While the Asians have embraced the Wal-Mart way of shopping, German bargain shoppers have snubbed the American retail giant, resulting in losses estimated at $200 million per year and the closure of at least two German Wal-Mart stores.

Other American discount chains have tested the global waters as well. Most recently, warehouse-style "big box" wholesale clubs have tried to break into markets across the globe – particularly in Asia – and have met with varying degrees of success.

Wholesale supermarkets had existed in Europe in the 1970s, but the first wholesale members' club in the United States was started back in 1976 by Sol Price when he opened his first Price Club store in San Diego, California. Price grew the business slowly, branching out into other California locations over the next few years.

Price built no-frills stores stocked to the rafters with merchandise bought directly from the manufacturer. Savings were passed to the customers, who each paid an annual membership fee. He also courted area businesses with offers of special membership deals and exclusive shopping times.

The idea worked. And like any good idea, it wasn't long before the imitators started sniffing around. One bold competitor even went so far as to pay Sol Price a face-to-face visit, pick his brain, and get the scoop on the inner workings of Price Club. The man was Wal-Mart's Sam Walton. In 1983, Walton opened his first Sam's Club wholesale operation in Midwest City, Oklahoma. By 1989, Walton had the largest wholesale club chain in the U.S., with 123 stores, each averaging 100,000 square feet.

The same year Sam's Club came onto the discount retail scene, so did another chain that would become a major player in the wholesale clubs business. After working for Sol Price for 24 years, Jim Sinegal partnered up with Jeffrey Brotman to open the first Costco store in Seattle, Washington.

Unlike its competitors, the Costco Wholesale Corporation made a decided effort to go upscale – in regards to both its stock and its members. Costco members were required to prove they had a steady income to qualify for the $35-a-year memberships, and in return would have access to all kinds of brand-name electronics, food, books, clothing, housewares, and more.

In 1993, Costco merged with Sol Price's The Price Company and within five years the PriceCostco (and, as of 1997, simply Costco) name was plastered on 289 warehouse storefronts worldwide.

Today, it is estimated that one in every four American households have a Costco membership and that each member drops approximately $94 per visit, which the average member does about every 10 days. The company has stores in the U.K., Canada, and Asia, and is expanding many locations to include gas stations, auto shops, and – like any good discount retailer – more square footage.

*America's Money-Saving Experts*, has built a following of millions (his radio show draws about four million listeners) and became a celebrity in his own right.

Maybe celebrity cheapskate isn't an oxymoron after all.

# Redeem Me!

*Coupon culture catches on*

**S**aucy screen legend Mae West once said, "A man in love is like a clipped coupon - it's time to cash in." But what West failed to mention in her pithy 1975 statement is that there are a lot of people - women in particular - who seem to care far less about a man's love than they do about saving a few cents.

Couponing, as it's now known, has been the preferred sport of household champions since the late 1880s when former wholesale druggist Asa Candler introduced the first coupons to promote his fountain drink Coca-Cola. After purchasing the formula for the beverage from Atlanta pharmacist John S. Pemberton for $2,300

Mae West.

in 1888, Candler set about marketing the new product. It was 1894 when he hit upon the coupon idea and proceeded to offer the public a free glass of Coca-Cola upon redeeming the handwritten, money-saving slips.

The first grocery store coupons made a splash the next year when breakfast cereal magnate C.W. Post offered shoppers a coupon for a one-cent discount towards his latest brand, Grape Nuts.

Coupons continued to gain momentum into the early twentieth century, but it wasn't until the Great Depression of the 1930s that they became a mainstay in many homes. With record unemployment, rations, prohibition, and the threat of war looming, consumers were determined to save pennies whenever they could.

Pinching pennies became ingrained in the culture and created habits that lasted long after the Depression ended. When supermarket chains started to pop up in the 1940s, coupons were an integral part of the mix, enabling food manufacturers to promote their products to larger numbers of shoppers than ever.

As the use of coupons grew, so did one very significant problem. Retailers frequently encountered difficulties getting the coupon value reimbursed by the manufacturer. In 1952, this particular complaint fell on the ears of market researcher A.C. Nielsen, Jr (yes, the same Nielsen known for the television ratings system that network executives live and die by).

Five years later, Nielsen had successfully convinced both manufacturers and retailers that having a middle-man - a coupon clearing house - dedicated to processing and reimbursing coupons would be the perfect solution. Nielsen Clearing House officially launched in 1957, becoming the first business of its kind, but certainly not the last.

By 1965, 50 percent of Americans were admitted coupon users. Numbers kept climbing into the 1970s (in 1975, 65 percent of Americans had the coupon bug), as did the diversity of manufacturers offering coupon discounts. Coupons were no longer the exclusive domain of food products and household goods.

Throughout the 1970s and '80s, coupons were everywhere - at the shops, in the mail, in magazines and newspapers. The abundance of coupons prompted serious savers to start coupon swap clubs and launch newsletters devoted to coupon-clipping tips.

Susan Samtur of Yonkers, New York, is known in couponing circles as the "coupon queen." She publishes the newsletter, *Refundle Bundle*, and has been clipping coupons for 30 years. Michele Easter, who lives in Bountiful, Utah, has been at it for over 20 years, and publishes the *Refunding Makes Cents* newsletter. In 2001, Easter explained the appeal of couponing to Eileen Powell of *AP Online*: "You're there in a store, and you pick up your favorite shampoo. You go through the checkout, put down your coupons and you get it for 25 cents. It's a high."

Easter goes on to explain in the same article, "Store Coupons Can Be Worth Millions," that the ultimate score in couponing is what she calls the "triple play," when a shopper has a coupon and a mail-in rebate card for a product that's already on sale.

But while Samtur and Easter were merrily clipping their way into the 1990s, general consumer interest in coupons was beginning to slide, and by mid-decade usage was at an all-time low. In 1995, less than two percent of manufacturers' coupons were redeemed, and soon companies began cutting back on coupons.

The media was quick to pronounce the coupon industry dead (or at least on its last legs), labeling the practice outdated and passé.

But even the most savvy consumer analysts couldn't have predicted the resounding comeback coupons were to make in 1999. The death of the coupon, it seems, was premature and greatly exaggerated.

The Internet changed everything. Although the first online coupons appeared in 1995, the concept took four more years to fully catch on. But when it did, it did big time. Online coupons caught on with the most affluent and influential living generation: the Baby Boomers. And just like that, coupons were back.

According to the Coupon Council of the Promotional Marketing Association (PMA) in New York, coupon distribution in 1999 rose for the first time in five years with 307 billion coupons floating around on paper and in cyberspace. The next year saw another impressive jump to 330 billion, and the figures rose again to 340 billion in 2001.

As of 2000, the PMA estimated that 77.3 percent of the American population used coupons. And surprisingly, it wasn't the lower income households that were the biggest clippers. While 72.2 percent of households with incomes under $25,000 annually used coupons, it was those homes that fell in the $50,000–$76,000 range that had the highest usage rate of 81.7 percent.

The surge of coupon usage in recent years translates into approximately $3.6 billion in consumer savings per year, with many of those savings being found on websites like *ValuPage.com*, *CoolSavings.com*, and *GroceryCoupons.com*. But with Internet coupons has also come Internet coupon fraud. Take the fake Starbucks coupon shenanigans, for example.

In July 2002, the coffee shop chain was deluged with customers looking to redeem the coupons they had received via email entitling them to a free 12-ounce Crème Frappuccino. The coupons were counterfeit, but by the time Starbucks had learned of the scam and alerted its stores, countless free beverages had been given out. And pity the grumpy customers who turned up hoping for a free Frap and were instead told it was all a big fake mistake.

"I can't tell you how many times I've been cussed out today," an unidentified Starbucks employee in Washington, D.C. told writer Dina El Boghdady of *The Washington Post.* "Some people are getting really mad even when I explain it to them."

Like everything else in life, if a coupon seems too good to be true, it probably is.

## The Sample Effect

*Great deals for skinny shoppers*

Anyone who doubts the theory of modern shopping-as-sport – and occasionally near-violent sport, at that – has never been to a sample sale. Not an imposter of a sample sale held somewhere in Middle America featuring bad mall cast-offs that was advertised prominently in the local newspaper, but a true-blue designer sample sale.

A real sample sale meets three specific criteria. One, it's almost always held in New York. Two, it's only ever advertised in very particular publications (i.e., *New York* magazine) or on certain websites (i.e.,

# From the Manufacturer to You

*Factory outlets are a bargain hunter's paradise*

**T**he year was 1936 and men's clothing manufacturer Anderson-Little hit upon the idea of selling off overruns, samples, and overstock directly to the public at warehouse locations in out-of-the-way areas.

The factory-direct concept was quietly adopted by apparel manufacturers in the 1940s and through the 1950s and '60s. But outlets as a shopping phenomenon didn't make a big splash until 1974 when Vanity Fair, the first multi-tenant manufacturer's outlet center, opened in Reading, Pennsylvania. Five years later, Belz Enterprises opened the first enclosed factory outlet mall in Lakeland, Tennessee, on the outskirts of Memphis.

Bargain shopping would never be the same.

A manufacturer's factory outlet is, by definition, a discount retail operation run by the manufacturer. An outlet is not the same as an off-price retailer (think T.J. Maxx or Winners), which receives its stock from a variety of manufacturers and then sells the goods off in its stores.

Throughout the 1980s, more and more factory outlet malls popped up each year. The malls were often located in suburban areas or a short drive from a major center, and many sported generic "village"-style architecture. In 1987, there were 108 factory outlet malls in the U.S.; by 1996 there were 329. In 1989, there were 4,500 outlet stores; by 2001, there were more than 14,000.

Belz, along with Tanger Factory Outlet Centers and Prime Outlets, were leaders in the field, all having gotten in on the ground floor of outlet mania. Today, manufacturer's factory outlets in the United States bring in more than $14 billion every year and, with the exception of a brief drop in sales in the mid-1990s, have proven to do well even in times of economic uncertainty.

The outlet concept grew and mutated into various forms, spreading across several continents, but finding its greatest success in its American homeland.

The "world's most upscale outlet shopping center"

*DailyCandy.com*'s Candy Sampler listings). Three, if you're bigger than a size six don't bother showing up.

The designer sample sale as we know it is a primarily American phenomenon with its roots in the 1970s, when such events were open only to the designer's employees and sometimes their friends and family. Design and manufacturing samples, showroom samples, and even one-off experimental pieces that never made it to the runway, were sold off at a fraction of the retail price.

It wasn't until the 1980s, however, that sample sales became generally accessible to the shopping public and were soon the worst best-kept secret on Seventh Avenue. Driven by word-of-mouth, those in the know were

Spree: A Cultural History of Shopping

(according to its press data) opened in Primm, Nevada in 1998. Situated close to the California border and just a 35-minute drive from the Las Vegas strip, Fashion Outlet of Las Vegas capitalized on the trend of outlet-mall-as-travel-destination. Complete with a gambling area, the mall was an immediate success, playing host to both individuals and tour groups looking for a designer discount at shops like Burberry, J.P. Tod's, and Versace.

Across the country, the first catalog outlet center opened in Wilmington, Delaware in 1999. The Shipyard Catalogue Outlet drew tenants from formerly catalog-exclusive retailers such as L.L. Bean, which was among the first to sign on to The Shipyard project, leasing 17,000 square feet.

Home shopping television channels QVC and the Home Shopping Network also got into the outlet act, opening stores of their own and breaking down the long-standing classifications of shopping breeds. Gone were the days when a retailer was pigeon-holed as *only* a department store, *only* a direct-mail seller, or *only* a home shopping channel.

Into the late 1990s, words like *diversification*, *convergence*, and the 1980s classic, *synergy*, were dusted off and ended up on the tip of every business executive's tongue. It wasn't good enough to be good at one thing anymore - and everyone had to try online retailing on for size.

Prime Outlets was the first (and only) of the bricks-and-mortar outlet developers to take on the Internet in any significant capacity. Amid a flurry of excited press releases, the company - which, it is estimated, controls more than 20 percent of the total outlet square footage in the U.S. - announced in October 1999 it would launch *eOutlets.com* the following spring.

Come March 2000, Prime Outlets had sunk $16.5 million into the project and had opened its first online outlet, for the Etienne Aigner women's wear brand. All was far from rosy, however, and on April 12, 2000, Prime Outlets revealed it had discontinued the initiative.

One major contributing factor to the swift demise of *eOutlets.com* was that the online outlet market - for designer fashion and accessories - had been cornered in 1998, by *BlueFly.com*. Prime Outlets was simply too late to the Internet party.

smugger-than-smug and reveled in their "fashion insider" status.

In the 1990s, when dates, times, and places of sample sales started popping up in magazines and on the Internet, bigger and bigger crowds were squashed into the often cramped office spaces where the sales were held. Any civility left in this particular shopping process had to go.

Shoppers argue with each other, struggle over clothes, grab items out of others' hands, and exchange profane insults. The room is jammed full of clothes on rolling racks and it's not unusual to see naked people everywhere (dressing rooms are unheard of). The standard office fluorescents make everything – and everyone – look bad and it's almost impossible to distinguish navy blue from black with any confidence, although chances are it's black if the brand is high-end and based in Manhattan.

But aside from the catty comments and aggressive jostling, the key for any sample sale shopper is size.

Like it or not, it's unlikely a woman will ever come across an item larger than a size six at a sample sale and even that's pushing it. Many designers create their samples using a size four standard, although more and more have been opting for a size two in recent years. The Sample Effect is dictated by designers who are influenced by fashion magazines and, most importantly, by models.

The body type of the day is the determining factor. How thin, how curvy, how flat-chested or thin-hipped the mannequins gracing the covers of the big fashion bibles like *Vogue*, *W*, *Elle*, and *Harper's Bazaar* are gives potential sample sale shoppers a pretty good idea as to whether or not to make the trek. In the 1980s, it was a curvy Cindy Crawford and samples were made in size six or eight; into the early twenty-first century, it's boy-body androgyny.

But regular-sized gals need not be entirely discouraged and shut-out from indulging in one of fashion shopping's great experiences – after all, there's always shoes and handbags.

But the future of outlet shopping is not necessarily online at all – it's overseas, in countries where outlet shopping is relatively new and pure.

Japan's first factory outlet mall, Tsurumi Hanaport Blossom, didn't open in the Osaka area until 1995. The U.K. and Europe also remained virgin territory until the early 1990s. In the U.K., there was only one factory outlet center in 1993; in 2000 there were 37.

The European market didn't take to the very American idea of outlet shopping right away and, even as it's gained popularity, has followed a different path.

Finding the boxy, warehouse-style factory outlet malls in the U.S. distasteful, the Euro malls are more aesthetically pleasing, placing considerable emphasis on design. Building an outlet business in Europe also proved a new challenge for developers (many of whom are American), due to rigid zoning laws, expensive land that is regularly priced at 10 to 20 times more than in the States, and there are laws which restrict retail practices with regard to sales and discounts.

At least before the European outlet market reaches its own critical mass, there are still discounts to be had. In North America, spotting authentic factory outlet bargains had become an endangered – and sometimes frustrating – pastime.

It's highly unlikely that those brands which have become omnipresent in the outlet world, with stores in practically every factory outlet mall, have so much overstock and so many samples. They don't. Taking advantage of the perception of savings many customers get from simply stepping foot in a manufacturer's outlet, certain brands are diluting the outlet shopping experience by creating goods specifically to be sent to outlet stores.

Think about it. There are only so many overruns and seasonal leftovers to go around. As the number of factory outlets increase, so does the difficulty in finding a real deal. But when a true bargain hunter does make a genuine score, the smug satisfaction is even sweeter.

# Second-hand Shopping

chapter

vi

# Going, Going, Gone

*A look at auctions through the ages*

**O**ne can accuse our ancestors of a lot of things, but political correctness isn't one of them.

Some scholars speculate that the practice of auctions may date back to Biblical times, but the first historically documented auctions took place around 500 BCE, and were conducted by the Babylonians. The annual auctions were not for land or animals or grain, but for women – more specifically, for maidens of a marrying age.

The auctions worked something like this. All the local men in the market for a wife would gather around the auctioneer (or herald, as he was known in those ancient times), who would lead the bidding process. First up were the best-looking, most beautiful girls who were likely to fetch top dollar. The women were then auctioned off one by one, in descending order of physical attractiveness. Then, to add to the already high humiliation factor, it was typical for the not-so-good-looking or disabled women to go for a negative amount; the girls' father had to pay the buyer.

The Romans, on the other hand, preferred their auctions with a bit of violence.

At the height of the Roman Empire, auctions were sometimes held right on the battlefield. Immediately after a victory, a Roman soldier would symbolically drive his spear into the ground and others would gather around to take part in an auction of the victims' things. If an auctioneer didn't happen to be on hand (these men would often follow soldiers out into the field hoping for just such an opportunity), the goods were carted back to the *atrium auctionarium* for later sale.

The Romans' habit of driving a spear into the earth as a symbol of victory led to the Latin term for early Roman auctions, *subhastare* (*sub*, meaning under; *hasta*, meaning spear). The word auction was later adopted, with its root being the Latin term *auctus*, meaning "to make an increase."

Spree: A Cultural History of Shopping

At auction - or *subhastare* - the *argentarius* (or person who organized, promoted, and conducted the auction) would sell goods on behalf of the *domus* (or person whose goods were up for grabs) and the *emptor* - the highest bidder - would walk away with the goods. The system was surprisingly civil. No shouting was permitted to indicate a bid; winking or waving were the preferred signals.

The Romans held auctions for all kinds of things, including slaves, and the proceeds were frequently used to finance further military actions. But perhaps the strangest of Roman auctions was for that of the Empire itself.

In March 193 BCE, the Praetorian Guard put the whole kit-and-caboodle on the block after the emperor Publius Helvius Pertinax was killed. Senator Marcus Didius Salvius Julianus came out ahead at the auction, paying 25,000 *sesterces* per guard. But his control over the Romans was short-lived, as he was beheaded less than three months later, when Rome was conquered by Septimus Severus.

After the Roman Empire auction fiasco, interest in auctions waned, and although the term did pop up for the first time in the *Oxford English Dictionary* in 1595, the practice was not again commonplace until the late seventeenth century when it was popularized by the British.

Early English art sales were held in coffee houses and taverns. At that time there were four ways of conducting an auction. Hourglass and candle auctions were ones during which the bidding would be limited by the length of time it took for the sand in the hourglass to run out or for the candle to burn.

Dutch auctions - which, reasonably, originated in The Netherlands - involved the auctioneer kicking things off with a high price, then whittling it down until there was a bidder. A variation of the Dutch auction was called "mineing." Once the price declined to a value a bidder was willing to pay, he'd yell, "Mine!" Then, unlike the traditional Dutch auction, the price would start to ascend again until the highest bidder (or "miner") won.

The hammer auctions of the seventeenth century were almost identical to the customary auction process used today. The auctioneer would command the crowd, taking bids in an effort to push the price as far as possible, then would use the hammer to signify a sale to the highest bidder.

Although it is believed that lists and descriptions of items up for auction at the tavern and coffeehouse art sales of the seventeenth century were distributed to bidders, the first true auction catalog was used in 1717 England for a sale of books. Catalogs were *de rigeur* by the time the world's two biggest auction houses – Sotheby's and Christie's – opened later in the 1700s.

Of the two, Sotheby's was on the scene first. Specializing primarily in fine art and artifacts, the auction house opened its doors on March 11, 1744, in London. Founded by Samuel Baker, its first sale was of a library

Christie's Auction House, circa 18th century.
*Courtesy Mary Evans Picture Library.*

of books owned by an English dignitary. Sotheby's enhanced its formidable reputation through the years by selling Napoleon's books after his death and, in the twentieth century, holding spectacular sales like the renowned Goldschmidt sale of 1958.

Celebrities Anthony Quinn, Kirk Douglas, Lady Churchill, and the writer Somerset Maugham attended in full evening dress (an evening sale had not been held at Sotheby's since the eighteenth century) to participate in a lively 21-minute sale of seven Impressionist and Modern paintings.

Sotheby's main competitor, Christie's, held its first sale on December 15, 1766. The auction, conducted by founder James Christie, included assorted household items such as linens, irons, and chamber pots. But things at the London auction house got a whole lot more interesting come 1874, when James Christie auctioned off books, jewelry, and furniture belonging to the French transvestite spy Charles de Beaumont. According to Christie's official history, the sale catalog described the notorious de Beaumont as "a lady of fashion and an officer of Dragoons."

After finding success in Britain, both houses sought to add to their auction empire by opening offices around the world – and infiltrating the U.S. was key.

Real estate auctions had been held in the United States since around 1740, but it was in 1865, following the end of the Civil War, that auctions reached a wider scope. Army colonels were given the power to conduct land sale auctions and even today, there is a tradition of calling an auctioneer "colonel."

Stateside, auctions were not always for real estate, tobacco, and livestock. American fine art auctions were pioneered by Hiram Haney Parke and G.T. Otto Bernet in the 1930s when the two founded Parke-Bernet Galleries in New York. The company rose to become the premier American auction house. Sotheby's opened its first office in Manhattan in 1955, but raised its profile in the U.S. considerably in 1964 when it purchased Parke-Bernet. Christie's opened its first New York saleroom in 1977 on tony Park Avenue, moving in 1999 to Rockefeller Center.

Throughout the twentieth century, Sotheby's and Christie's jostled for the titles of biggest, richest, and best. In 1987, Sotheby's created a sensation when it auctioned off the jewels of the Duchess of Windsor at its Geneva salesroom, raking in over $50 million. In 1990, Christie's set the record (which stands to this day) for the most expensive item ever sold at auction when Vincent van Gogh's *Portrait of Dr Gochet* went for $82.5 million.

Such heady figures coupled with the booming auction business had Christie's and Sotheby's riding high through the 1980s and '90s, but in January 2000, the reputations of both auction houses were tarnished by scandal. The U.S. Justice Department launched a probe into conspiratorial price-fixing allegations between the two houses that rocked the auction world.

Between the two, Christie's and Sotheby's controlled more than 90 percent of the art auction market, which was estimated to be worth $4 billion per year. The chairman of Christie's, Sir Anthony Tennant, was forced to resign after the scandal broke, and although he was indicted on anti-trust charges, refused to appear in the United States and could not be extradited.

Sotheby's and Christie's settled civil suits for $256 million each and Sotheby's pleaded guilty to price-fixing (which brought in an estimated $15 million a year). Sotheby's agreed to pay $45 million in retribution, but the company's chairman (who had also resigned as a result of the investigation), Alfred Taubman, was not off the hook and was prosecuted for his role in the scheme. He was found guilty by a jury in December 2001 and was later sentenced to one year plus one day in jail, and fined $7.5 million. He served nearly ten months in prison and was released early, on May 15, 2003, on account of his good behavior.

As U.S. District Court Judge George Daniels said at Taubman's sentencing: "No one is above the law."

# Scam Artists, Royalty, and Patron Saints

*Inside pawnbroking's colorful past*

egend has it that that cute kids' ditty, "Pop Goes the Weasel," doesn't really have anything to do with a skinny little rodent poking his head out from a hole in a musical wind-up box. The tune, which dates back to the seventeenth century, has more than 20 different versions of lyrics, but the most common relates to the practice of pawning.

Popping the weasel was once English cockney for pawning one's coat. A "weasel" was a bobbin-like tool used by shoemakers that, according to music expert Tom Miller in Cecil Adam's "The Straight Dope" newspaper column, "popped" when a spool of thread was full. This knowledge helps to make sense of certain versions of the nursery rhyme.

Many scholars who interpret the historical meaning of nursery rhymes point to a version of the lyrics from the late nineteenth century in which a silk maker or cobbler – depending on the interpretation – sells his "weasel" to a pawnbroker in order to pay for drinks at the local pub. That bar, referred to in various versions of the song, was likely The Eagle freehold pub on Shepherdess Walk in London. As the song goes: "Up and down the City Road/In and out The Eagle/That's the way the money goes/Pop goes the weasel."

Pawnbroking has been around since ancient times and was the first source of modern consumer credit. The House of Lombard in the late Middle Ages is frequently cited as the first registered money lender, but pawnbroking can be traced back 3,000 years before that, to the Buddhist monks in ancient China who would pawn the belongings of monks who had passed away.

A pawnshop on Beale Street, Memphis, 1939.
*Photo by Marion Post Wolcott, courtesy Library of Congress.*

Spanish Queen Isabella.

## What I Did On My Summer Vacation

*Treasure seekers flock to the world's largest garage sale*

Call it what you will – a garage sale, a yard sale, a boot sale. Every summer, pack rats comb their homes for little-used items, set up a few tables in their yard or garage, post a few homemade signs advertising the address, and open for business. Garage sales are simple, practical, and present an opportunity to pocket a few bucks. And none is bigger than the 127 Corridor Sale held every August in the southern United States.

The sale, that spans 450 miles of highway

But it was the House of Lombard in England and the de Médici family in Italy that drew attention to pawnbroking. The House of Lombard was said to have been visited by such dignitaries as King Edward III in the fourteenth century, and Queen Isabella of Spain is believed to have pawned her crown jewels to finance Christopher Columbus's journey to America.

Both the Lombards and the de Médicis featured the three golden balls as their symbol. The three golden balls have been the international logo of pawnbrokers since the Middle Ages, but the symbol actually dates back to Saint Nicholas.

Best known for his role in history as the inspiration for Santa Claus, St Nick is the patron saint of children, but also of bankers, brewers, brides, coopers, jurists, perfumers, seafarers, scholars, robbers, travelers, maidens, and pawnbrokers.

According to a Russian Orthodox story, Nicholas, who was renowned for his work with the poor, secretly bestowed three small bags of gold coins upon a man whose three daughters would otherwise have been sold into slavery. Those three bags became the three golden balls of pawnbroking, and pawnbrokers from the Lombards and de Médicis to those of the twenty-first century look to the patron saint to bless their business.

A pawnbroker's sign.

Patron saints and royal customers were not often associated with the pawn shops of twentieth-century America. Although pawnbroking arrived on the shores of the States with the first settlers, it was in the early 1900s that the practice grew to become a major source of consumer credit – and the then-unregulated industry began to cultivate a bad reputation.

Because anyone could set up a pawn shop, sell whatever they wanted for any price, charge outrageous interest (sometimes 300 percent), or set unreasonable terms of loan, pawnbroking became a haven for shady businessmen selling stolen goods. This stigma dogs the

110

pawnbroking business to this day, but thankfully, things have changed.

According to the National Pawnbrokers' Association, more than 75 million people in the United States do not have a bank account or credit card and are the pawnbroker's prime customer. Modern pawnbroking loans average from $50 to $100 with interest rates about five-to-six percent per month. Some of the most commonly pawned items are jewelry, guns, electronic equipment, and musical instruments, and all items must have serial numbers recorded and filed with the local police department.

Typically, a customer will receive one-third to one-half of the pawned item's value from the broker. They then have three or four months to pay off the debt and reclaim their property. If the debt is left unpaid, the pawnbroker has the option to renegotiate and renew the loan (provided all interest has been paid) or sell the item in his shop.

It is estimated that 70 to 80 percent of goods pawned are redeemed, while the rest end up in pawn shop windows. The industry is working hard to erase the dishonest image associated with pawnbroking, invoking tough new laws to protect customers and – one can be sure - praying to St Nick.

between Covington, Kentucky and Gadsden, Alabama, was originally conceived by former Fentress County, Tennessee official Mike Walker in 1987 to encourage drivers to take some of the area's less traveled roads.

Starting just south of Cincinnati, treasure hunters encounter hundreds of roadside vendors as they follow the highway, which winds south through Kentucky, then Tennessee, makes a tiny dip into Georgia and winds up in southern Alabama. Most of the vendors are clustered on the Cumberland Plateau in Tennessee and, as much as some of the residents complain about the traffic during the sale, it's very good for business.

Land owners on the 127 Corridor rent parcels of roadside property to vendors from around the country and many hotels and motels on the route are booked solid up to a year ahead. The four-day sale drew more than 400,000 people in 2000, and was expanded to nine days in 2003 due to popular demand. It has even attracted the attention of *Martha Stewart Living* magazine and, most importantly, brought the old adage "one man's trash is another man's treasure" to life.

# Flea Market Showdown

*Two markets vie for the titles of oldest, biggest, and best*

At first glance, the number of commonalties between Paris, France and Canton, Texas, seem to add up to a big fat zero. The city of Paris boasts a population of 2.1 million; Canton is a town of less than 3,000. Paris is French, Canton is American or, more aptly, Texan. Canton has six motels; the number of *hotel* rooms in Paris is approximately 75,000.

But the two centers do share one thing: each plays host to one of the earliest and largest flea markets on the planet.

The Marché Aux Puces de Saint-Ouen is widely regarded as being the first true flea market, where vendors rented stalls to sell their goods. The term flea market does indeed come from the French *marché aux puces* and, when literally translated, means "market of the fleas." It is said that the merchandise at early Parisian markets was infested with fleas and other nasty bugs and the name was coined as a result.

Marché aux Puces de Saint-Ouen. *Illustration by L'Assiette au beurre, 1910.*

Paris was not only crawling with fleas in the latter half of the 1800s, it was also crawling with *biffins*, *chiftires*, and *pecheurs de lune* (or "moon fishermen"). These scruffy, homeless men sifted through trash in search of treasure and were dubbed "rag and bone" men. The city officials, however, were less than enthused with the presence of the rag and bone men and excised them from the city center in an effort to clean up the neighborhood.

But the enterprising men did not stop hunting for goods to resell and instead relocated to the various gates leading into the center of town. Curious folk began to flock to the areas just past the gates of Montreuil,

Vanves, and Clignancourt to check out the wares the rag and bone men had unearthed.

Eventually, in 1885, the makeshift markets that peppered the periphery of Paris's core were organized into one central market and the flea market was born. Just like the markets of today, the vendors at Saint-Ouen were required to pay a fee to exhibit their goods, and customers were expected to haggle.

The growth and success of Saint-Ouen resulted in an increase of flea markets in the French capital. Around 1920, the Malik Market opened with 100 stalls; five years later, the Biron Market opened with 200. Saint-Ouen, however, maintained its reputation as the biggest and the best.

Today's Marché Aux Puces de Saint-Ouen covers over 17 acres and attracts 120,000–

Marché aux Puces de Saint-Ouen. *Illustration by La Baionnette, 1916.*

150,000 visitors each weekend. It also bills itself as the world's largest antiques market, a title eerily similar to that of a market across the Atlantic in Canton, Texas.

Sixty miles southeast of Dallas, Canton would likely fit the bill of sleepy little American town if not for its giant flea market. Covering about 400 acres, the town's First Monday Trade Days claims the title, "world's oldest and largest flea market."

Local lore has it that in the 1850s, a U.S. circuit judge made his monthly stop in Canton on the first Monday of the month. Area residents would gather in town on those days to check out the court action and perhaps - if they were lucky - get to witness a hanging or two. Because they were heading into town anyway, many sought to kill two birds with one stone (so to speak) and bring with them any goods they had to sell or trade. Soon, the town square was bustling with consumer activity and hence, a market grew organically.

In 1965, the First Monday market expanded to a six-acre parcel of land a couple of blocks away. And as the market continued to swell, so did the amount of land it ate up with stalls.

Presently, more than 3,000 vendors set up at Canton's First Monday Trade Days, and the sale itself is no longer on the first Monday of the month. Instead, it's held the weekend prior to the first Monday. In the off-season (the summer and winter months), approximately 100,000 shoppers peruse the market. That number jumps to about 300,000 in the spring and fall, and sales at the Canton market undoubtedly make a tidy contribution to the total U.S. flea market sales, which are estimated to be $5–10 billion per year.

So, which is biggest? Technically Canton. Which is best? From the accounts of many hardcore collectible collectors, Paris. Which came first? That's a toss-up.

From a consumer perspective it doesn't much matter – both are old and big and impossible to cover in just one day. And as long as they're full of treasures and not fleas, shoppers will keep on coming.

# Charity Cool

*How thrift store shopping became fashionable*

F ashion was not a consideration when the Salvation Army organized its Household Salvage Brigade in 1890s London. Rather, the venerable Christian charity put unemployed men to work collecting discarded household items, books, and clothing in an effort to provide jobs and pass the salvaged goods on to the needy.

The practice of recycling used items for charity blossomed in the first half of the 1900s, spreading across the U.K. and into North America. But charity shop shopping as we know it today didn't appear until mid-century. The English organization Oxfam International claims its first charity shop – opened in 1948 on Broad Street in Oxford – was the first such store in the U.K.

Oxfam filled its stores with donations from the community, reselling the goods at low prices and using the profits to fight global poverty and suffering. The patrons of charity – or thrift – shops were primarily the poor; people who could not afford the luxury of buying new merchandise.

The first hint of the merger of thrift and fashion was in the late 1960s when the free-spirited "hippie" movement emerged along with communal living and messages of peace. Like many organic youth movements (whether it be '60s hippies, '70s punks, or the grunge kids of the early 1990s), a look evolved and was ultimately co-opted by the mainstream who habitually rejected the politics and focused on the fashion.

Diane Keaton in *Annie Hall* (United Artists, 1977).

## Everything Old is Cool Again

*Vintage shopping the modern way*

Models and Hollywood actresses love it, regular fashionwise folk troll thrift shops, flea markets, specialty stores, and websites to get it. Designers borrow heavily from it and you'd be hard-pressed to pick up a fashion magazine without finding evidence of it. Yet, vintage shopping is a relatively new phenomenon.

When photographer Annette Del Zoppo and her business partner, Parke Meek, opened the first vintage clothing store in the U.S. in the late 1960s, it was impossible to predict how the market for vintage clothing would grow. Del Zoppo and Meek, who both had worked for stylish mid-century design couple Charles and Ray Eames, opened their shop, Ephemera, in Los Angeles, selling vintage apparel and famously outfitting the band Sweetwater.

Serious vintage shopping remained very much a niche market until the 1980s when celebrities started turning up to public events in unique vintage couture and flea market finds. As vintage cool evolved, so did the shopping opportunities.

One of the most notable vintage stores opened just outside of downtown Las Vegas in 1989. The Attic started out as just that, the attic of Victor and Mayra Politis' used appliance store. Victor would purchase broken-down appliances from non-profit agencies, fix them up, and resell them in his shop. During his frequent visits to suppliers he noticed heaps of used clothing and started snapping up garments to sell from the attic of his store.

By 1993, Politis called it quits in the refurbished appliance business and began concentrating full time on vintage clothing. Soon, The Attic was touted as "the largest vintage clothing store in the world."

With its kaleidoscopic exterior and myriad racks stocked with items from the 1940s through the '70s, The Attic became a must for fashion aficio-

In 1977, the first poster girl for thrift shop chic arrived, with no ties to youth movements or to poverty. In fact, she wasn't a real person at all, but a character on the big screen. Playing the title role in Woody Allen's *Annie Hall*, Diane Keaton became a fashion icon, pairing oversize men's suit jackets with long skirts, boots, and hats. Keaton and her onscreen alter ego made the eclectic, thrift shop look fashionable, although thrift shopping amongst the middle and even upper classes had yet to shed its undesirable stigma.

Thrift stores were equated with poverty, neediness, smelliness, filth, and beyond a select group of fashion-forward hipsters, thrifting was not an acceptable shopping activity. Scouring the racks for vintage or antique finds had become customary in certain circles, but thrifting in general didn't hit mainstream North America until the 1980s.

If you could pinpoint one individual who made the most significant impact on the rise of thrift-as-fashion, it would have to be Madonna. When the provocative pop singer burst onto the world music scene in 1983 with her self-titled debut album, then released *Like A Virgin* one year later, she quickly cultivated a loyal following of young female fans eager to imitate her signature ragamuffin, thrift shop style.

Another musical thrift style muse surfaced in 1991 when Hole front-woman Courtney Love took to the stage in baby doll dresses and smeared lipstick, bringing what was dubbed the "kinderwhore" look to the fore. Love, along with her late husband, Kurt Cobain of the grunge posterband, Nirvana, influenced a shift in the thrift shop fashion look. From Love's thrift shop slips to Cobain's laid-back, disheveled style, the twosome had suburban kids around the world rifling through thrift store racks.

While Love and Cobain were tearing up the stage in their thrift shop finds, Los Angeles-based artist Jim Shaw was trolling charity shops for finds of his own. Since the 1970s, Shaw had collected kitsch and often very bad paintings found in thrift stores, never paying more than $35 for a piece. Ultimately, he amassed quite a collection (called Thrift Store Paintings) which has continually toured worldwide since the early '90s and is in part responsible for sparking interest in "bad art."

By the mid-1990s, thrift store culture was firmly

entrenched as an acceptable modern shopping practice, and by the end of the decade two popular independent publications had been launched.

Pittsburgh, Pennsylvania resident Al Hoff was the first with the debut of her *Thift Score* 'zine in 1994. A long-time thrifter who was at it years before it was fashionable, Hoff shared her finds, thoughts, and advice with fellow thrifters, eventually authoring a *Thrift Score* book for publisher HarperCollins in 1997.

1997 also saw the launch of *Cheap Date.* Founded by British editor Bay Garnett and her fashion stylist friend Kira Joliffe in London, *Cheap Date* soon attracted high-profile supporters and contributors, particularly in the fashion industry. Models like Karen Elson and Sophie Dahl were among those who appreciated *Cheap Date*'s anti-"lifestyle magazine" stance and aesthetic. *Cheap Date*, the book, was released in 1999.

The integration of thrift to fashion was complete when, in the late 1990s, the very charity stores which had been branded with such a negative stigma started isolating the items the staff felt could fetch top-dollar from the fashion conscious thrifter. Oxfam took things a big step further when it launched its Oxfam Origins (later renamed Oxfam Originals) stores to cater specifically to trendy thrift store shoppers, making true thrift shop bargains all the more rare and coveted.

nados travelling through Vegas. Awareness of the store grew even greater when, in May 1998, it was featured in a Visa television commercial that aired during the series finale of *Seinfeld*.

The Attic, like many real-world vintage stores, started to face stiff competition from the increasing number of websites devoted to vintage in the late 1990s. Oregon-based *RustyZipper.com* was the first online vintage store, opening in March 1996 and remaining an industry leader. Between such vintage websites and online auction houses like eBay, many vintage shops have either packed it in or have joined the throng online.

The feelings of many vintage shoppers have been mixed. It's certainly easier than ever to source that exact piece from that exact period from the comfort of home, but the thrill of the chase has been diminished. Alas, no shoppers, it seems, can ever truly have it all.

An Oxfam store in London.

# The Little Company That Could

## Charting the rise of eBay

**V**ery few people did the dot-com thing right. Pierre Omidyar was the exception to the rule.

On Labor Day 1995, the French-born Omidyar launched an online auction website he called eBay. By day, the computer science grad from Tufts University worked at General Magic in California's tech hub, Silicon Valley, and tinkered around with his hobby in his off-hours. The "person-to-person trading community" (or so eBay brass like to call it) took off and in 1996 Omidyar resigned from his day job to devote his time exclusively to eBay.

It was a simple concept. People with something to sell could put the item up for auction on the site and other eBay members could bid. The seller set a minimum price, wrote and designed the posting, and paid eBay a small placement fee (typically 25 cents to two dollars) and a success fee which was determined by the final closing price.

To a great extent, the community policed itself and, in fact, it was eBay members who suggested Omidyar start charging the placement fees that came into effect in February 1996.

Before the web came along, Internet users bought, sold, and traded goods through postings on message boards. The boards, however, were text-driven and populated primarily by computer-savvy young men on the hunt for computer hardware and software. A more diverse membership was attracted to eBay, and most auctions soon incorporated photos so potential buyers could get a better sense of the item they were bidding on.

By summer 1997, just shy of its two-year anniversary, eBay was in the black. The dot-com boom was in full swing, and most web companies were busy drumming up millions from venture capitalists to finance their often flighty and nonsensical ideas and business plans.

And eBay was no exception. In September 1998, the company posted its initial public offering (IPO) at $18 per share; the stock closed at $47.38 at the end of the first day.

Impressive IPOs weren't unusual in the heady days of the dot-com boom, but eBay had something most of the others didn't: staying power. It was, as they say, the real deal, with the only thing fake about it being that infamous Pez story.

In his 2002 book *The Perfect Store: Inside eBay*, writer Adam Cohen debunks the famous story of how eBay got its start. It had been repeatedly reported that Omidyar was inspired to start the company when his then-girlfriend, now wife, Pamela Kerr, complained of having trouble connecting with other Pez candy dispenser collectors to trade with. In Cohen's book, eBay public relations woman Mary Lou Song fesses up to fabricating the story to hook reporters on the eBay story.

Professional ethics aside, Song's story worked and the eBay/Pez tale has been circulating ever since. The Pez myth rose in tandem with the company's profits. After going public in 1998, Pierre Omidyar made the unusual move of stepping aside to make room for whip-smart CEO Meg Whitman, who had previously held executive posts at Disney and Hasbro. Omidyar, who is worth more than $5 billion, relocated to Paris, busying himself by plotting eBay's expansion strategies, and in 1999 *Time* magazine named him Man of the Year.

Meg Whitman, meantime, was gaining a reputation as one of the brightest CEOs around, having shepherded eBay's profits from $47 million in 1998 to $749 million in 2001.

High profile Internet brands like Amazon and Yahoo! did their best to horn in on the online auction market, but eBay was too far ahead in the race for either to even dream of catching up. But being the biggest and most profitable meant being more vulnerable to scams and criticism.

Clever hackers have been known to tap into the online identity of eBay members and go on reckless bidding sprees. Some psychologists have witnessed a rise in the number of "eBay addicts," whose compulsion is similar to that of problem gamblers. Courses designed to exploit the eBay system teach how to charge exorbitant shipping and handling fees, and other users have attempted to auction distasteful (and often fake) items such as remnants of the collapsed World Trade Center towers.

But eBay scams and exploitation are relatively rare, considering it has more than 50 million members. In fact, its democratic system of buying and selling goods is almost old-fashioned and quaint, and sometimes very funny.

In November 2002, a man from Orange County, California auctioned off his services in an ad titled "I Will Go Shopping for Jeans With You." George, of item #983171300, was pictured sitting on a sofa, clad in boxer shorts and posing like the muscled he-man he wasn't. Bidding began at one cent, with interested parties undoubtedly sucked in by the tempting description of the merchandise:

"This auction is for a 100% pure Man. He lives in Orange County and wants to go shopping with you. High bidder agrees to pick him up in Newport Beach so he can go shopping with them. He will carry bags and give expertise fashion advice. He can also go out to eat if you would like him to, his treat. This item measures 5'9" and is stocky build. The item you are bidding on likes designer jeans, candle light dinners, and long walks on the beach. Please, serious bidders only. I prefer PayPal but will also accept money orders, checks, and food stamps."

After seven days and seven bids, George's services were sold. He went for 55 cents, proving that shoppers really can find it all on eBay.

# Shopping for a Living

chapter

**vii**

# Pulling the Strings

*Celebrity fashion stylists yield real power in Tinseltown*

**H**ollywood fashion stylists give a whole new meaning to the term "power shopping." Armed with killer client lists and a nose for new and press-stirring looks, the once-anonymous men and women who dress L.A.'s prettiest have become celebrities in their own right.

It used to be that stylists were strictly behind-the-scenes, dressing models for editorial photo shoots, buying props for film sets, and making sure that bowl of Cheerios being filmed for a commercial looked absolutely perfect. (By the way, that's not milk, it's white glue.) But of the legions of food stylists, prop stylists, and fashion stylists employed by various creative industries, it's the Hollywood fashion stylist who has become the biggest star.

Salma Hayek.

And of those stars, none shines brighter than Phillip Bloch.

A former Jordache Jeans model with a pencil moustache and a penchant for wearing berets, Bloch has worked with some of the biggest names in the movie business. Halle Berry, Salma Hayek, Sandra Bullock, and Jada Pinkett Smith have all been Bloch's clients, and he has helped them choose just the right ensemble for the Oscars, the Golden Globes, and other high profile events.

Sandra Bullock.

But when Bloch finds the time to attend to a starlet's every image-driven whim is a mystery.

He has been a contributing editor at *In Style* magazine and a mem-

Jada Pinkett Smith.

ber of Joan Rivers' Golden Hanger Awards committee, the members of which assess the best of Hollywood style annually for the cable channel E! In 2000, Bloch got involved with the charitable Community Closet program in Los Angeles. In an effort to assist women re-entering the workforce after spending time on welfare, Bloch would perform 32 career clothes makeovers per day aboard a 53-foot-long bus.

Phillip Bloch.

He frequently pops up delivering snappy soundbytes on television shows like *Entertainment Tonight* and even provided live, color commentary alongside film critic Roger Ebert on the pre-show telecast of the Academy Awards in 2001. In January 2002, he became the first fashion editor for online auction site eBay, which promised, "Philip will rock your closet and hook up your style!!"

Mega-browed billionaire Donald Trump hired Bloch to re-style his Miss Universe pageant and somewhere along the way, Bloch even managed to write a book, *Elements of Style: From the Portfolio of Hollywood's Premier Stylist.*

The rise of Hollywood stylists has been fast and furious. Bloch, for example, moved from New York to Los Angeles in 1994 where he had achieved success in a more traditional styling career – pulling together the fashion for magazine spreads and advertisements. Around the same time, more Hollywood stars were starting to employ stylists to help them cobble together looks for big events. And as the stakes in the annual Oscars who's-wearing-what-designer grew, so did the demand for and power of these shopping elite.

Giorgio Armani was the first designer to recognize and fully exploit the advertising potential of having an A-list star decked out and photographed in one of his designs on Hollywood's biggest night. In 1990, Armani set up an L.A. office and set about courting actresses to wear his clothes to big events.

Other designers followed suit, but soon encountered a power shift. Many stars began relying on their stylists to do their fashion bidding for them, rifling through the best the fashion world had to offer, eventually whittling the choices down to a small selection for the star to pick from. And so the practice of designer-courting-stylist began, and it wasn't long before Bloch and his contemporaries were assigned front-row seats at designer fashion shows.

Giorgio Armani.

The best peek into the domain of the most powerful stylists is witnessed in September Films' 2000 documentary, *Dressing for the Oscars.* The British film chronicles the frenzy of pre-Oscars fashion negotiation and captures the dynamic that has evolved between designers and stylists. They need each other, but it's clear from the film that stylists like Bloch and the decidedly low-profile Jessica Paster are the ones who wield the real power.

The power and profile of celebrity stylists such as Bloch prompted a wave in interest in styling as a career, with schools from New York's prestigious Fashion Institute of Technology to the International School of Design in Orlando, Florida offering styling classes and/or programs.

Love him or hate him (he's often the target of catty comments on industry message boards due to his self-promoting ways), Phillip Bloch: Stylist to the Stars, is entitled to at least a bit of the credit for bringing stylists' jobs out from behind-the-scenes and empowering them with influence.

Let's just hope they use that power for fashion good, not evil.

## Shopping on the Inside

*Personal shopping for prisoners*

In a November 2001 article by Alan Feuer in *The New York Times*, Adrienne Smalls was dubbed the "L.L. Bean of the New York Prison System." Smalls doesn't sell preppy staples like Fair Isle sweaters and duck boots; she sells toothpaste, deodorant, sheets, and socks to prisoners incarcerated in New York state jails.

The Bronx-based woman started her Small Quality Packaging Corporation in 1999 with $500 she raised through her family, then a $25,000 loan from the Bronx Overall Development Corporation. As a representative of the organization told the *Times*, Smalls paid the loan back right away and by all accounts her personal-shopping-for-prisoners business has been a smashing success. She was even named the entrepreneur of the month by the Harlem Venture Group in summer 2001.

Inmates, and their nearest and dearest, can choose from a list of reasonably priced items and Smalls will deliver the goods. Sometimes a prisoner orders something for himself, but often it's friends and family members planning a prison visit who engage Smalls' services.

Shopping for prisoners is a tough gig. Each correctional facility has its own rules and restrictions regarding what can (and what cannot) be brought into the prison. Adrienne Smalls makes it her business to know all the ins and outs of the dos and don'ts, and passes the valuable information on to those who may not know that items must be hermetically sealed, contain not a drop of alcohol, and that certain colors of clothing are generally banned, as they are

www.prisonhelp.com

associated with prison staff or other law enforcement officers.

Smalls and her son Michael, who helps run Small Quality Packing Corp and the website *PrisonHelp.com*, know a thing or two about what prisoners want. Both mother and son spent time behind bars: she did three years from 1989 to 1991 for hitting a police officer, while he spent 1993 to 1998 in jail for a drug offense.

Whether it's Smalls in the Bronx or a sleek and polished personal clothing shopper in Manhattan at Barney's New York, personal shopping is personal shopping. And the key to success is knowing the needs and wants of the clientele – from $4.50 Dred Lock Shampoo to a pricey Jean Paul Gaultier suit.

## Somebody's Watching You

*Mystery shoppers keep retailers in line*

**C**all it shopping on the sly. A regular Jane or Joe enters a store, browses around, fingers the merchandise, maybe asks a few questions or tries something on, then makes a purchase. It's an everyday scene at an everyday shop, except for one rather significant detail: the store and its employees have just been "shopped."

Mystery shoppers, who have been around since the early 1900s when banks and stores hired private investigators to catch dishonest employees in the act of stealing, are the anonymous faces whose job it is to police the retail world. They may look and act just like real shoppers, but they are, in fact, shopping with purpose.

A retailer will outline its objective to a mystery shopping provider agency and the agency will, in turn, find a shopper who fits the demographic bill. The shopper is then given detailed instructions as to what to watch for and will most likely be required to answer a questionnaire or write a report describing their experience.

Up until the 1990s, employee theft was the main reason mystery shoppers were hired. Throughout the twentieth century, mystery shoppers were used to keep a close eye on just how a clerk rung in a sale. (When was the register opened and closed? Were all items entered or was the tally simply quoted, leaving the cash free to be pocketed? Would an employee accept an expired coupon?) And the sneaky job has had all kinds of names: integrity shoppers, secret shoppers, and spotters among them.

The term mystery shopper is said to have been coined in the 1940s by WilMark, the first company in the

United States to offer such services to retailers in an organized fashion. The term stuck and the industry grew.

The first hint the public had that mystery shoppers shopped among them came in the 1970s and early 1980s when the Atlanta firm Shop 'n' Chek became a media darling. Founded in 1972 by Carol Cherry, the company today uses more than 100,000 shoppers and completes almost half-a-million client evaluations in North America each year.

Today's mystery shopper, while still often hired to help prevent theft, is also called upon to evaluate customer service. This shift in focus resulted in a boon for would-be mystery shoppers, but also prompted the industry to band together to prevent bogus companies from sullying its image.

In 1998, the Mystery Shopping Providers Association was founded, and lists over 250,000 registered shoppers. It is estimated that the industry generates over $1 billion in revenue worldwide every year, and the numbers keep climbing as retail competition heats up.

The Internet has played an important role in the growth of the industry. For 20 bucks, there are ebooks a wannabe mystery shopper can download to learn the so-called tricks of the trade, and pop-up ads that promise easy work and big bucks abound.

Legitimate mystery shopping agencies have used the Internet to expand their business and seek out new shoppers. Most list territories in which they are seeking shoppers and the desired demographic profiles. But mystery shoppers will not find their fortune secretly evaluating retailers' attitudes and practices. They are paid by the hour (usually $10-15) and work can be sporadic.

The unpredictable work schedule and the small paychecks, however, are worth it for many mystery shoppers: they live the dream of being paid to shop.

# *Life in the Biz*

*Professional shoppers reveal what it's like*

## Gwendolynn Gawlick,
## MYSTERY SHOPPER

**1. How and when did you get into the mystery shopping business?**

I heard whispers about it about five or six years ago – I knew it existed, but I didn't know how to find it – so I really started doing research and I found one firm and [took it] from there. Then I started doing research on the Internet and that really helped. Nowadays, all the mystery shopping firms are on the Internet.

[The process] is fairly straightforward: you have an application, you fill it out, and then they call you for jobs. It's a contract job and it can take three or four weeks for them to call you depending on the company.

I did it because I could do it on my own time – so I didn't have to be in an office. It isn't great money, but I got to eat out a lot for free, which I liked, and I could do it around my general [errands] of the day. When I was doing a lot of it I was making a couple hundred dollars a month, which is not a lot of money. If you were actually trying to make a full-time living you'd have to work your butt off. But it's not meant to be a full-time job, it's meant to be something that people do in their spare time.

**2. How do you describe your job and its responsibilities?**

Basically, you're usually doing customer service evaluation, so you're paying very, very close attention to detail and reporting it to the mystery shopping company, who then reports all the data to the client.

**3. What are the key skills and traits you believe are necessary to succeed as a mystery shopper?**

The primary thing about mystery shopping – it sounds really basic – is timeliness. [The contracts] are very often done in a very short time frame and have to be reported in a very short time frame so you have to be really reliable. You do it when you say you're going to do it and you get the material in. The second thing is an ability to really pay great attention to detail - pay attention to detail and then remember it.

### 4. What are the most common misconceptions about mystery shopping?

One of the biggest misconceptions is that you get to buy things and keep them and you almost never get to do that. Almost always you have to evaluate customer service in the purchase and in the return.

So many more people seem to be aware of mystery shopping today and want to do it.

### 5. How have you seen the image of your business change since you began?

There is more competition to get the jobs and I think that the average Joe is more aware that [mystery shoppers] are around. It used to be that employees had no idea we even existed and they didn't know there are mystery shoppers coming in once a month.

[For people who want to do it, getting hired is based on] partly your demographic, partly whether you have any experience, and partly by the way you fill out the application. If you can't fill out the application correctly, they're going to assume that you're not going to be able to fill out the reports very well. My best advice would be to go to the Internet and mount an organized search. Write down the names of 10 top companies and then apply in the way they ask you to apply.

<br>

## CHRISTINA MCDOWELL,
## PERSONAL SHOPPER, HOLT RENFREW CANADA

### 1. How did you become a personal shopper for Holt Renfrew?

Holt Renfrew has had a personal shopping service for more than 10 years, just not as a [separate] department - that was launched almost four years ago. That's how they connected with me. I would come in with my private clients [from my own personal shopping business] and they got to know me.

## 2. How do you describe the job of a personal shopper and its responsibilities?

It's very much a service-based business. In retail you're seeing less and less service, people complaining when they go into stores that nobody is there or that nobody knows what they're doing. For me, it's the ability to read and interpret my clients and their lifestyle. I then have to be able to source out appropriate product. I'm always looking – always looking.

There's very much a psychological part to this business – really understanding the person-to-person [dynamic] is necessary. One of my biggest kicks with my clients is when I see a transformation. I get very excited when I see someone come in with her head kind of down and by the time I take her through the whole process she says, "I've just had the best time," and feels great about herself and goes out there and knocks them dead. I won't let anyone say it [personal shopping] is superficial because it absolutely is not – it's about the way they [clients] actually feel when they leave here.

## 3. What are the key skills and traits you believe are necessary to succeed as a personal shopper?

A clear knowledge and expertise in the business, since this is very much a professional service. [You need] a strong sense of people skills, obviously, and a flair and panache in fashion. And discretion is a huge part of the job. It can be very intimidating [for someone to consult a personal shopper for the first time] and one thing I like to do is make my clients feel comfortable immediately because they come in and go, "Oh god, this is private, it's personal, and you're looking at me." They have their self-deprecating approach to their body and their image and I just turn it around right away as much as possible.

## 4. What are the most common misconceptions about personal shopping?

I get approached by people saying, "I want your job, I want your job," thinking that anybody can do it because they have an interest in fashion or they like shopping. It's so much more. I'm an image consultant, although it's changed somewhat to personal shopping in that that is what they've defined the department [at Holt Renfrew]. For me wardrobe and image styling is really what I'm doing.

**5. How have you seen the personal shopping business grow and change during your years in the business?**

The profile is getting higher, but there are still a number of people who have no idea what it is, but once they do they go, "Wow, I didn't know that existed." And that we at Holt Renfrew offer it as a complimentary service - my private clients were used to me charging them - there is great value in it. [Clients] realize the difference between shopping from department-to-department or person-to-person as opposed to having a comprehensive approach to shopping with one person intimately.

The business has steadily grown since I started. People say once they've used it they don't know how they could do it without you - there's almost a dependency thing. And that could be a style savvy client or one that has no clue or no interest [in fashion] - it's the way that I pull it all together for them.

## KIRSTEN BOWEN, DIVISIONAL DIRECTOR: WOMEN'S CONTEMPORARY FASHION, INTIMATE APPAREL, AND HOSIERY, HOLT RENFREW CANADA

**1. How and when did you get into the buying business?**

I've always been in retail - I've been with Holt's for 14 years. I started on the selling floor and I just moved my way through. [Buying] was always a long-term goal. [The store] ended up helping me out with my education - I took fashion merchandising - and then went in on a co-op placement, then was an assistant buyer, an associate buyer, a buyer, and then a divisional.

**2. How do you describe the job of a buyer and its responsibilities?**

We're always in the showrooms, we're always at the trade shows. Being contemporary and being the fastest division in the company - the fastest turning - we're always looking for the latest, hottest line to bring in first to Canada. We have to have our ear to the ground on what's happening.

[Being a buyer is about] finding the best product first and bringing it to the customers because they expect to go into the store and find the best possible edit of what's out there. That's our responsibility so we go all over the world to do that. We also negotiate the best deals with the suppliers for the company and make sure the product arrives on time. We place the order, we work with the suppliers, we find out when it's leaving their factory so we know when it's going to hit our distribution center, and then we make sure it's going out to the right stores. We follow the process all the way through.

Many people [representing the lines] call you, so you have a lot to sift through. We have buying offices in New York and Europe who tell us about all the new lines. Then like every customer, you read *In Style*, you read *Vogue*, you find out what's happening. And the Internet has done wonders. You don't have to wait anymore - you can see [the clothes] the day after the runway show happens or even an hour after and it's fun to forecast what the hot new trend will be.

### 3. What are the key skills and traits you believe are necessary to succeed as a buyer for Holt Renfrew?

You have to have a lot of passion for what you do - it's a very emotional business. You have to have a lot of dedication, perseverance, and patience because there are many things you do that aren't as glamorous or as fun as when you deal with the design side. You have to balance out the greatest things with what a customer will actually buy in each market. You also have to divorce your personal taste from that of what will sell.

You have to be very organized and you have to know retail math because when you're in negotiation for a price or for a deal you always have to know what the implications are. At the end of the day it's all about whether you are going to make money on it, and [it's your job] to figure that out. There is a lot of behind-your-computer work. Minimal time is actually spent out in the market - you always want more. It's not all about picking product

### 4. What are the most common misconceptions about buyers?

The hours are very long and sometimes very grueling and very emotional - we're all passionate - and sometimes the pressure is high. Everything is a rush. It's not as glamorous as people think it is.

**5. Do you have any career advice for wannabe fashion buyers?**

There are people who come in from the outside and people who work their way through [the ranks of the store]. I think the best buyers do come from the [sales] floor because they see the customer side and they know the process. Sales associates are your front line so they are your most important selling tool, and having been there and done it you know the importance of it and the importance of keeping customers informed and romanced and happy, and how much that can impact your business. Also coming through the ranks as an assistant and then an associate you also know the little things you don't think are important, like how to order supplies or use the FedEx machine or how to process an order – you just know every aspect.

Going into a fashion merchandising program is always a good way [to start], but it's nothing like what you get on the job. [You have to] get into an office and volunteer to get a realistic picture of what the job is, of what pace you operate at, of the ins and outs and the back scenes of the business because that I think sobers many people – some love it and expect it and others are just done – they're not interested.

The education is always good to have, but truthfully I found I got the most out of on-the-job experience and working my way through, but it is generally easier to get in with a degree. Did it really help me? Did I really need it? Probably not, but it certainly helped me get my foot in the door.

# Shopping and the Media

chapter
viii

### 1.
### BEING A DEPARTMENT STORE MAGNATE WAS ONCE CONSIDERED THE EPITOME OF SUCCESS

The money-grubbing tycoon has long been a big screen fixture. He's often a greedy and tyrannical boss who enjoys making his employees tremble with fear and, more often than not, gets his comeuppance before the closing credits. The only thing about this enduring character that seems to change is the arena in which he made his fictional fortune.

His character's chosen industry usually reflects the social and economic times. In the 1980s, he would have been a Wall Street power trader; in the 1950s, an oil tycoon. During the Great Depression of the 1930s, there's a very good chance a cinematic magnate would have owned a department store – or at least been the ne'er-do-well son of one.

A variation on the big-meany department store magnate surfaced in the 1927 Clara Bow comedy, *It*. "It," in this case, meant sex appeal and Bow's salesgirl character, Betty Lou, uses it to get her hooks into store owner/man-about-town Cyrus Waltham (Antonio Moreno).

Clara Bow and Antonio Moreno in a scene from *It* (1927).

Three years later, in *Our Blushing Brides*, a pair of New York City department store clerks/flatmates, take up with the rich, nasty sons of the store's owner. Level-headed Gerry Marsh (Joan Crawford), fares a bit better than her pal Connie (Anita Page), who commits suicide after being unceremoniously dumped by the younger brother David: at least she lives.

Depression-era London is the backdrop for *Looking Forward* (1933). Teetering on the brink of losing the family business, department store owner Gabriel Service Sr (Lewis Stone) finds his life has turned into a melodramatic mess after firing his best employee, Tim Benton (Lionel Barrymore), and finding out his money-hungry wife (Benita Hume) has left him for another man. But because Gabriel (or "Angel" as he's nicknamed) is a sympathetic, down-on-his-luck, good guy tycoon, everything works out okay for everyone.

Department store heirs are at the center of two '30s films, *Vagabond Lady* (1935) and *My Lucky Star* (1938). Boring John (Reginald Denny) and fun-loving Tony (Robert Young) are the two sons of department store owner, R.D. Spear (Berton Churchill), and battle over pretty young thing Josephine (Evelyn Venable) in *Vagabond Lady*.

In the musical *My Lucky Star*, it's Cesar Romero who's playing daddy's boy. As George Cabot Jr, Romero enlists the help of sales girl Krista Nielsen (Sonja Henie) to enroll at the local university as part of a dubious plan to advertise the store's fashions on campus. Expulsion, love, singing, and dancing ensue.

Sneaky department store owner, J.P. Merrick (Charles Coburn), goes undercover as a shoe salesman to infiltrate the ranks of his employee union organizers in 1941's *The Devil and Miss Jones*. But instead of breaking up union plans, Merrick soon finds himself wrapped up in the personal lives of his employees (who, naturally, have no idea that he's their boss posing as a lowly fellow sales clerk), along the way discovering love, romance, and the true meaning of capitalism.

## 2.
### SALES CLERKS HAVE INORDINATELY DRAMATIC PERSONAL LIVES

Want drama? Need angst? All you need to do is get yourself a job in a store. Since the 1916 film *The Shop Girl*, sales clerks - particularly women - have been subjected to all kinds of on-screen tragedy and suffering.

Just before taking a position as a San Francisco sales girl, Louise Elliott Medlin (Bette Davis) gets married, pregnant, dumped, survives a big earthquake, and miscarries in *The Sisters* (1938).

In George Cukor's 1939 classic, *The Women*, perfume sales girl Crystal Allen (Joan Crawford) has a torrid affair with the wealthy husband of society dame Mary Haines (Norma Shearer), who - as all wronged women should - hightails it to Reno upon discovery of her husband's infidelity.

## Must-See Movies

### *Five shopping scenes not to be missed*

#### BREAKFAST AT TIFFANY'S

Audrey Hepburn's Holly Golightly window shops in front of the famed jeweler Tiffany & Co in early morning Manhattan in the first scene of Blake Edward's 1961 classic, setting the tone for the romantic tale of love, money, and an impeccably dressed high class escort.

Audrey Hepburn in *Breakfast at Tiffany's* (1961).

#### COMMANDO

Director Mark Lester's 1985 film features an unusually violent, yet comical, scene in which raging Colonel John Matrix (played by beefy Arnold Schwarzenegger) decides to do some late-night shopping for guns 'n' ammo by driving his tank of a vehicle through the front of a store while growling in his thick Austrian accent, "Let's go shopping!"

#### PRETTY WOMAN

Julia Roberts is hooker-with-a-heart-of-gold Vivian Ward in Garry Marshall's

1990 film that made her a huge box-office star. Vivian's "John," Edward Lewis (Richard Gere), takes her on a no-holds-barred shopping spree on L.A.'s posh Rodeo Drive to make over her street hooker look, transforming her into a modern-day princess.

### GENTLEMEN PREFER BLONDES

Howard Hawks directed screen legends Marilyn Monroe and Jane Russell in the 1953 comedy about two man-hungry singers en route to Paris by boat. It is in Paris that Russell's Dorothy Shaw and Monroe's ditzy Lorelei Lee embark on a shopping extravaganza that will make viewers swoon.

### WINDOW SHOPPING

A French musical set in a mall, Chantal Akerman's 1985 kitsch comedy features several shopping theme scenes that must be seen to be believed. It's a little West Side Story, a little Fast Times at Ridgemont High, a lot of unrequited love – and plenty of singing.

It's all musical high jinks and shenanigans for Debbie Reynolds and Eddie Fisher in *Bundle of Joy* (1956). Reynolds plays fired shop girl Polly Parish who finds an abandoned baby on her doorstep, while Fisher does a turn as Dan Merlin, the store owner's helpful son.

Fast-forward four decades and movie buffs will discover that not much has changed. The clothes are different, there aren't many musical numbers, but the shop clerk drama/angst factor is still the same.

Kevin Smith's 1994 breakthrough effort, *Clerks*, revolved around the bored, disaffected lives of New Jersey convenience store workers Dante Hicks (Brian O'Halloran) and Randal Graves (Jeff Anderson). And, if nothing else, modern cinema has taught us that the perfect employment for quirky, self-absorbed over-analyzers is in a record shop, thanks to films like *Pretty in Pink* (1986), *Empire Records* (1995), and *High Fidelity* (2000).

## 3.
## SHOPPING MALLS ARE THE CENTER OF TEEN TURMOIL

The late twentieth century marked a new era in shopping cinema: the teen mall movie. Granted, it is not essential for a teen mall movie to take place exclusively at the mall; the mall simply must figure as a key location and the film must evoke that intangible teen mall spirit. It also helps if the movie is set in Southern California.

Amy Heckerling's early '80s masterpiece, *Fast Times At Ridgemont High* (1982), meets all the requirements for a teen mall movie, and stars the likes of Sean Penn, Phoebe Cates, Judge Reinhold, and Jennifer Jason Leigh. While Penn's ever-stoned Jeff Spicoli doesn't venture to the mall, the suburban L.A. shopping center serves as a meeting and socializing hub for the rest.

While the *Fast Times* folk were busy discussing fellatio, delivering fast-food chicken, and contemplating losing their virginity, in another part of town - namely, the San Fernando Valley - another SoCal mall shopping phenomenon was unraveling on screen. The valley girl craze quickly spawned songs, books, and films - most notably *Valley Girl* (1983) and *The Vals* (1982). With more gnarly "likes," "totallys," "tubulars," and "awesomes" than you can count, the gals of the valley girl films grow surprisingly weary of teen mall life, discovering that there is indeed more to life than shopping: there are boys!

The mall continued to play a supporting role in teen movies throughout the remainder of the 1980s and into the '90s, with even the animated teenager Judy Jetson getting some mall action in 1990's *Jetsons: The Movie*. But by the mid-1990s, the mall was back front and center. Director Amy Heckerling once again defined a decade of teen mall movies with *Clueless* (1995), starring Alicia Silverstone as Cher Horowitz, a mall-shopping, Jane Austen *Emma* wannabe with a heart of gold.

Alicia Silverstone in *Clueless* (1995).

Released the same year was Kevin Smith's *Mallrats*. An exception to the Southern California rule, *Mallrats* featured an ensemble cast (including Ben Affleck and Shannen Doherty) and was set in a suburban shopping mall in New Jersey. The film, which was a critical and box office dud, is summed up with its tag line: "They're not there to shop. They're not there to work. They're just there."

## 4.
### HIDING OUT OR GETTING TRAPPED IN THE SHOPS IS EASIER THAN YOU'D THINK

In the real world, after-hours life at the mall is not nearly as exciting as it is in the movies. Being trapped inside the walls of a store or mall has become a cinematic cliché, even prompting the writers of the animated television series, *The Simpsons*, to develop such a story line (involving Bart and his friend Milhouse) in the May 2000 episode, "Last Tap Dance in Springfield."

On the big screen, there has been no shortage of wacky goings-on long after the last customer has left. In the 1933 animated short, *We're in the Money*, toys, dolls, and – you guessed it – money, come to life and perform the famous song. Another animated short, this time starring none other than the Pink Panther, finds the sleuthing cat hiding out in a department store. In *We Give Pink Stamps* (1965), the Panther messes with the head of the unwitting store janitor to amuse himself as he whiles away the overnight hours.

The night janitor is also at the center of the largely forgettable 1991 teen flick, *Career Opportunities*. The

## Modern Shopping Lit 101

### *Five must-read shopping books*

*Mallworld*
BY SOMTOW SUCHARITKUL
(AKA S.P. SOMTOW)

It's shopping, futuristic, sci-fi style in Sucharitkul's 1981 novel, *Mallworld*. The Mallworld of the title is a planet-sized shopping mall populated by odd characters and feeds a hyper-consumer culture. The mall, which is a huge tourist attraction, never closes and offers shoppers just about any kind of experience they can imagine.

*Mallworld* includes seven of Sucharitkul's stories set in the futuristic and darkly creepy mall society. Indeed, the mall is not a pleasant place, as evidenced in stories titled "The Dark Side of Mallworld," "The Jaws of

Mallworld," and "The Vampire of Mallworld."

The later edition of *Mallworld*, published in 2000 as *The Ultimate Mallworld*, featured new stories in the series, including "Bug-Eyed in Mallworld" (also known as "The Mallworld Falcon" in some editions). Nearly 20 years after its initial publication, things at Sucharitkul's massive mall, however, had not improved.

Author Rudnick, who is best known for writing the films *Jeffrey*, *Addams Family Values*, and *In and Out*, takes readers on a week-long shopping spree in the New England fall in his second novel, 1989's *I'll Take It*.

Protagonist Joe Reckler, a 26-year-old Yale grad, accompanies his mother and two aunts on their annual New England Autumn Leaves Tour. But the true motivation for the wacky family road trip is shopping. The foursome each consider themselves seasoned shoppers and pop into stores all along the way to Maine (where, naturally, they must check out L.L. Bean). Trouble is, as much as Joe's favorite gaggle of gals love to shop, they're not quite as fond of paying, resulting in all kinds of comic high jinks.

town hottie Josie McClennan (played by a pre-Oscar winning Jennifer Connelly), falls asleep in the dressing room of a pre-cool Target store, and wakes to a nearly empty store, trapped inside with only town loser, Jim-the-janitor (Frank Whaley), to keep her company.

But in the 1990 horror film, *Elves*, there's no nice-guy janitor to banter with. Instead, there's an evil Nazi elf and bad-ass Santa to contend with.

Joe Pesci and Daniel Stern's bumbling criminals are young Kevin McCallister's (Macaulay Culkin) motivation for hiding out after-hours in New York City's biggest toy shop in the second installment of the Home Alone series, *Home Alone 2: Lost in New York* (1992).

Award-winning Canadian director Gary Burns puts a different spin on mall entrapment in his 2000 film, *Waydowntown*. The movie finds four friends voluntarily sequestering themselves indoors on a bet, spending much time in an office/mall labyrinth working, smoking pot, and tracking a shoplifting boss.

## 5.
## MALLS ARE SCARY

There are two kinds of scary: there's attempting to shop at a Wal-Mart on a Saturday afternoon scary and there's movie mall scary. The latter usually means someone is going to die – or, at the very least, some bad stuff is going to go down.

In the first sequel to *Night of the Living Dead*, the plot of *Dawn of the Dead* (1978) involves four people barricading themselves in a deserted mall to escape the evil biker zombies wreaking havoc outside. Twenty years later, the made-for-TV film, *Terror in the Mall*, again proves that malls are scary when a group of people – including former *Melrose Place* actor Rob Estes and soap opera actress Shannon Sturges – spend some quality time in an empty mall with an escaped killer.

It's back to disgruntled undead types in the slasher flick, *The Phantom of the Mall: Eric's Revenge* (1989). Eric Matthews (Derek Rydall), haunts the mall that now sits on the property his house once stood on before it was burned to the ground – while he was in it – by evil mall developers. And in 1994's futuristic, sci-fi film, *Shopping*, Jude Law and his now-estranged wife, Sadie Frost, go on "ram-raiding" sprees as Billy and Jo, driving cars into store windows.

But without a doubt, the best of the worst scary shopping films is *Chopping Mall* (which, incidentally, also picks up the award for Best Shopping Cinema Title). The 1986 film has teens getting inventive with merchandise to fend off the evil, malfunctioning robot guard in the local mall they've been using as a party space after-hours. The little-seen movie isn't a cinematic masterpiece, but regardless, it's clear a considerable amount of thought went into its handful of hilarious tag lines. Pick your favorite; collect them all.

- "At Park Plaza Mall the security force isn't just tight, it's terrifying!"
- "Buy or Die."
- "Chopping Mall: Where they slash their prices – and their customers!"
- "Shop 'til you drop - dead!"
- "Where shopping can cost you an arm and a leg."

## 6.
## SOMETIMES MANNEQUINS ARE REAL

It would be impossible to address the subject of shopping cinema without paying tribute to the *Mannequin* movies. Entertaining in the so-bad-it's-good tradition, the first film, *Mannequin* (1987), stars *Porky's/Sex and the City* actress Kim Cattrall as artist Jonathan Switcher's ideal woman - except for the fact that she's a mannequin he sculpted. His creation - Emmy - ends up coming to life (as an Egyptian woman from 2154 BCE, no less) after a series of nutty coincidences result in Jonathan working at the very department store in which Emmy is displayed in the window.

And because this premise was so excellent, four years after the release of *Mannequin*, audiences were treated to *Mannequin 2: On the Move*. This time around both Emmy and Jonathan are long gone and the sequel's plot centers around Jessie (Kristy Swanson). She's not exactly a mannequin, but a 1,000-year-old statue of a farmer's daughter who comes to life and falls in love with Jason Williamson (William Ragsdale), a dead-ringer for Jessie's true-love, the prince of the fictional kingdom she came from.

*Silvermeadow*
BY BARRY MAITLAND

Silvermeadow is not an English estate or the name of a horse, it's a mall – a big, huge English mall in Essex where very bad things happen.

Published in England in 2000, and the U.S. in 2002, suspense writer Maitland takes readers behind the scenes at the fictional Silvermeadow mall as seen through the eyes of the author's recurring characters, Detective Chief Inspector David Brock and Sergeant Kathy Kolla of Scotland Yard.

A bank robber who got away years prior (and in Maitland's book *The Marx Sisters*) is rumored to have turned up at Silvermeadow, so the two are quickly on the case, using the mysterious disappearance of a teenage mall worker as an excuse to investigate the happenings at the mall. But they get more than they bargained for when the missing girl turns up dead and it becomes clear that the goings-on at Silvermeadow are not necessarily what they seem.

*Mall*
BY ERIC BOGOSIAN

The mall is quite literally the scene of the crime in playwright/actor Eric Bogosian's 2000 novel, *Mall*. Hepped up on speed,

Mal kills his mom and then heads straight for the suburban mall where he continues to kill. Mal's crazed actions cause the lives of Bogosian's bored and disaffected characters to intersect in unusual ways.

Danny, a well-to-do Yuppie, is caught masturbating in the J.C. Penney department store. Donna, the housewife with the hot body, is responsible for Danny's arrest, but eventually ends up in a hotel room with young Jeff, whose day has been filled with acid and episodes of unrequited love. All of this goes down as the mall burns spectacularly and Michael, the Haitian mall security guard, hunts the killer in the dark.

THE *Shopaholic* TRILOGY
BY SOPHIE KINSELLA

Shopping is both fun and frustrating for Sophie Kinsella's heroine Rebecca Bloomwood in the first of the *Shopaholic* series,

## Department Store Follies
*Television exaggerates and ridicules the stories behind the scenes*

**I**f one were to believe everything seen on TV, it would have to be assumed that department stores are crowded with malicious, back-stabbing employees, or run by a bunch of buffoons, or else populated after closing by creepy living mannequins who like to belt out songs by Stephen Sondheim.

Television, thankfully, is not reality (no matter what anyone says), there are no creepy singing mannequins, and buffoonery does not run rampant in department stores across the land. That doesn't mean, however, that such antics aren't fun to watch.

In 1966, ABC aired the hour-long television special, *Evening Primrose*. Based on a short story by John Collier and featuring the music of Stephen Sondheim, it told the story of a reclusive writer (played by *Psycho*'s Anthony Perkins) who moved into a department store to avoid the world outside. But, as luck would have it, the department store turns out to be inhabited by a society of strange people who by day disguised their presence by serving as the store's mannequins. And, being a Sondheim vehicle, there was singing, with the most famous tune being "If You Can Find Me I'm Here."

The department store show took a very different turn in the early 1970s with the debut of the British comedy *Are You Being Served?* The show's 13-year run began with a pilot in 1972 and followed the comic adventures of the staff at the fictional Grace Brothers Department Store. With men's wear sharing floor space with the ladies in the women's unmentionables department, classic British farce ensued.

So successful was the show that in 1977 an *Are You Being Served?* feature film was produced. In the film, Grace Brothers undergoes a renovation and ships its staff of characters off to Spain for a vacation which, of course, goes horribly wrong, and sets the stage for yet more high jinks.

The cast on the set of *Are You Being Served?* (1972-1985).

Only 69 episodes of the original series were made, but there were several attempts to expand and continue the franchise. In 1980, an Australian version of the series was produced, but failed, and an American version, *Beane's of Boston*, suffered the same fate. Even the original team couldn't get it right when, in 1992, many of the old gang reunited to star in *Grace & Favour*, a series that found the former Grace Brothers' staff running a rural hotel *à la Fawlty Towers*.

Success was not in the cards for the 1985 prime-time soap opera, *Berrenger's*, either. Hoping to ride the wave of *Dynasty/Dallas/Knot's Landing*-style TV melodramas, *Berrenger's* was set at a fancy New York department store - Berrenger's - that was run by a rich, back-stabbing family full of secrets. Starring Hollywood B-list favorites such as Jeff Conaway, Donna Dixon, and Jack Scalia, *Berrenger's* lasted a pitiful 12 episodes, from January 5 to March 9, 1985.

The only American series at least partially set in a department store to draw viewers was *The Drew Carey Show*. Starring stand-up comic Carey, the sitcom first aired in 1995 and quickly gained a loyal following. Carey, with his thick glasses and loveable nerd persona, played the assistant director of personnel at a Cleveland department store.

While the show's action was divided between Drew's work and home lives, the audience couldn't get enough of the garish Mimi (Kathy Kinney), Drew's nasty, conniving coworker. With her thick blue eye shadow and gaudy print dresses, the goings-on behind-the-department-store-scenes would often take center stage, undoubtedly causing at least a few viewers over the years to wonder whether there was a Mimi working in the offices of their local department store.

*Confessions of a Shopaholic*. Original published in England in 2000, the book washed up on North American shores in 2001, retitled (its English title was *The Secret Dreamworld of a Shopaholic*) and ready to cause a stir.

The misadventures of shopping addict/financial journalist Becky hooked legions of fans, and Kinsella – who once worked as a London financial journalist herself – was soon at work on the second installment, *Shopaholic Takes Manhattan*, released in 2002.

This time around Becky has temporarily relocated to New York with boyfriend Luke, and is quickly immersed in the world of sample sales, museum shops, and Barneys. And her spending habits manage to get her in more trouble than ever – that is, until book three.

The latest *Shopaholic* book, *Shopaholic Ties the Knot*, finds Becky planning not one, but two weddings. There's the simple, homey ceremony at her parents' house in England, and then there's the full-scale Sleeping Beauty theme blow-out at New York's Plaza hotel. And weddings, as everyone knows, require a lot of shopping, something that Becky knows best.

## Shopping to Win

### The evolution of the shopping game show

### MISSUS GOES A-SHOPPING

John Reed King hosted the first commercial daytime series on CBS. *Missus Goes A-Shopping* (which was later revamped and retitled *This is the Missus*) was based on a popular radio program and made its TV debut in 1944 in a prime time slot. The show ran in the evenings until early 1946 and was included in the daytime schedule in November 1947, where it remained until January 1949.

Broadcast live from supermarkets in Manhattan, the female-only contestants on *Missus Goes A-Shopping* answered grocery shopping related questions, raced about the store, and tried to outdo each other by performing various stunts in an effort to be crowned the day's winner.

### THE PRICE IS RIGHT

Bill Cullen, the original host of *The Price Is Right*, circa 1960.

Long before Johnny Olsen, the late *Price is Right* announcer of the 1970s and '80s, ever commanded contestants to "Come on down!" there was a much more sedate version of television's longest running game show. NBC first put *The Price is Right* on the air in 1956. In the original show, there was no crazed cheering or big prize wheel to spin, only four contestants using their market knowledge to outwit the each other by estimating the price of a featured product without going over the "actual retail price."

*The Price is Right* was popular for many reasons. Female viewers could play along with original host Bill Cullen and the four contestants while their husbands enjoyed the eye candy of the show's trademark merchandise models. The show was so successful, in fact, that NBC added a prime time version just one year after its daytime debut.

All did not remain so rosy, however, and in 1963, the show jumped networks to ABC. And after two years

Bob Barker with Nikki Ziering, Claudia Jordan, and Heather Kozar, at the 30th anniversary of *The Price Is Right.*

the network pulled the plug on *The Price is Right*. Seven years passed before yet another network – CBS – decided to give the show another shot.

The new team included host Bob Barker, "Come on down" announcer Johnny Olsen, and merchandise model Janice Pennington, who remained with the show until 2000. The show itself was also re-energized with a lively studio audience, a slew of mini shopping-related games, and contestants who won the initial pricing round participating onstage in hopes of making it to the final Showcase Showdown.

## SUPERMARKET SWEEP

During the original two-year run of *Supermarket Sweep*, a lot of couples did a whole lot of running. Contestants on the ABC shopping game show, which was on the air from December 1965 to July 1967, were expected to do just what the name of the show implied: sweep through the supermarket loading a shopping cart as quickly as possible.

Two teams of two were given a limited amount of time to get not only as much merchandise in a shopping cart as they could, but the merchandise that had the highest value, as that tally would determine the winner.

An updated version of the short-lived show turned up again in 1990, when *Supermarket Sweep*'s original creator, Al Howard, resurrected the concept. The new *Supermarket Sweep* featured a $5,000 "bonus round" and aired on the Lifetime cable channel before moving to PAX, where contestants can still be found racing about the grocery store to this day.

## SALE OF THE CENTURY

It was a simple concept: answer general knowledge questions and win cash and the opportunity to purchase goods at low discount prices. The formula worked during the five-year run of *Sale of the Century* from 1969

## Playing to Win

### *Gamers get shopping*

The shoot-the-aliens/ninja fighting/car racing world of video games is not an arena where you'd expect to find much evidence of shopping. But further to the theory that shopping has indeed become a sport in which there are winners and there are losers, there are a handful of shopping video games.

It's all about the mall – shopping in it, building it, trying to get out of it – in the four shopping-related games, *Mall Maniacs*, *Mary-Kate and Ashley: Magical Mystery Mall*, *Diva Starz Mall Mania*, and *Mall Tycoon*.

1999's *Mall Maniacs* is a shopping cart racing game, a twist on traditional car racing games in which quick eye-hand co-ordination and good navigational skills are a must.

*Mall Tycoon*, released in 2002, is yet another entry into the crowded market of "Tycoon" games spurred by the success of *Roller Coaster Tycoon* in 1999. Like its close cousins (there's *Zoo Tycoon*, *Car Tycoon*, and even *Fast Food Tycoon*), *Mall Tycoon* challenges players to set up their own mall and run the business in hopes of turning a profit. Players set store rents, lease space to tenants, and take a cut of the shops' profits, all while trying to lure customers to their mall.

The folks behind both *Mall Maniacs* and *Mall Tycoon* used existing and familiar video game templates to create somewhat forgettable gaming experiences, entering a saturated market aimed at an equally maxed-out consumer: the teenage boy.

Teenage boys and video games may be synonymous, but the emerging market of teen and preteen girl gamers has had game developers rethinking strategies and targeting product (or "pink" games in industry-speak) at this last great bastion of virgin video gamers.

Tech-savvy young ladies are the market for the shopping-theme games, *Mary-Kate and Ashley: Magical Mystery Mall* for Sony PlayStation and *Diva Starz Mall Mania* for Sony Game Boy.

The Mary-Kate and Ashley of the *Magical Mystery Mall* are none other than teen actors and merchandising moguls, Mary-Kate and Ashley Olsen. Former child stars of TV's *Full House*, the fraternal twin girls have built a multi-million dollar empire around their image. There are Mary-Kate and Ashley videos, dolls, books, clothes, and,

to 1974, but when viewer interest waned the show was chopped from the NBC schedule in 1973, and lasted in syndication for only one year.

Like so many game show successes, *Sale of the Century* came back. After its final failings in the U.S. market, Australian producer Reg Grundy bought the rights and took the idea Down Under, where it became a smash hit. Convinced the show could find a new audience in the States, Grundy brought it back to NBC in 1983. *Sale of the Century* remained on the network's schedule until March 1989, but the syndicated American version of the show, which began in 1985, is still on the air.

## WHEEL OF FORTUNE

It's hard for shoppers not to get a little teary-eyed when reminiscing about the old *Wheel*, the one that started in 1975 with host Chuck Woolery. The original *Wheel of Fortune* involved contestants competing to solve a mystery word or phrase by spinning a giant money wheel and guessing letters that may or may not be revealed as part of the answer.

Sure, it sounds eerily similar to the modern *Wheel of Fortune*, but the big difference lies in how the grand prize was distributed. Originally, the winners of the day's show had the chance to take their winnings and "shop" in the various *Wheel of Fortune* boutiques. From cars to toaster ovens, watching the winners' choices was often the highlight of the game. In fact, the working title of the show was originally *Shopper's Bazaar*.

The shopping bazaar concept was nixed in 1987 and the final prize changed to cash, but that hasn't stopped *Wheel of Fortune* from becoming one of the most successful game shows in history, its name familiar around the world.

In addition to a children's version of *Wheel of Fortune*, there's been a U.K. version, an Australian version, a New Zealand version, and even an Israeli version titled *Galgal Hamazal*. But it's unlikely that the show host and letter-turning hostess of any of the international versions of *Wheel of Fortune* could ever eclipse that of Pat Sajak and Vanna White.

Sajak took over from Chuck Woolery as host in 1981 and – despite a brief (and spectacularly unsuccessful) sojourn into the world of late-night talk shows – is one of television's most recognizable faces. Letter-turner/model Vanna White, who was once a contestant on *The Price is Right*, has barely uttered an on-air word since she started on *Wheel of Fortune* in 1982, but no matter. The TV game show has made her a star.

## HOME SHOPPING GAME SHOW/BARGAIN HUNTERS

Hoping to cash in on the home shopping TV craze of the mid-1980s, the syndicated shopping game show *Home Shopping Game Show* and ABC's *Bargain Hunters* debuted in 1987. The *Home Shopping Game Show* started its run June 15 and had contestants vying to place letters in a scrambled word to win featured merchandise that – and here's the gimmick – viewers at home could call an 800 number to order.

*Bargain Hunters*, which started July 6, was labeled a *Price is Right* rip-off from day one. Contestants were shown merchandise and had to decide whether the price on the item made it a bargain or not. And viewers at home could – get this – call a toll-free number to order the items featured.

Neither show caught on and both called it quits in September 1987.

## SHOP 'TIL YOU DROP

Since 1991, married couples have been going up against each other on *Shop 'Til You Drop*, performing stunts, answering trivia questions, and aspiring to win the third "Shopper's Challenge" round of the game show. Winners of the Shopper's Challenge are let loose on the 10-store shopping mall set to – what else? – shop 'til they dropped.

The show has been knocking around for more than a decade. It first aired on the Lifetime cable channel from 1991 to 1995, then was picked up in 1996 for two years by the Fox Family Channel and was renamed *The New Shop 'Til You Drop*. After its run ended in 1998, PAX began airing reruns of the show before producers Scott Stone and

as of 2000, a video game.

In *Mary-Kate and Ashley: Magical Mystery Mall*, players must work their way through five levels of play (including a fashion level where the player must help the twins pick outfits for an in-store fashion show) or be doomed to stay in the mall indefinitely. Successful players will be permitted to go home at the end of a long shopping/working day.

Mary-Kate and Ashley Olsen's *Magical Mystery Mall* game (Dualstar Entertainment).

That the reward for "winning" *Magical Mystery Mall* is getting to go home is a touch confusing. Wouldn't the Olsen twins prefer it if all preteen girls were trapped in the mall – especially their mall – eternally?

The goal of 2001's *Diva Starz Mall Mania*, on the other hand, is to get the bug-eyed, big-headed Mattel dolls ready for a fashion show. This would obviously require a trip to the mall and, apparently, six levels of simple gaming play. Players pick out music, clothes, and snacks (and, inexplicably, pets) to get the Starz through their turn strutting their stuff on the runway.

*Mall Mania* isn't brain surgery, rocket science, or even visually impressive. It's also unlikely to be the last we've seen of the shopping video games. For as long as there are 10-year-old girls like the unnamed reviewer of *Mary-Kate and Ashley: Magical Mystery Mall* who posted her thoughts on *Amazon.com*, there will be always be room for one more. "This is my favorite game," the girl stated. "I can't wait to get more Mary-Kate and Ashley games for Christmas."

David Stanley (*Popstars*, *The Mole*) started making new episodes for the network in 1999.

## MALLMASTERS

It probably seemed like a good idea at the time. In 2000, Stone Stanley Entertainment struck a deal with the Game Show Network to produce 65 episodes of *Mall Masters*. Filmed at the giant Mall of America in Bloomington, Minnesota, the show had contestants guessing at survey results and answering questions based on categories named after the mall's stores. All this and assistance from everyday shoppers via the show's "Mall Cam" resulted in a confusing concept that left viewers scratching their heads and asking, "Huh?"

## A Song to Shop By

*"When the Special Girlfriend" tells a tale of*
*love, shopping, and lesbianism*

In the 1982 song, "Valley Girl," Moon Unit Zappa parodies the shopping habits of mid-'80s Southern California teens with lines such as, "There's the Galleria/And like all these really great shoe stores/I love going into like clothing stores and stuff/I like to buy the neatest mini-skirts and stuff."

The song, included on her father Frank's album, *Ship Arriving Too Late to Save a Drowning Witch*, was a huge radio hit and drew attention to the mall culture of the time, mocking it mercilessly, but making its point. Reference to shopping in song was especially popular in the 1980s and 1990s, as clusters of malls cluttered the North American landscape. But few of those references were at all positive. In two decades, more than two dozen songs were released featuring a shopping theme in either its title or content.

On the 1986 album, *Sounds from True Stories*, the Talking Heads had "Mall Muzak." Goth-rock band, The Voluptuous Horror of Karen Black, had the track "Shopping Spree" on their 1998 release *Black Date.* Both the Pet Shop Boys and the Jam have recorded songs titled "Shopping" (the Pet Shop Boys on 1987's *Actually*; the Jam on the 1982 EP, *Beat Surrender*). And no reminiscence of shopping pop would be complete without mentioning everyone's favorite overgrown cheerleader, Toni Basil, and her 1983 song, "Shoppin' From A to Z."

Since most talk of shopping or malls in modern song has been negative, it's a refreshing pleasure to encounter a ditty that celebrates shopping or – most specifically – celebrates the act of shopping and bonding with a very special friend.

It's not everyday someone pens a song paying homage to girl-on-girl shopping love, but in 1927, Russian composer Mischa Spoliansky did just that. Spoliansky emigrated to Germany in 1905 to study music and found himself involved in the daring Berlin Cabaret (or "Kabarrett" as it was called, to distinguish it from the tawdry

## When the Special Girlfriend

*Mischa Spoliansky*

When the special girlfriend
meets her special girlfriend
for a little shopping
shop to shop they're hop-
ping
shopping without stopping
There's no greater pleasure
than to shop together
and the special girlfriend
tells the special girlfriend:
You're my special girlfriend
Oh you're my favorite
girlfriend
my sweet and pretty
girlfriend
I trust in you my girlfriend
to keep our secrets,
girlfriend

When the special girlfriend
meets her special girlfriend
with great tenderness she'll
tell her friend she's special
oh my special, oh my
special girlfriend

– So what does my special
girlfriend say about that?
– Well, I can only tell you
one thing . . . if I didn't
have you, we'd get on so
well . . .
– awfully well . . . it's almost unbearable how
well we get on together .
. . there's only one other
person I get on so well
with
– with my sweet little man
– oh yes, with your sweet
little man . . .

O my man, what a man
but a man's just a man
Still a man with a frau
when he can sure knows
    how
Just last week her boyfriend
had her in a whirl
that romance is over
she's dropped him for a girl

– Well, your sweet man is
    a little pushy
– oh yes?
– yes, absolutely
– why? . . . how come . . .
– well, he does these
    things . . .
– oh, I don't approve of
    that at all . . .
– well, come on, let's kiss
    and make up
– okay love, let's make up

Just last week her boyfriend
had her in a whirl
that romance is over
she's dropped him for a girl

When the special girlfriend
meets her special girlfriend
with great tenderness
she'll tell her friend she's
    special
oh my special, oh my
    special girlfriend

strip club "cabarets" of the time) scene.

Originally written in German and titled "Wenn die beste Freundin," Spoliansky's "When the Special Girlfriend" was sung and recorded by the high priestess of 1920's Berlin Cabaret, Marlene Dietrich. The song resurfaced over the years in live performance, but it was singer Ute Lemper who drew attention to the tune once again when she included it on her 1997 album, *Berlin Cabaret Songs*.

Marlene Detrich.
*Courtesy Library of Congress (LC-USZ62-772424).*

Lemper's English version of the song (she recorded the album in both English and German) also appeared in the hit indie film, *Kissing Jessica Stein*, in 2001.

"When the Special Girlfriend" tells the story of two young women in love who not only love each other (rather than their dullard boyfriends), but love to shop together. It illustrates in song the bond many women - lesbian or not - feel when shopping with a good friend, making it the best shopping karaoke tune around.

# Shoppers Get Lucky

*American shopping magazine takes its cues*

*from the Japanese*

The media snobs scoffed and snickered when American publishing giant Condé Nast unveiled the first test issue of *Lucky* magazine in May 2000. A banner above the title on the cover read: "The New Magazine About Shopping" and it was exactly that.

No celebrities, no supermodels, just apparel, accessories, beauty products, and a touch of home décor content. Readers could spend an evening curled up with *Lucky* poring over pages of shoes and handbags or marveling at the one-skirt-five-looks type features. The magazine even provided a page of color-coded, easy-peel stickers at the front so readers could mark *Lucky*'s pages with an enthusiastic "Yes!" or a not-so-sure "Maybe?"

With stickers, page after page of pictures, no famous models, and – heaven forbid – next to no celebrity photos, *Lucky* didn't seem poised for success. Critics likened it to a catalog, rather than a magazine, primarily because everything featured in the publication was accessible.

Unlike most fashion magazines, every item showcased in *Lucky* was available to readers, and the description of each piece included a phone number to call or a website to visit to make the purchase. But for all the skepticism and its unusual formula, *Lucky* worked.

Created by Condé Nast editorial director James Truman and editor-in-chief Kim France, *Lucky* – which is aimed at women in their 20s – drew heavily from Japanese teen magazines, most notably, *Cutie*.

*Cutie*, as the cover of every issue declares, is a magazine "for independent girls." Or make that: independent girls who love to shop. *Cutie*'s readers need not know a word of Japanese to appreciate the content. There are no articles, only photos and the occasional *manga* comics spread.

*Lucky*'s Truman and France have repeatedly acknowledged the influence of *Cutie* and similar publications such as *McSister*. Both had reportedly been fans of Japanese *johoshi* magazines which, like *Cutie*, are classified as "information magazines" in their home country. Newsstands are cluttered with *johoshi* magazines for girls and for boys. Some feature only haircuts. The magazines effortlessly mix fashion and style with shopping, something North American women clearly wanted, but didn't know they needed until *Lucky* came along.

Since its 500,000-copy launch, *Lucky* has grown to a circulation rate of about 800,000 per issue as of late 2002. It is arguably the most successful new American magazine of the twenty-first century to date and proves that avid shoppers will triumph over media snobs every single time.

# The Fame Game

## Meet the queen bees of Kmart

Famous for: gracing the pages of *Sports Illustrated's* annual swimsuit issue (she holds the record for the number of appearances in the issue at 12 times); guest appearances on TV shows like *Melrose Place*; fitness videos and pin-up calendars.

Kathy Ireland.

Success story: In 1994, Kmart introduced the Kathy Ireland swimwear and bodywear collection. The line soon expanded to include women's sportswear, girls' wear, maternity clothes, and eventually, fitness equipment; annual revenues are estimated at $500 million.

*Name: Jaclyn Smith*
Birthdate: October 26, 1947

Famous for: playing Kelly Garrett in the 1970s TV hit *Charlie's Angels*;

# Selling Celebrity
### Kmart leads the way with three powerhouse star brands

Jaclyn Smith.

**I**t's hard to imagine Martha Stewart, Jaclyn Smith, and Kathy Ireland having much in common. But the women do share one significant link beyond the fact that they each have worked as a model: all three have partnered with discount department store Kmart to market goods bearing their name. In fact, it is widely acknowledged that without the celebrity labels, Kmart's financial woes that began in the mid-1990s would have been far greater.

Celebrity branding on any large scale is a relatively new concept that wasn't embraced by either marketers, stores, nor the celebrities themselves until the late 1980s. Shoppers, on the other hand, were always fond of the celebrity sell.

Fragrance was one of the earliest industries to employ the use of big names to sell their products. In the 1960s, Brut hired boxer Muhammad Ali and NFL quarterback Joe Namath to pitch for their product. Twenty years later, celebrities weren't just endorsing a cologne, they had started to lend their name to it, sometimes selling $40 to $50 million worth of the stuff.

Some achieved greater success than others. In 1986, Michael Jackson's trio of scents, Unwind, Heartbeat, and Wildfire, tanked miserably. Others, like the TV-inspired *Dynasty* fragrance, Carrington, caused near riots when the show's stars, Linda Evans and John Forsythe, made promotional appearances.

Singer Julio Iglesias and dancer Mikhail Baryshnikov went for the high-end consumer with the debut of their respective fragrances in 1989. Both Iglesias' Only and Baryshnikov's Mischa - the Scent, sold for about $200 an ounce.

But the grand dame of celebrity brand smells is Elizabeth Taylor. The actress introduced her signature fragrance, Elizabeth Taylor's Passion, in 1986, a men's fragrance of the same name in 1989, and Elizabeth Taylor's White Diamonds followed in 1991. In subsquent years she added four more fragrances to her repertoire: Diamonds & Emeralds, Diamonds & Rubies, Diamonds & Sapphires, and Black Pearls. But White Diamonds in particular struck a note with women, and by 1996, the scent was pulling in $50 million per year and has consistently ranked as one of the top 10 selling fragrances in the U.S.

More recently, singer/dancer/actress Jennifer Lopez has made a successful entry into the celebrity scent arena with Glow. Lopez had already built a thriving business selling her signature J.Lo clothing line to young women, just as her infamous ex, Sean "P. Diddy" Combs did with his highly profitable Sean John line.

Fragrance counters, clothing stores, and even supermarket aisles are today littered with celebrity names, from Paul Newman's all-proceeds-to-charity line Newman's Own (salad dressing, popcorn, lemonade, and sauces) to mini-moguls Mary-Kate and Ashley Olsen's youth sportswear and accessories line sold exclusively at Wal-Mart.

Martha Stewart.

But a celebrity name doesn't guarantee profits. In the end, the stars have to be selling something consumers want and an image they're eager to buy into. Kmart, on this front, seemed to have the magic touch, sometimes taking unlikely celebrities and finding extraordinary success.

later, many made-for-television movies

Success story: One of the first celebrities to put her name to a line of clothing (especially a line of clothing sold at a discount department store), Smith's affordable collection debuted in 1985. Her brand of apparel has become the third most recognizable sportswear label in the U.S. and results in about $300 million in yearly sales. According to a survey by trade publication *Women's Wear Daily*, Kmart's Jaclyn Smith collection falls only behind Liz Claiborne and the Gap in sales.

### Name: Martha Stewart
*Birthdate: August 3, 1941*

Famous for: cooking, crafting, and saying, "It's a good thing"; also known as a hard-nosed, perfectionist business woman

Success story: In 1987, Martha Stewart signed on with Kmart as a consultant and spokeswoman. It wasn't until 10 years later that the retailer introduced Stewart's brand-name line of home furnishings and accessories, Martha Stewart Everyday. The line, which includes about 5,000 pieces each year, brings Stewart's just-so style to the mass market and is Kmart's number one brand, raking in an estimated $1.5 billion annually.

# Spend Like a Star

*Shopping, celebrity style*

Greta Garbo.

## Before They Were Stars

*Sales clerks who became someones*

You've got to start somewhere, even if you're destined to become one of the richest, most famous press darlings around. Retail jobs are ideal fillers for a girl on the fast-track to fame, and were once a no-brainer launching pad for a local modeling career.

Notoriously reclusive actress Greta Garbo wasn't always so shy. She worked as a shop assistant, then went on to model hats for the PUB Department Store in her native Sweden.

Before landing her first (tiny) movie role in 1954's *The French Line*, Kim

It's every shopper's dream: to have the means to buy all the cars, clothes, gifts, and knick-knacks on the slightest of whims. The rich and privileged classes do it quietly and with discretion. The rich and *famous* do it all under the watchful eye of the press. Increasingly, attention is drawn to the shopping habits of the stars.

Magazines like *In Style* showcase goods purchased by famous folk that readers too can own by dialing up the accompanying toll-free number or hitting a website. Tabloids take blurred, long-lensed photos of celebrities darting in and out of shops, bags in hand. Television shows like *Entertainment Tonight* broadcast items about who was out shopping where and what they bought.

The seemingly insatiable curiosity about celebrity culture has risen in tandem with the proliferation of shopping-related media stories and the evolution of shopping as sport, so it only makes sense that the three have intersected in the early twenty-first century.

One of the most public shopaholics who has, in interviews, called herself just that, is Sharon Osbourne, of MTV's reality series, *The Osbournes*. Beyond the cussing and the rock 'n' roll family feuds, the show has allowed viewers a peek into the world of a very serious shopper. All of the Osbournes have achieved celebrity status thanks to their participation in the show, but mother Sharon has become a full-fledged shopping star.

In the September 2002 issue of *Harper's Bazaar*, writer Kristina Richards tagged along on a shopping spree with Mrs Osbourne. The resulting article, "$30,000 in Three Hours," paints a picture of a determined woman who loves to shop and knows what she likes.

"I don't get the same buzz unless I pay for it," she told Richards of her preference for paying for an item rather than have the store or designer give her things for free. Osbourne also turns up her nose at sales and shared her musings about buying quality over quantity in the

*Bazaar* profile, "If you buy well you'll always look good – even when you're dirt poor."

Sharon Osbourne dropping $28,875 in the space of three hours is nothing compared to rap star L'il Kim's definition of shopping spree. In the September 23, 2002 issue of *Us Weekly*, she told writer Jennifer Tung that the most she ever spent at once was $80,000. And it only took her one hour to do it.

Stylist Derek Khan, who has worked with L'il Kim, also told the magazine that the flamboyant star can "easily destroy a Versace boutique in one whirlwind shopping spree – I've seen her literally purchase an entire rack of clothing. She's the biggest diva shopper I've ever encountered."

Other celebrities *Us* has pegged as big shoppers include Gwyneth Paltrow, Sarah Jessica Parker, and, of course, Madonna.

The number of times the "Material Girl" label has been trotted out to describe the pop star must number in the hundreds of thousands. But such influential style-setters have to shop, right? And, according to media reports, make sure that their nearest and dearest look just as good as they do. According to *Us Weekly*, Madonna spends an alleged $50,000 annually on daughter Lourdes' clothes and employs a personal stylist for the grade school girl.

Unabashed Madonna fan Britney Spears also shares her idol's passion for shopping. The summer 2002 special edition magazine, *Britney: The Most Important Days of Her Life* quotes the singer as saying, "I'm such a girly-girl, I just love shopping and buying clothes."

Spears is such an avid shopper that Internet company Yahoo! and Pepsi teamed up in June 2001 to bring fans closer to the star by inviting them to log on to watch Spears and her then-boyfriend, 'N Sync's Justin Timberlake, shop in Manhattan. The webcast gave viewers the opportunity to watch as Spears and Timberlake shopped, as well as the chance to purchase many of the items the two bought for themselves.

But celebrity shopping chatter and gossip is not all fun and frivolous.

After causing a public spectacle shopping at the Forum mall at Caesar's Palace in Las Vegas over the 2002 Thanksgiving weekend, actor Ben Affleck and fiancée

Novak worked as a teen department store model. Skip ahead decades later and you'd find Oscar-winning actress Geena Davis working at an Ann Taylor store in New York after earning her drama degree from Boston College. She also did time as a Saturday window model for the store before landing an agent and booking considerably bigger gigs.

Writer John Steinbeck was no model, but he did work as a sales clerk to get by after dropping out of Stanford in 1925. And just one year earlier in

Gloria Swanson.

1924, there was another unlikely sales clerking tale unfolding. Gloria Swanson, who decided to get all Method for her role in the film *Manhandled*, went undercover as a Macy's salesgirl, but was soon recognized and was forced to cut her experiment short.

Research was probably the last thing on the minds of actress Joan Crawford and singer-songwriter Joni Mitchell when they did their respective time in the shops – Crawford needed the money for dance lessons in Kansas City, while Mitchell was saving up the $140 required to join the union that regulated musical performers in Toronto.

Even some of the women revered as style icons once worked behind the counter. As a teenager in Georgia, Julia Roberts sold shoes at a mall. After spending a year studying to be a court reporter, Michele Pfeiffer wound up working as a check-out clerk at Vons, a California grocery store. No Doubt vocalist Gwen Stefani worked selling clothing at the Broadway Department Store in Anaheim with bandmate and former flame Tony Kanal.

And who's to say that working as a sales clerk can't in fact *work* for your future career. When she was a Connecticut teenager, actress Chloe Sevigny drew media buzz for her style sense while working at the clothing boutique Liquid Sky in Manhattan's SoHo district. You just never know.

Jennifer Lopez incited media speculation that Affleck was having trouble controlling his spending. London's *World Entertainment News Network* reported that "friends" of Affleck were concerned because the actor supposedly spent $500,000 that weekend on gifts of jewelry, cars, and clothes for Lopez and her mother and sister.

But that's nothing. Affleck is a rank amateur compared to the king – or should that be queen – of celebrity shopping, Elton John. The over-the-top English pop singer has admitted his shopaholic status, claiming to have spent, between January 1996 and July 1997, £290,000 on flowers alone. He's also partial to pricey jewelry and anything Versace. Some of Sir Elton's extensive collection of Versace (and Prada . . . and Gucci . . . and so on), however, was sold at great discounts in December 2002, with all proceeds going to charity. The singer's fourth "Out of the Closet" sale featured more than 17,000 items, the monies going to benefit the singer's HIV-AIDS organization.

But that kind of extravagance and excess is what celebrity shopping is all about. As the old saying goes, if you've got it, flaunt it.

# Imelda and Andy

## A tale of two shoppers

L et's talk shoppers. Famous shoppers. Legendary shoppers. *Infamous* shoppers. Let's talk about Imelda and Andy.

A former first lady of the Philippines, Imelda Marcos is best known for her extravagance, spending, and the extensive collection of designer shoes she amassed while her late husband Ferdinand was in power.

The Pop Artist Andy Warhol was on the other end of the shopping spectrum. He loved to shop and before his death in 1987, had accumulated a variety of huge collections that rivaled that of Imelda's shoes, and included ceramic cookies jars and World's Fair souvenirs. But unlike Imelda, Andy was notoriously thrifty.

The pair actually met once, in 1982, at a White House dinner, but who's to know if they talked shopping. We do know that others *have* talked. The spending habits of both celebrated shoppers have been dissected, denied, exaggerated, and marveled at. Let's dive into that saucy melange of hearsay, rumor, and fact.

### IMELDA'S STORY

First, we have to clear up this business about the shoes. Various press reports put the tally of Mrs Marcos' shoe collection at 3,000, 2,700, or 1,220 pairs at the time she and her husband were ousted from power in 1986. Imelda scoffed at these figures, claiming they all got it wrong. In fact, she publicly declared, "I did not have 3,000 pairs of shoes. I had 1,060."

Regardless, the public had little sympathy for a woman who could go for nearly three years without wearing the same pair twice. But outrage regarding Imelda's shopping was nothing new. This was, after all, the woman who reportedly once said, "Win or lose, we go shopping after the election," and believed that one day the term "Imeldific" would make it into the dictionary. By her own definition it would mean "ostentatious extravagance."

## Busted!

*Celebrities caught exhibiting bad shopping behavior*

It's embarrassing enough being nabbed for pinching a CD or a lipstick, or getting locked up for credit card fraud, but imagine the humiliation of having your shopping slip-ups chronicled by the media. Some celebrities don't have to imagine – they've lived it. Let their stories serve as a cautionary tale to any would-be stars with a checkered past or a penchant for stealing. Here's the dirt.

**Who:** Ol' Dirty Bastard (AKA Big Baby Jesus, AKA Russell Jones)
**Claim to fame:** Founder of hip-hop group Wu-Tang Clan
**Busted for:** Allegedly shoplifting a pair of $50 Nikes from a store in Virginia Beach in July 1998;

Mr Dirty Bastard made matters worse for himself when he didn't show up for court – three times; a judge issued a warrant for his arrest, but the rapper was often busying himself with other issues like getting shot in a supposed home invasion and being arrested for possession of crack cocaine and uttering death threats.

**Who:** Jennifer Capriati
**Claim to fame:** Pro tennis champ
**Busted for:** Allegedly stealing a $15 ring from a store in Tampa, Florida in December 1993; she was not prosecuted.

**Who:** Joan Collins
**Claim to fame:** Played rich-bitch Alexis Carrington on the 1980s prime time soap, *Dynasty*
**Busted for:** Allegedly stealing makeup from a department store.

**Who:** Coolio (AKA Artis Leon Ivey Jr)
**Claim to fame:** Rapper known for songs like "Gangsta's Paradise"
**Busted for:** Stealing $940 worth of clothing from a clothing store in Boblingen, a suburb of Stuttgart, Germany, as well as for assaulting the store's manager in November 1998; was convicted of both crimes the next month and ordered to pay $30,000 in damages and perform six months community service.

Imelda Marcos.

The extent of Imelda's very real ostentatious extravagance was revealed when her possessions (including the famous footwear) kept at the Marcos' 54-room Malacanang Palace were seized and itemized. Few were impressed with the shoes, the jewels, the dresses, the 200 size 42 girdles, and the 500 size 38 bras, one of which was bullet-proof.

American congressman Stephen J. Solanz told *The New York Times* in March 1986 that "compared to Imelda, Marie Antoinette was a bag lady."

*Newsweek* writer Russell Watson wasn't so kind. "Enriched beyond the dreams of any normal person's avarice, she accumulated possessions with a single-minded lust that calls to mind those ancient Romans who gorged themselves, then vomited so they could gorge again," he wrote.

Poor Imelda. Exiled to Hawaii with an ailing husband (who would die in 1989), she complained to the media that she was cash-strapped and forced to shop at J.C. Penney. But there was a time when the solidly middle-American, value-priced goods at J.C. Penney would have likely brought Imelda great shopping pleasure.

Born Imelda Romualdez on July 2, 1929 in Manila, Imelda grew up in Tacloban, in the province of Leyte, without fancy shoes, gowns, or wealth. At the age of 23, when the former beauty queen returned to Manila after studying education at university, she only had five pesos to her name.

But what Imelda lacked in cash, she made up for in connections. Her lawyer father arranged for her to stay with influential political friends. It was 1952. Two years later, after an 11-day courtship, she married Ferdinand Marcos, who was then a member of the House of Representatives. But the shopping fun didn't really begin until her husband became president in 1965.

Imelda, very conscious of her impression as first lady, indulged in shopping sprees to Rome, Paris, and

New York, snapping up clothes and shoes at a rate even *Sex and the City*'s Carrie Bradshaw could only dream of.

As a result, by the early 1970s, Filipinos were starting to question the excesses of their first lady. Imelda frequently tired of defending her lavish spending in the press, claiming that the people of her country expected her to look "like a million dollars" and wouldn't respect her if she dressed down.

Her bad image only got worse. In 1975, *Cosmopolitan* magazine speculated that Imelda was perhaps the richest woman in the world. Two years later, it was reported that she went on a $40,000 shopping binge in Honolulu without even bothering to try anything on. Another report had Imelda and a gaggle of friends demanding Bloomingdale's in New York be closed for a private shopping extravaganza, then marching through the store pointing to desired items and saying, "Mine. Mine. Mine. Mine."

Her mine, mine, mine days came to an abrupt halt in 1986, when not only were she and her husband forced to flee their home country, but were also hit with what would be the first of many fraud, embezzlement, money laundering, and graft charges in both the Philippines and the United States.

In 1991, Imelda was permitted to return to the Philippines and set about crafting a new image for herself by running twice – unsuccessfully – for president. She did, however, land a seat in the House of Representatives in 1995.

Internationally, she's kept a relatively low profile since her return home, although now and then the over-the-top Imelda everyone thinks they know emerges. She threw a swanky 70th birthday bash for herself in 1999 and invited her perennially tanned old friend George Hamilton to escort her. And in early 2001 she attended the opening of the Marikina City Footwear Museum, which has over 200 pairs of her seized shoes on exhibit. Smiling for reporters and reminiscing about her beloved shoes, she quipped, "They went into my closets looking for skeletons, but thank god all they found were shoes, beautiful shoes."

A display of some of Imelda Marcos' shoes.

**Who:** Shannen Doherty
**Claim to fame:** Played bitchy Brenda on *Beverly Hills 90210* and a witchy sister on *Charmed*
**Busted for:** Writing almost $32,000 worth of bad checks while starring on *90210*; as a result, the California United Bank garnisheed her wages.

**Who:** Stephen Fry
**Claim to fame:** Dry and witty English actor/writer best known for British imports like *Jeeves and Wooster* and Robert Altman's *Gosford Park*
**Busted for:** Credit card fraud as a youth in England; served three months in Pucklechurch prison for the crime. He went on to study at Cambridge.

**Who:** Zach Galligan
**Claim to Fame:** Starred as Billy Peltzer, alongside the big-eye furball Gizmo, in the 1984 film, *Gremlins*
**Busted for:** Alledgedly nabbing a *Deep Purple* CD from a Tower Records store in Los Angeles in January, 2003.

**Who:** Olga Korbut
**Claim to fame:** Olympic gold medal-winning gymnast
**Busted for:** Shoplifting $19 worth of groceries from a Publix grocery store in Norcross, Georgia in January 2002; Korbut reportedly swiped figs, cheese, chocolate syrup, Earl Grey tea, and seasoning mix. Instead of facing a trial, Korbut volunteered to enter a pre-trial diversion program costing $330.

**Who:** Hedy Lamarr
**Claim to fame:** Austrian-born actress who was best known for her role in 1954's *Samson and Delilah*
**Busted for:** Shoplifting at the May department store in 1966; she was acquitted by a jury, but the negative publicity left her career in tatters. Lamarr was arrested again for shoplifting in Florida in August 1991 and received one-year probation; she died in 2000 at 86

Andy Warhol.

Anyone who has read *The Andy Warhol Diaries*, published in 1989, two years after his death, knows that the legendary Pop Artist and media sensation was obsessed with money, merchandise, and shopping.

Like Marcos, Warhol loved to collect things (and people, for that matter). But for every shoe or designer dress Marcos had stashed in her closet, Warhol had more cookie jars, more pieces of folk art, and more World's Fair souvenirs.

The artist's possessions filled all but two rooms of his five-storey Manhattan townhouse at the time of his death, and the cataloging of his things was still in progress at the end of 2002. He left behind 608 cardboard boxes, time capsules of things he had saved through the years. He started the practice in 1974 and saved a wide range of items, including a piece of cake from Caroline Kennedy's sixteenth birthday in 1973, an uneaten pizza, $14,000 cash, and a dress that once belonged to screen siren Jean Harlow. Archivists also discovered a mummified Egyptian foot.

He loved to shop. He claimed to visit a flea market, attend an auction, or pick up something at an antiques shop every single day. To label him a pack-rat would be a gross understatement.

Selections of his famous collections finally went on display at the Andy Warhol Museum in Pittsburgh in 2002. The exhibition and accompanying book were fittingly titled "Possession Obsession" and gave the public a closer look at Warhol's shopping quirks and eccentricities regarding money.

Warhol loved that he had money. Not having grown up with much, he relished the fact that he could spend to his heart's content. He believed in cash – not checks or credit cards – and he hoarded it. He was accused of being stingy and cheap, but also of being a fabulous shopper. In his 1975 book *The Philosophy of Andy Warhol (From A to B and Back Again),* he spent an entire chapter musing about money.

"Cash. I am not happy when I don't have it. The minute I have it I have to spend it. And I just buy STUPID THINGS," he wrote.

And whenever he bought those "stupid things," he always made sure to get a receipt.

Paranoid of a tax audit, Warhol was vigilant in keeping every receipt for everything he bought, no matter whether the item was eligible for a tax write-off or not. In his *Diaries* he meticulously lists his expenditures, down to the 25-cent pack of gum purchased at the corner store.

Eventually, the receipts became another collection and Warhol, by his own account, took great pleasure in amassing them. A passage in *The Philosophy of Andy Warhol* sums it up best:

"When I have fifty or sixty dollars in my pocket, I can go into Brentano's and buy *The Life of Rose Kennedy* and say, 'May I please have a register receipt?'

And the more receipts I get, the bigger the thrill. They're even getting to be like money to me now.

And when I go to the numbers-racket greeting card store in the neighborhood because it's late and everything else is closed, I go in and I'm very CHIC. Because I have money. I buy *Harper's Bazaar* and then I ask for a receipt. The newsboy yells at me and then he writes it on plain white paper. I won't accept that. 'List the magazine, please. And put the date. And write the name of the store

**Who:** Bess Myerson
**Claim to fame:** Miss America 1945 who went on to work as a public speaker, game show host, and the New York City cultural affairs commissioner
**Busted for:** Stealing $44.07 worth of goods from a Pennsylvania drug store in 1988; Myerson pleaded guilty and was fined $100 in addition to court fees. But according to writer Shana Alexander's 1990 book, *When She Was Bad: The Story of Bess, Hortense Sukhreet and Nancy,* her 1988 arrest was not her first shoplifting bust; Alexander asserts that the former beauty queen was caught with sticky fingers in Harrods in London in 1970, but the incident was "hushed up."

**Who:** Rex Reed
**Claim to fame:** Powerful movie critic for *The New York Observer*
**Busted for:** Swiping three CDs from a Tower Records store in New York in February 2000 – one Peggy Lee, one Mel Torme, and one Carmen McRae; a judge ordered the charges dropped that April if Reed managed to stay out of trouble for six months.

**Who:** Simon Rex
**Claim to fame:** Porn star-turned-MTV VJ-turned-actor
**Busted for:** Credit card fraud and forgery at the age of 17 in San Francisco and was sent to juvenile hall.

Winona Ryder.

at the top.' That makes it feel even more like money. The reason for doing it is I want that man to know I am an HONEST CITIZEN and I PAY MY TAXES."

For a man who made a career of manipulating and selling commercial images like Campbell's Soup cans and boxes of Brillo soap pads, he placed a great deal of importance on honest consumerism.

If Warhol had lived into the 1990s, he may very well have been branded a shopping addict or at the very least a compulsive collector. He may not have liked to spend a lot, but he did love to spend and remains a leading candidate for the Shopping Hall of Fame. Anyone who felt it necessary to complain about the stores he wanted to visit not always being open when he wanted to visit them is worthy of inauguration.

As he wrote in *The Philosophy of Andy Warhol*, which was published long before shoppers could get their fix seven days a week, "I hate Sundays: there's nothing open except plant stores and bookstores."

# Shopping and Gender

chapter
x

# Girl Power

*The tenuous relationship between shopping, women,
and the feminist movement*

"**G**o out and buy!"
Nineteenth-century feminist Elizabeth Cady Stanton fought for many things – divorce reform and the right of women to work outside the home among them – but it was her command to hit the shops that set off the first wave of women's consumerism. In her 1852 speech, Cady Stanton decreed it time for women to insist on the right to spend the family's money. Women everywhere heeded her advice and thus, the modern female shopper was born.

Elizabeth Cady Stanton with daughter Harriot, 1856.
Courtesy Library of Congress (LC-USZ62-48965)

It seems strange to think of shopping as a feminist activity when today a woman who says she enjoys shopping is often branded as frivolous, superficial, and perhaps a little dumb. But Cady Stanton's cry to take control of the household income was more about empowerment than it was about shopping for shoes with girlfriends.

At the time, Cady Stanton and her friend, fellow feminist Susan B. Anthony, were proposing radical changes to the oppressive patriarchy of the 1800s. Women were relegated to the home on a day-to-day basis and not permitted to work outside the house. Embracing shopping and consumerism got them - quite literally - out of the house, into stores, and into the company of other women.

The parlors of early department stores in England and France were popular meeting places for women to get together, relax, enjoy each other's company, and discuss the issues of the day.

The social aspect of women and shopping coupled with the assertion of female economic power garnered impressive results. "It was the first form of women's liberation," writes American retail anthropologist Paco Underhill in his 1999 best-selling book *Why We Buy: The Science of Shopping*. Women were indeed liberated from the home by this newfound activity, and by 1915, 90 percent of spending in the U.S. was controlled by women and 90 percent of department store customers were female.

For turn-of-the-century women shopping was, for the most part, a responsibility rather than an enjoyable exercise. Shopping was typically about keeping her family clothed and fed, but the rise of commercial advertising in the 1920s sought to introduce women to a new kind of buying: leisure shopping.

Marketers enticed women with a manufactured lifestyle that dictated beauty products as essential to femininity, and that new and more were better than old and few. According to the advertising spin doctors, shopping for shiny new products was *fun.*

The campaign worked, and by the time the post-Second World War suburban era rolled around, shopping was completely feminized. In the century that followed Elizabeth Cady Stanton's directive to women to shop and buy, shopping had gone from a male activity to one that was not only considered distinctly female, but inspired snickers and derision if a man shopped for anything outside the realm of "manly" items like tools or cars. While he may have worn the pants in the family, he was certainly not supposed to buy them.

Paco Underhill put it this way: "Shopping is still and always will be meant mostly for females. Shopping is female. When men shop they are engaging in what is inherently a female activity." Feminist writer Germaine Greer sums up the difference between male and female shoppers succinctly in her book *The Whole Woman* by stating that "men don't shop, even for their own underpants."

The postwar suburban wife was the shopper. She bought the groceries, the clothes, the toys for the children. All this shopping resulted in a great deal of time and effort on the part of women, but it did not result in respect.

In his 1964 book, *The Impact of Women*, author Henry Galus writes: "The American wife is often a baffling chameleonlike irritant to her 'practical male' because of her extravagant buying of prestige items, on one hand, then becoming the penny-pincher *extraordinaire.*"

One of Galus' sources in the book, Mayo Clinic consultant Dr Walter T. Alverez, takes the insults even

## Battle of the Sexes

### *Shopping stats and facts*

• According to a study conducted by Bruskin Research for the Woolite Fashion Forum in 2001, the average American woman owns almost 40 sweaters or T-shirts and 24 pairs of shoes

• Working women generated 42 percent of all mall sales in 2000; working men accounted for 23 percent (source: Stillerman Jones & Company, "National Benchmarks of Shopping Patterns and Trends, 2000")

• Healy & Baker's annual "Where People Shop" report found that European men visit shopping centers 25 times per year, while women do the Euro mall only 22 times

• Eighty-six percent of women check the price tag before they by, according to retail anthropologist Paco Underhill in his book *Why We Buy*; only 72 percent of men do. Underhill also found that men want to get in, get what they need, and get out of a store as quickly as possible. To that point he says that 65 percent of men who try on clothing will buy the garment, while only one-quarter of women will

*The Stepford Wives (1975).*

further with his characterization of female shoppers. "They spend $10 worth of energy on a 10-cent task," he is quoted as saying. "Then they come home so terribly tired that they shriek at their children and fuss at a perfectly good husband."

The image of the housewife-shopper was a popular target of the first generation of modern feminists, who took to task the stereotype that had so quickly evolved.

• A Pew Internet & American Life Project survey revealed that 58 percent of all online holiday shoppers in 2001 were women

• Women control or influence more than 80 percent of consumer spending according to data published in "Understanding the Female Shopper's Mystique" by Cynthia McCracken, *Shopping Center World*, May 1, 2000

• Young modern men shop more frequently (and more like women) than their fathers. WSL Strategic Retail's 2001 study, "How America Shops," showed that men between 18 and 34 make 3.6 shopping trips per week; women the same age make 4.1

• More than 70 percent of men say that price is the most important consideration when buying clothing, according to a Cotton Incorporated's Lifestyle Montior study in 2002

In her ground-breaking 1963 book, *The Feminine Mystique*, Betty Friedan wrote of the 1950s housewife: "Many women no longer left their homes, except to shop, chauffeur their children, or attend a social engagement with their husbands."

Like the social engagements and the chauffeuring, shopping had become a duty, and one, it was widely assumed, that they enjoyed. One of the best comments regarding the traditional role of the housewife-shopper was the 1975 film *The Stepford Wives*. Based on the book by Ira Levin, the movie tells the tale of Joanna Eberhart (played by Katherine Ross) who moves with her family from Manhattan to the seemingly perfect suburb. But, as the movie posters teased, "Something strange is happening in the town of Stepford."

Joanna and another Stepford newcomer, Bobbie Markowe (played by Paula Prentiss), notice that their fellow Stepford wives are unnaturally consumed by housework, child-rearing, and shopping. They are "perfect wives" who have no interests beyond keeping their husbands happy. Sure, they're creepy automatons, but they know how to please their men – and how to navigate the aisles of the local supermarket effortlessly. And that, apparently, is enough.

In 2003, plans to remake the movie, starring Nicole Kidman and Bette Midler as Joanna and Bobbie, were announced. That the film's premise and message was still relevant and timely almost 30 years later is most telling.

First-generation modern feminists fought to combat

the housewife-shopper image and convince the masses that shopping was an arduous activity. Unfortunately, that was one thing few were interested in buying.

Feminist Germaine Greer made waves with her 1970 book *The Female Eunuch*, then again in 1999 with its sequel, *The Whole Woman*. In the latter work, Greer devotes a chapter to the relationship between women and shopping, placing particular emphasis on the house-wife-shopper. She writes that home-makers "have been programmed to believe that shopping is recreation and there is no greater female festival than a whole day's shopping" and that "when a women is not working in her home or with her children she is working at shopping."

Shopping, according to Greer, is work, not leisure or sport, and women have been brainwashed into thinking it is. "Women are supposed to be possessed by a lust that can only be satisfied by shopping; left to their own de-vices they will shop till they drop," she states. "Shopping is actually exhausting work for which women are trained from infancy."

Many women would likely agree that certain shop-ping experiences are more about work than others. Grocery shopping, for example, is not an activity either men or women look forward to. Nor is wading through the racks of a big department store in search of those elusive perfect-fitting pair of pants or, god forbid, a bath-ing suit.

Like Germaine Greer, futurist Faith Popcorn be-lieves that shopping can be work for women. But she takes a different stance on the subject in her 2000 book *EVEolution: The Eight Truths of Marketing to Women*. Popcorn more or less accepts shopping as part of the av-erage female's role and encourages marketers, advertis-ers, and store owners to take on the challenge of making shopping easier.

"Rarely fun, never leisurely, shopping in a large department store is more a necessary evil so why can't department stores make the experience more painless, even productive for women," Popcorn writes, then prais-es businesses that have instituted changes that result in a simpler shopping experience.

Much of Popcorn's simplification theory is based on time and the fact that women today have little of it to spare. Instead of asking women to stop shopping or

• A 2001 study of holiday shopping habits by De-loitte & Touche showed that only 40 percent of men had at least three-quarters of their holiday shopping done by Decem-ber 24

• Nearly 70 percent of cat-alog shoppers are female, according to a 1999 survey by *Catalog Age* magazine to examine any oppressive or "anti-feminist" stereotype they may or may not be perpetuating, she speaks to the businesses that rely on female shoppers to stay alive. "Smart companies have begun to realize that a minute saved is a sale earned," she writes.

The hardcore feminist line that all shopping is oppressive drudgery is a hard sell. As much as second generation modern feminists such as Susan Faludi would like women to champion the belief that women's shopping and consumerism is primarily motivated by

Gloria Steinem.

such evils as envy of other women, low self-esteem, and a seductive image concocted and reinforced by the advertising industry, others like Faith Popcorn and feminist icon Gloria Steinem have adopted a more moderate - and realistic - approach to finding a balance between feminism and shopping.

While visiting Toronto for Feminist Expo 2000, Steinem "urged women's groups to set up booths in shopping centers because that's where the women are," according to reports in the *Toronto Star*, and made the bold assertion that "what the black churches were to the civil rights movement in the South is what shopping centers will be to the women's movement."

Steinem appealed to feminists to take to the malls to spread the good word. She acknowledged that the shopping mall was a woman's domain without passing judgment regarding *why* they were there – whether it was to carry out a mundane task like buying toilet paper and toothpaste or a leisurely excursion of browsing and buying.

The social and leisure aspect of the female shopping experience is a polarizing subject for many feminists. On one hand, it's hard not to notice the parallels between the shopping-as-empowerment message of the latter 1800s and the assertion of shopping independence and power of the lipstick feminists who emerged in the late 1990s

They are the characters in *Sex and the City*, the real-life women who publish and read *Bust* magazine, and they are women who aren't ashamed to admit they enjoy spending an afternoon shop-hopping with a girlfriend.

The hum-drum everyday shopping for groceries and the like is just as much a chore for them as it is for any other woman. They, however, find guilt-free pleasure in leisure shopping.

It's okay to shop, it's okay to indulge in nice things and fabulous shoes, and shopping doesn't necessarily equal stupid. In fact, the underlying message is often about financial freedom and confidence. The women flaunt that they don't need a man to pay for things; it's their money and they will spend it as they see fit.

From Elizabeth Cady Stanton to *Sex and the City*'s Carrie Bradshaw and the 150 years of female voices who have sounded off about shopping in between, the connection of shopping to feminism has no set boundaries, only individual definitions of where and why a line should be drawn. One camp insists on branding shopping as ultimately anti-feminist and oppressive, the other claims leisure shopping as an empowering pastime. But as the debate rages, it's unlikely that many modern women give the subject much thought, for, as nearly all the experts will agree, she's too busy shopping for toilet paper and toothpaste at the mall.

## Shopping Talk

### *Famous musings on shopping and gender*

"I've found out it's fun to go shopping. It's such a feminine thing to do."
– actress Marilyn Monroe (1926–1962)

"A successful man is one who makes more money than his wife can spend. A successful woman is one who can find such a man."
– actress Lana Turner (1920–1995)

"Men are obsessed with cleavage, women are obsessed with shoes."
– comedian Jerry Seinfeld

"When women are depressed they either eat or go shopping. Men invade another country. It's a whole different way of thinking."
– comedienne Elayne Boosler

"Shopping seemed to take an entirely too important place in women's lives. You never saw men milling around in men's departments. They made quick work of it. I used to wonder if shopping was a form of escape for women who had no worthwhile interests."
– U.S. factory personnel manager, economist, and educator Mary Barnett Gilson on working as a salesclerk in *What's Past is Prologue* (1940)

# From Sluts to Snobs

*How early salesgirls got such a bad reputation*

**"T**here is the cheesy boutique full of cotton-jersey dresses that will lose their shape during the first wearing, full of smarmy smiling salespeople who are so eager to help, so perky, so friendly that you *must* punch them in the face. The kind of salesperson who, when you try on a cotton-jersey dress that turns you into an elephant, squeals 'fabulous!' The kind of salesperson who thinks a cheap patent-leather belt will cover cretinous tailoring.

"Then there are the boutiques full of clothes that make you see god. Boutiques full of clothes of such exquisite elegance, such brilliant frivolity that tears come to your eyes and your insides contract with yearning. Boutiques full of salespeople who want you dead."

Writer and humorist Cynthia Heimel summed up the extremes of the typical Manhattan shopping experience as such in her 1989 *Vogue* article, "Fear and Clothing." But as countless women can attest, Heimel's two salespeople can be found working retail in any North American city.

But whether it's the endlessly upbeat clerk or the snotty saleswoman, chances are she's not fending off job offers from madams, wreaking havoc on her digestive system due to poor quality food, or on the brink of a full moral breakdown on a daily basis.

That was not always the case.

Salesgirls of the early 1900s were often seen in a most unsavory light. Employment opportunities for women were, for years, limited to the traditional careers of teacher, nurse, or seamstress, and working as a salesgirl in the department stores that had recently sprung up across the continent was viewed with much skepticism.

The women were frequently young, attractive, perhaps a little naïve, and, for whatever their individual reason, in need of a steady paycheck, however low. They were well groomed (adhering to strict standards set by their employer), underpaid, and even wore makeup

"A woman will buy anything she thinks a store is losing money on."
– journalist Frank McKinney Hubbard (1868–1930)

"It was the first female-style revolution: no violence and we all went shopping,"
– feminist Gloria Steinem on the fall of the Berlin Wall, as quoted in *Newsweek* (December 18, 1989)

"It was easy to see how upsetting it would be if women began to love freely where love came to them. An abyss would open in the principal shopping street of every town."
– Australian writer Christina Stead (1902–1983) in her novel *For Love Alone* (1944)

at a time when makeup was considered the domain of prostitutes and performers by god-fearing, puritanical conservatives.

The perils and moral challenges of being a salesgirl seem exaggerated and almost laughable today, but at the time were of serious enough concern to provoke Reverend R.J. Campbell to publicly warn that shopgirls were ripe to be led into a lives of prostitution. The Vice Commission of Chicago – a hub of early American department stores – also warned of the dangers of the job when it asserted that the typical six-dollar-a-week wage tempted shopgirls into a life of prostitution as a way of supplementing their income.

In a report released around 1910, the Vice Commission revealed that "the investigation of 119 women who had gone wrong, and who were found leading immoral lives in houses, dancehalls, and on the streets, shows that 18 women came from department stores."

The Vice Commission study was quoted in the 1911 study issued by the Juvenile Protective Association of Chicago titled "The Department Store Girl." The study sent undercover female investigators to interview a sampling of 200 department store salesgirls in February 1910, when about 25,000 women worked as clerks in the Chicago area.

The women, it found, were on average 19 years old (although some salesgirls would begin work as young as 12) and had all sorts of trouble to contend with. Madams from "disreputable houses" would recruit new hires from department stores with promises of extra cash. Sometimes they would send male business associates to do the dirty work, and if a girl said she was not interested in this type of work, he would report her to her male boss, claiming she had been rude to him in his guise as customer, an offense for which she could be fired.

The bosses were no treat either. Almost always men, the young salesgirls had come-ons and propositions to deal with. Long before the term sexual harassment was coined, it was common that "the man higher up" would effectively force the salesgirls into accepting his advances if she wanted to keep her job.

In addition to the madams and the store managers, salesgirls worked what was then considered long hours: about 10 hours a day. The Chicago report emphasized

"Women are born to shop. ... Men are born to invest, and are then evasive and deceitful about their losses and gains."
– writer Asa Baber

"Ever since Eve gave Adam the apple, there has been a misunderstanding between the sexes about gifts."
– writer Nan Robertson in *The New York Times* (November 28, 1957)

"How men hate waiting while their wives shop for clothes and trinkets; how women hate waiting, often for much of their lives, while their husbands shop for fame and glory."
– psychiatrist Thomas Szasz

## Gay Rites

### *Shopping with the pink dollar crowd*

They're here, they're queer, and they have emerged as an influential and desirable group of consumers. Gays and lesbians account for between six and 10 percent of the U.S. population, and according to experts, they have no problem exercising their spending power.

The gay community controls about $450 billion spending dollars each year, according to a study conducted by the University of Georgia in 2002. The same study found that gay consumers have an average annual household income

the hardships: long work days and wages so low the salesgirls could barely afford to eat. One of the study's investigators could not continue with her plan to eat as a typical salesgirl for one month.

The study, which had measured the experiences of salesgirls working in downtown Chicago versus those working in the outlying areas, concluded that if a woman was resigned to working as a salesgirl, she was much safer – both mentally and physically – in the suburbs. The immoral temptations were found mostly downtown and the advantages of working on the outskirts were numerous. There were no madams, many of the girls lived in the suburban areas so the commute to work was not long, and they could go home for a nutritious lunch.

The heart of the big city was no place for a nice girl to make a living and asserting her independence in such a way was just a dangerous lark. She was, after all, still just a woman.

Used with permission. ©2003 Coors Brewing Company, Golden, CO 80401.

# Real Men Don't Shop

*Myths and truths about the male shopper*

ity the heterosexual North American male who likes to shop: he is publicly mocked and ridiculed, his masculinity is considered suspect, and his very existence is questioned. A man is expected to whine about accompanying his wife/girlfriend/sister/mother on a shopping spree and is not to have any comprehension of leisure shopping. Men, it seems, are not shoppers. They are buyers and even that is a role they assume only when absolutely necessary.

But the mythical male shopper – the one who actually enjoys shopping – is out there. He's just a hard man to find and may well be closeted, hiding his fondness for shopping from the world.

Who can blame him?

Edward Bok, editor of *Ladies Home Journal* from 1889 to 1919, once wrote, "If a man is at all reasonable, one shopping trip is about all he wants in a lifetime." Nearly a century later, retail anthropologist Paco Underhill wrote in his 1999 book, *Why We Buy: The Science of Shopping*, "If I owned The Limited or Victoria's Secret, I'd have a place where a woman could check her husband – like a coat."

Shopping was and is women's work (and women's passion), and from Bok's editorial quip to the views of modern shopping experts like Paco Underhill, it's easy to see how a male shopper could develop a complex. Not only is he supposed be born equipped with an anti-shopping sensor, he is repeatedly reminded of his allegedly preprogrammed dislike of the mall and everything it stands for.

In 2001, Khabi Mirza, an editor at the trade publication, *Menswear*, told Andrew Tuck of the *Independent on Sunday* that men only "know one or two brands and do not enjoy leisure shopping. You see girls shopping on a Saturday and they will look at all the clothes in every shop. Men just go to one or two places, get what they want, and leave."

of more than $60,000 and they're probably college educated. And since they aren't as likely to have children as their heterosexual counterparts, they have more disposable income to burn.

The University of Georgia study, and a national survey conducted by Witeck-Combs Communications and Harris Interactive, showed that gay consumers were very particular when it came to two things. One, they had a preference for products and brands that advertise directly to them. Two, they liked to indulge themselves with nice things.

In the Witeck-Combs study, 39 percent of respondents said they prefer to purchase products from companies that advertise in the gay media. There's no room for the wink-wink, nudge-nudge advertising of yesteryear – gay consumers want to be courted by businesses who aren't afraid to come out and go after their considerable dollars.

US Air, Subaru, Coors Light, Johnny Walker Red Scotch, and Jaguar have openly marketed to gay consumers in recent years, while United Airlines just dipped a baby toe into the so-called "pink market" before abandoning the initiative.

Perhaps the airline should have thought twice about that decision.

According to the University of Georgia study, more than three-quarters of gay consumers believe in indulging themselves and more than half prefer to buy top-of-the-line goods. They like luxury and travel and when they see something they want, they tend to snap it up. Plus, they're considered one of the most loyal consumer groups around.

It all adds up to a marketer's dream – but they have to make the commitment to going pink before they'll see any gay green.

Mirza's statement is in line with popular thinking about men and shopping, but some researchers have recently begun to question the accuracy of the stereotype. New York's WSL Strategic Retail found in 2001 that American men aged 18–34 shop nearly as much as women in the same demographic.

In 1999, London's Retail Intelligence urged merchants to turn their attention to male shoppers whom, their data revealed, weren't so much put off by shopping, but whose business was rarely courted by stores. The firm's report, "Men & Shopping: Unlocking the Potential," claimed that while men may have a solid wham-bam-thank-you-ma'am reputation as shoppers, they are more than open to the seduction and enticement retailers have been heaping on female shoppers for decades.

Encouraging men to shop is a tricky business, however. They've had the message "real men don't shop" beaten into their brains for so many years, it's quite possible they may be suffering from a collective case of low shopping self-esteem. Retail analysts have yet to study the psychological damage repeated negative messages regarding shopping may have had on generations of men, but it's not difficult to understand how male shoppers may experience feelings of shame and embarrassment.

Not only do they receive repeated messages that they don't shop, male shoppers have been told that when they do shop they can't get it right. In her 1995 article for *The Dominion* titled "Why Men Simply Can't Shop," writer Helen Bain summarized the results of a shopping study conducted by New Zealand Market Researchers Mattingly & Partners like this: "They spend too much, buy ridiculous and unnecessary items, buy the wrong items, skip the most important ones, and take too long."

That's more than enough to hurt a male shopper's feelings.

# The Dark Side of Shopping

*chapter*

**xi**

# Shoppers Who Steal

*Inside the minds of shoplifters and kleptomaniacs*

Politically correct types take note: kleptomaniacs are definitely shoplifters, but most shoplifters are not kleptomaniacs. In other words, it is both politically and medically incorrect to label someone who steals a "klepto." Whether they be the teen truant who lives down the block and steals chocolate bars at the corner store or the movie star who suffers a very public arrest for swiping loads of designer clothes from a fancy department store, chances are if they steal, they're a shoplifter, not a member of the tiny percentage of the world's population that fits the clinical definition of kleptomaniac.

A rare psychiatric disorder causes true kleptomaniacs to steal, but not because they need or even desire the items they pinch. Their acts are not premeditated; it's an impulse reaction, a compulsion similar to other addictions like alcoholism and drug dependency. They often steal to relieve an overpowering sense of tension and anxiety, and experience a rush from the act of theft, but are quickly left deflated, with feelings of guilt. Sometimes, a kleptomaniac's guilt is so encompassing that they will even return to the scene of the crime and attempt to return the merchandise to the shelves.

A Victorian era shoplifter.
*Drawing by E.Mars.*

Evidence of kleptomania dates back to the mid-1800s, not coincidentally at around the same time as the rise of commercial shopping and the Industrial Revolution. In fact, a rash of what was labeled kleptomania late in that century was witnessed among middle-class and well-to-do Victorian women. It was known as a "women's disease" and the term was tossed around casually, with no distinction made between kleptomania and shoplifting.

It was believed that the women who stole were biologically predisposed to do so simply because of their gender, and as a result, the female "klepto" became the butt of many jokes and the target of comedy sketches of the time. The women who stole didn't do so out of need or want but because they were so entranced by the orgy of consumer delight that was the department store. Shopping was a spectacle and although many female shoppers of the day did indeed make legitimate purchases, they also frequently pocketed extra items that were not paid for.

It's unlikely that all – or even a majority – of the light-fingered women were textbook kleptomaniacs, but rather shoplifters who stole because modern consumer society was still in its infancy and the rules were unclear. As Elaine S. Abelson points out in her definitive 1989 book on the subject, *When Ladies Go A-Thieving: Middle Class Shoplifters in the Victorian Department Store*, many women when caught would offer the excuse that "everyone is doing it."

Everyone may have been doing it then, and kleptomania was written off as a female condition that couldn't be helped, but today it is estimated that only one percent of shoplifters are kleptomaniacs. And even when the term is evoked in medical or legal situations, there is always an expert skeptical of its validity.

In the case of Beverly McGill, an Ogden, Utah woman who was arrested in 1998, experts were split regarding her diagnosis (and subsequent defense) of kleptomania.

McGill, the common-law wife of a police officer, stole daily, even using her children as decoys. She knew the blind spots of various stores (the areas that a security camera can't see), she was known to put electrical tape over alarm sensors, and eventually was caught with over $250,000 worth of stolen merchandise in her home.

The stolen goods filled a warehouse of the Ogden Police Department, and three large trucks were necessary to cart all the goods away. The prosecution in her case alleged that she was a personal shoplifter who stole on demand, taking orders from clients and selling the merchandise for profit. When her home was searched, police found a vast array of items – from 102 scented candles to five bridesmaid's dresses.

Her common-law husband confessed he knew of her habit (how could he not?), but couldn't stop her. As a result, he was found guilty of theft by concealment, served six months in jail, and lost his job as a police officer. McGill, too, was found guilty and is serving a 15-year sentence.

Whether McGill fit the definition of kleptomaniac

# Scary Stuff

*A roundup of shopping fears, hauntings, and psychic activity*

### SEX SHOP HOME TO PARANORMAL PANDERERS

Standing on the site of a former brothel, the Pillow Talk sex shop in Kent, England is said to be haunted by the prostitutes who were once employed there – and messy prostitutes at that. Shop owner Alan Butler and his staff became convinced of the ghostly activities after arriving to work only to find lingerie and other naughty items strewn around the store like, as Butler told one newspaper when the story broke in spring 2002, "an orgy's taken place."

### TOY STORE CALLS IN FAMOUS MEDIUM TO TALK TO THE DEAD

Noted psychic Sylvia Browne was called in to sniff out the ghost that had been haunting a Sunnydale, California Toys "R" Us for years. The building, which was built in 1970, was reportedly home to a spirit from day one. Employees at the toy store heard voices, experienced phantom touches, and encountered disrupted merchandise in the aisles.

Browne held her first

séance at the store in 1978 and claimed to meet the Toys 'R' Us ghost, a ranch hand named Johnny Johnson who bled to death after an accident with an axe in 1884. Browne returned to the store to work her psychic magic many times over. The store – and the story – has become legendary in the area, with people visiting it in hopes of catching a glimpse of the mischievous spirit.

### DRUG STORE PSYCHIC NABS SHOPLIFTERS

According to *Charles Berlitz's World of Strange Phenomena Volume One*, Canadian drug store chain Shoppers Drug Mart hired psychic Reginald McHugh to catch shoplifters in the 1980s. McHugh would feel a shoplifting sensation when spotting certain people and, according to a documentary film crew who was trailing McHugh on the job, had uncanny success in ferreting out the law-breakers.

is up for debate. Certainly, she displayed certain traits, but when a typical kleptomaniac steals the act is unplanned, and McGill undoubtedly knew she was going to steal when she hit the shops armed with electrical tape, her two daughters in tow to throw security watchdogs off her scent.

But like any mental illness, there is no test that can offer indisputable proof of kleptomania, which is perhaps one of the reasons kleptomania and compulsive or addictive shoplifting is misunderstood.

Shoplifters, unlike their kleptomaniac cousins, have an agenda when they hit the shops. A small number of shoplifters steal out of need, and it's usually staples such as food and clothing that they're after. But only an estimated one in 10 shoplifters fall into this category, according to the *Allure* magazine article "Crimes of Fashion" by Simon Dumenco, published in April 2002. The other 90 percent is comprised of a hodge-podge of thrill-seeking teenagers, drug addicts, and professionals who covet pricey designer goods to enhance their lifestyle, and shoplifters with obsessive-compulsive personalities.

Statistics are sketchy. Stores don't often care to speak publicly about shoplifting issues, but the Retail Theft Trends Report in 1999 stated that teenagers account for 25 percent of all shoplifters and only one in 35-to-50 is caught.

One of the reasons stores are so reluctant to divulge shoplifting data is that it is believed much of the retail theft in the United States is an inside job, with store employees doing the stealing. The 2001 National Retail Security Survey conducted by the University of Florida estimated that the average non-employee shoplifting incident resulted in a loss of $195.75; for store employees that number jumped to $1,445.86 per incident.

Retailers will acknowledge, however, that shoplifting is a bigger – and more costly – problem than ever before. The National Retail Federation pegs shoplifting loss at about $10 billion each year in the U.S. alone, and numbers are on the rise, jumping more than 21 percent from 2000 to 2001.

To combat shoplifters, merchants invest in sophisticated security systems, although it's usually only the big chains with big money that can afford a team of floorwalkers, consultants to redesign their space to best deter thieves, electronic sensor tags, and a bevy of security cameras and monitors. Although there are no hard numbers, it is widely believed that department stores, discount chains, drug stores, and supermarkets nab the highest number of shoplifters.

Regardless of a store's security system, there will always be shoplifters. Unlike the rash of female shoplifters in the 1800s, today's shoplifter is just as likely to be a man as a woman. More than half are under 25 and don't be surprised if they're wearing oversize clothing, carrying empty (or nearly empty) shopping bags, and - yes, the cliché does prove to be true - wearing sunglasses. The highest number of shoplifting incidents take place on Fridays and Saturdays, in the early afternoon; the most commonly stolen item in the U.S. is lipstick, though CDs and jewelry are also popular.

Incidents of shoplifting rise during the holiday season and during times of economic recession, but not necessarily for the reasons you'd think. Shoppers may be pressed for cash, maxed out on their credit cards, or unemployed, but it's often stress that triggers stealing.

Like kleptomaniacs and compulsive shoppers, the majority of shoplifters (the 90 percent who are not motivated to steal out of poverty) experience feelings of tension, anxiety, and stress before stealing, then a release - a high - during and immediately following the act. The next phase is guilt or depression, which leads back to the tension, anxiety, and stress that prompted them to shoplift in the first place.

Shoplifters differ from kleptomaniacs in that they are completely conscious of their behavior, perhaps even planning a day of thievery before heading to the mall. They may study security systems, learn the ideal time to steal from a certain store, or bring along helpful tools to aid the removal of sensor tags.

However creative, naïve, or clever a shoplifter may be in eluding capture, they probably had some sort of plan when they walked into the store.

Shoplifting is not in itself a psychological disorder, but habitual shoplifters often suffer from depression, come from abusive homes, and have self-esteem issues or anxiety related troubles. According to the organization Cleptomaniacs & Shoplifters Anonymous, the common motives

Macrophobes have to avoid heavy shopping days because of their fear of long waits in line and Bibliophobes are frightened of books, so bookshops are obviously out of the question, and anyone afflicted with Gallophobia (also known as Galiophobia and Francophobia) will never know the pleasure of shopping in Paris due to their fear of France. But perhaps the most paralyzing of shopping phobias is Chrometophobia (or Chrematophobia): the fear of money.

for shoplifting include "feelings of anger, revenge, or entitlement, to fill a sense of emptiness due to grief or loss, to try to make life seem fair, or as a thrill or high to escape problems, numb feelings, or ease depression. As Michael Nuccitelli, executive director of New York's SLS Wellness Center, told *Allure*'s Simon Dumenco, "Shoplifting means something negative is going on inside."

And whatever is going on inside the minds of shoplifters is certainly more powerful than any existing deterrent. Most shoplifters aren't even caught, let alone punished, and those who are rarely see the inside of a cell. Most offenders are fined and put on probation. Many will steal again.

Until recently, there was little support available for shoplifters, but support groups like Cleptomaniacs & Shoplifters Anonymous (which was founded in Detroit by recovering shoplifter Terrance Schulman) and advocacy groups such as Shoplifters Alternative strive to educate retailers, the public, and the shoplifters themselves about the problem and the reasons behind it.

Bedford's Bookshop. A Bibliophile's nightmare.

# Shopping Till They Drop
# (Or At Least Drown in Debt and
# Alienate Their Families)

*Compulsive shoppers are real-life shopaholics*

**C**ompulsive shoppers can't get any respect. Many members of the medical community roll their eyes when it is suggested that the impulse control disorder may get its very own classification in a forthcoming edition of the bible of mental disorders, the *American Psychiatric Association's Diagnostic and Statistical Manual of Mental Disorders*. At home, the compulsive shopper is often wracked with guilt, is usually in debt, and has frequent run-ins with family members regarding his or her – although it's nearly always a her – shopping habit. It's not even safe when a compulsive shopper settles in for a little late-night telly.

During his opening monologue for an episode of *The Tonight Show*, host Jay Leno joked, "Stanford University has developed a cure for compulsive shoppers. No matter what you buy, it makes your ass look big."

Funny? Maybe. Accurate? Not quite.

Researchers at Stanford University are indeed leading the charge when it comes to developing treatment for compulsive shopping disorders, but there has been no talk of big bums. Rather, the research team led by Dr Lorrin Koran, MD, has been studying whether the antidepressant drug Celexa can help control the destructive behavior. But the Stanford study of Celexa is not all it seems.

Anti-depressant medication Celexa.

As of early 2003, there had been three studies – including the Stanford one – that tested the effectiveness of Celexa on compulsive shoppers. What has caused some members of the medical community to question the motives (although not the findings) of the studies is that all three were funded by the pharmaceutical company that makes Celexa, Forest Laboratories, Inc. Both Stanford and Forest Laboratories have waded into a murky area of medical research, and one that's become increasingly common.

Critics charge that when drug companies fund studies it is possible that the status of rare and perhaps marginal ailments and disorders are exalted, and work their way into the general public's consciousness. Such is the case, skeptics contend, with recognizing compulsive shopping disorder as an official mental disorder.

The debate over drug company-funded testing of Celexa (and, as of December 2002, another Forest Laboratories anti-depressant, Lexapro) will undoubtedly continue, but those who suffer from the disorder are unlikely to care who has paid for what – as long as it works.

The results of the Stanford Celexa study, which monitored 24 mostly female compulsive shoppers over a 12-week period, found that 71 percent of the participants saw major improvements or stopped the behavior altogether. It's promising news for those who can't control the urge to buy.

Compulsive shopping is hardly a new thing. A German psychiatrist identified the condition a century ago. It was named oniomania and it has no known cure.

A study in the *Journal of Consumer Research* found that today between two and eight percent of American consumers are in danger of becoming compulsive shoppers. Most sufferers are female, educated, and middle-aged or younger. In her 1990 book, *Women Who Shop Too Much: Overcoming the Urge to Splurge*, author Carolyn Wesson theorizes that many compulsive shoppers were childhood victims of abandonment and neglect by their parents and that creative, or right-brained, people are more at risk.

While it's easy to dismiss Wesson's assertions as cliché and argue that blaming your parents for your very adult faults is so very early-'90s, psychiatrists do believe the behavior can be triggered by a need to feel special and to combat loneliness, as well as a hope that shopping will somehow change them for the better.

But compulsive shopping satisfies none of those needs and therefore the shopper's behavior may escalate.

Like compulsive shoplifters, compulsive shoppers are caught in a cycle of anxiety: endorphin-fueled highs and guilt-ridden lows. The cycle occurs no matter what kind of compulsive shopping pattern an individual follows. For example, there are those who have to shop every day, even if there is nothing they need. Then there are those shoppers who hit the mall to seek comfort or solace after becoming upset or depressed. Finally, there are those who buy many units of an unnecessary item. All three compulsive shoppers are prone to shop in secret as the condition worsens, debt increases, and relationships with family members and friends become strained.

Just as there is no cure for compulsive shopping, there is no one cause. Cases can stem from sociological factors, a biochemical imbalance, or psychological issues. Whatever causes a person to compulsive shop, the problem can be alleviated by first identifying the triggers, and then avoiding them and learning other coping mechanisms.

Because much of a compulsive shopper's spending is typically put on plastic, compulsive shoppers are instructed to use cash only. They are also encouraged to keep a spending diary detailing all of their purchases. Malls, of course, are out of the question. And: never shop alone. There are also organizations like Shopaholics Limited and the 12-step group Debtors Anonymous that are specifically set up to assist problem shoppers.

But before you get visions of rooms full of weepy women sharing their deepest shopping secrets with each other, it's important to note that although statistics show that the majority of compulsive shoppers are female, men are certainly not immune to the disorder.

"Men more than women seem to buy specialty items compulsively, focusing their spending in an obsession to acquire the 'best' or all examples of a product or gadget."

Sound familiar?

Well, that's one way writers Sally Coleman and Nancy Hull-Mast characterize the male version of compulsive shopping in their 1992 book *Can't Buy Me Love: Freedom From Compulsive Spending, Money and Obsession.*

Male compulsive shoppers may spend wildly to impress a woman, habitually trying to buy love. The behavior may also be triggered by feelings of inferiority when a woman they are involved with makes more money than them.

But whether the compulsive shopper is male or female, ultimately, the condition boils down to power (or lack thereof) and insecurity, crushing debt, and the quest to be liked. Eventually, taking a little pill may alleviate that overwhelming urge to spend, but it's never going to solve the deeper problem – or afford compulsive shoppers any more respect.

# It's Enough to Make you Sick

*Evidence of shopping bulimia is on the rise*

**W**e all know about bulimia, the eating disorder that results in a person bingeing wildly on food, then promptly vomiting. We all know about shopping. But shopping bulimia? That's a new one.

The term started popping up in books and magazine articles in the late 1990s, with psychologists defining the affliction as a form of compulsive shopping disorder, an addiction that can be hard to shake.

Like many compulsive shoppers and shopping addicts, shopping bulimics spend excessively. The thrill of shopping provides a rush, much in the same way any addict's indulgence in their particular vice does. But the shopping bulimic doesn't stop at spending.

Wracked with guilt, the bulimic shoppers return the goods they bought - sometimes the very same day.

In England, a study released in 2002 showed that shopping bulimia affected mostly women, and that designer clothing was one of the most popular items to be purchased, then returned. Tamira King, the author of the study, questioned 530 women in department stores about their shopping habits. The PhD student at Brunel University's school of business discovered that more than half of her interviewees admitted to returning items they didn't really want or couldn't afford.

In September 2002, King told the *Daily Telegraph* that "those who displayed dysfunctional shopping behavior tended to be shopaholics - people who repair their moods by going shopping and then feel guilty. This is where we see the parallel with disorders such as bulimia."

Many women cited the desire to live out a celebrity-dressing fantasy, even if it was just around their own home for a couple of hours. Others bought and returned clothes that were too small, perhaps experimenting with a bit of wistful-thinking-themed shopping bulimia. Some women did actually wear the clothes out before returning them, but shopping bulimia often stems more from the need of a shopping fix than out of the need for an outfit to wear to the company Christmas party.

There is no measure of what percentage of compulsive shoppers are shopping bulimics, but the research done so far indicates that the numbers of women who suffer from the disorder is on the rise.

In 1998, when shopping bulimia was first attracting attention, *USA Today* writer Craig Wilson was surprised to learn that so many women (and women he knew) were old pros at returning merchandise and quoted a friend who called the practice "shopping bulimia."

The disorder has turned out to be more serious than Wilson's light-hearted look at the subject then implied, but the defining signs remain the same: "You shop, and then you return," Wilson wrote. "You get the high of the purchase and then the cleansing of the return. We regurgitate merchandise."

# Shopping the Globe

## chapter xii

**D**esigner handbags, Italian roadsters, and bejeweled platinum watches are all well and good, but the ultimate status shopping - at least for the ladies - has got to be haute couture.

Twice a year, the fashion press flock to Paris to cover the theatrical fashion shows which often feature equally theatrical clothes. But for all the media exposure haute couture gets, there are only an estimated 3,000 women around the world who can (and do) lay down the cash for the ultimate made-to-measure garments.

Those 3,000 women are carrying on a rich tradition that began in the late 1700s when Marie Antoinette would commission hoards of dresses – usually in her favorite colors of lavender and lilac – from royal couturier and milliner, Rose Bertin. Antoinette, (or "the Austrian whore," as the French revolutionaries were fond of calling her), had a particular flair for fashion and in addition to her penchant for wearing sheer cotton dresses in the summer, was known for her extravagance and excess, making her the ideal couture customer.

Her dressmaker Bertin is often credited as being the first couturier, as well as the mother of accessories, as she created shoes, gloves, and hats to accompany the queen's dresses. But Bertin's name did not appear on a hand-stitched label inside the garments, nor did she have a namesake couture house. It took nearly a century before haute couture evolved beyond a royal clientele and began to resemble the phenomenon we know today.

Rose Bertin, couturier to Marie Antoinette and "Ministre de la Mode" (Minister of Fashion).

## Shopping Fun and Fireworks for the Whole Family

*Dubai's annual Shopping Festival draws millions*

Win a Rolls Royce. Hang out with the Smurfs or maybe the characters from *Sesame Street*. Check out the fireworks, the highbrow sporting events, and shop, shop, shop.

What better way to spend quality time with the family than at the Dubai Shopping Festival?

Since 1996, the wealthy beach-front city in the United Arab Emirates (UAE) has been hosting a month-long celebration of shopping and spectacle. Originally conceived to stimulate trade and tourism, the festival was

Charles Frederick Worth.

The first designer label, from Charles Frederick Worth.

Expat Englishman Charles Frederick Worth is acknowledged as the first commercial couturier. He set up the first haute couture *atelier* in Paris in 1858, displaying his high-end designs to high-end customers. Not one to be satisfied with simply designing dresses to order, he adopted a take-it-or-leave-it attitude and was indeed the first to sew a label bearing his name into his creations.

Following Worth's lead, other couturiers began popping up in Paris and soon haute couture (which is French for "high fashion") was influencing fashion on a grand scale. But their influence led to the industry's first knock offs, prompting Worth to found the *Chambre Syndicale de la Confection et de la Couture Pour Dames et Fillettes* in 1868.

The *Chambre Syndicale* was an assembly of couturiers who, though competitors in business, were united in fighting the common goal of design piracy.

The influence and popularity of haute couture grew throughout the late 1800s and into the twentieth century, but its growth was stunted and delayed twice as a result of the First and Second World Wars. But that didn't mean couture wasn't still on the minds of even the most unlikely of people.

During the occupation of Paris in the Second World War, the Nazis reportedly hatched a bizarre plan to move the prestigious couture houses to Berlin. The plan, quite obviously, was never brought to fruition due to its cost and impracticality (and possibly, its sheer craziness).

Haute couture flourished in the years following the war, the most notable impact being made by Christian Dior in 1947. Dior's New Look, marked by its round shoulders, nipped-in waist, and flared skirt, would set the template for women's fashion well into the next decade.

The 1950s were the heyday of haute couture. Gabrielle "Coco" Chanel was experiencing a renaissance, Hubert de Givenchy debuted his first collection in 1952,

encouraged by the Crown Prince of Dubai and UAE Defense Minister His Highness General Sheikh Mohammed bin Rashid Al Maktoum and quickly grew to become the mother of all shopping festivals.

Other Middle Eastern countries and cities followed Dubai's lead (there are shopping festivals held in Egypt, Lebanon, and Abu Dhabi), but none match its scope or its spectacle.

The port city, which has a population of roughly 850,000 people and the only seven-star hotel in the world, the Burj Al Arab, pulls out all the stops each winter, showcasing its finest wares and entertainment.

The festival is promoted as a wholesome, family affair, with lots of activities for the kids. Dubai's internationally recognized sporting events, like the Dubai World Cup (which is the richest horse race on Earth) and golf's Dubai Desert Classic, often take place during the Shopping Festival, giving the millions of visitors yet more incentive to make the trip.

And there's the shopping and the sales and the lack of taxes and those world-record-making raffles.

Dubai has long been a favorite shopping destination of the upper classes. Its shops are filled with tax-free luxury goods, particularly jewelry and exotic carpets. During the festival – which during its first years was held in March, but now runs from mid-January to mid-February – prices are cut 20–50 percent. In its inaugural year, the festival attracted 1.6 millions visitors; in 2002, 2.68 million people took in the shopping fun. Europeans, in particular, have attended in increasing numbers every year, although shoppers from all over the world have been known to make the winter trek to Dubai.

Aside from its obvious (shopping) component, the festival is known for two very different things: raffles and family values.

During the festival, outrageous prizes are drawn for on a daily basis. In 2000, a Rolls Royce Silver Seraph was given away during every one of the festival's 31 days. The next year, 31 lucky winners walked away with two Lexus cars and 100,000 Dirhams cash (about US$2,700). In addition, one kilogram of gold was drawn for daily and on the festival's closing day, one prize of 10 kilograms of gold was awarded. And, finally, keeping with the perpetual theme of the festival, One World, One Family, One Festival, 31 families won vacations.

Since its inception, family has figured prominently at the Dubai Shopping

and young wunderkind Yves Saint Laurent was causing a stir.

The heady days of the 1950s could not last forever, though, and haute couture experienced a significant decline in the latter half of the century. In 1946, there were over 100 official couture houses in Paris; in 2002, that number stood at 12 after the retirement of Yves Saint Laurent.

The *Chambre Syndicale de la Confection et de la Couture Pour Dames et Fillettes* (renamed the *Chambre Syndicale de la Haute Couture*) still regulates the industry and is the governing body that decides which houses are permitted to call themselves haute couture and which are not. The basic qualifying rules include that 50 new designs be created for each of the designer's two collections per year and that a house must employ a minimum of 20 full-time workshop staff.

Couture houses have long operated at a loss, and their relevance has long been questioned. But couture isn't about those 3,000 women who can afford the exorbitant prices (which range from about $15,000–60,000 per ensemble); it's become about the brand and the image.

While such a tiny percentage of women shop off the runway, millions can work cologne, cosmetics, or moderately priced items like sunglasses into their budgets.

Survival of haute couture is dependent on new customers and with an increasingly aging clientele, it's going to be hard to replace them. To this end, many designers have turned to Hollywood for exposure and potential customers.

The marriage of Hollywood and haute couture is nothing new. Audrey Hepburn was a muse and close friend of Givenchy; Brigitte Bardot was a fan of Louis Feraud. Today you may find Madonna in Jean Paul Gaultier or Elizabeth Hurley in Versace. Houses are keen to lend dresses to celebrities for high-profile events like the Academy Awards, gambling that the media exposure is going to be worth the expense and that countless women will be lined up at the perfume counter the next day.

But without paying clients, the future of couture is dubious, regardless of Hollywood exposure. Perhaps couturier Cristobel Balenciaga was ahead of his time in 1968 when he boldly proclaimed, "There's no one left to dress."

Spree: A Cultural History of Shopping

# Shopping Mecca: Hong Kong

## Faking it in the Far East

**F**orget Cabbage Patch Kids. How about a Rice Paddy Baby? There are "Country Cousins" and "Shortgrains" to choose from. According to an advertisement for the Hong Kong made dolls, "these little 'Mainlanders' hold China passports and are ready for new adventures in distant lands if sponsors can be found."

The adoptable Rice Paddy Babies clearly draw inspiration from the Cabbage Patch Kids dolls that took the world by storm in the 1980s. But inspiration is one thing – low-rent copies are another entirely.

Just ask Jean Claude Van Damme. Well, not the action actor himself, but the character he plays in the 1998 film, *Knock Off.* Van Damme is Marcus Ray, the former "king of the knock offs," who's determined to go legit with the help of business partner/undercover CIA agent, Tommy Hendricks (Rob Schneider). Together, the pair own V-Six Jeans and are embroiled in typical action-packed shenanigans (including ass-slapping with an eel) all set against the backdrop of Hong Kong's counterfeiting underworld.

*Knock Off* is not classic cinema, but makes a point about the rampant counterfeiting industry in Hong Kong. After his fake Puma sneakers (spelled "Pumma") fall apart, Van Damme's Marcus Ray exclaims, "What kind of a scumbag would sell knock offs?"

A lot of scumbags, that's who. Fakes, forgeries, knock offs. Whatever you call it, counterfeiting is big business, an industry worth anywhere between $250 and $1,000 billion each year worldwide (considering the illegal nature of the business, it's impossible to accurately gauge its scope). It is estimated that fakes account for nearly 10 percent of all world trade. And Hong Kong, both as a manufacturing and sales hub, has long been at the center of the action.

Festival. The One World, One Family, One Festival theme has been used on and off since 1996. There were a couple of years, however, that the festival adopted an alternate theme, though it was always just as sweet. For example, in 1998, the theme was Children of the World, and the Smurfs, Winnie the Pooh, and the *Sesame Street* gang all had their own shows. Then in 2000, the theme was To Mother With Love and a prize of US$10,000 was bestowed upon the lucky woman who won The Ideal Arab Mother Award. According to Dubai Shopping Festival press materials, the award was given to the most "exemplary mother" they could find.

It's all good, clean fun.

Stanley Market in Hong Kong.
*Courtesy Hong Kong Tourism Board.*

## To Be the Best

There is serious shop-
ping, and then there is
*really* serious shopping.
The shopping that takes
place for 11 weeks each
summer in Hong Kong
most certainly falls into
the latter category.

It's the HSBC Mega Hong
Kong Sale. The event takes
destination shopping to a
whole new level and
has translated the concept
of shopping-as-sport quite
literally.

Sponsored by the Hong
Kong Tourism Board, eager
contestants gather for a
five-hour shopping blitz,
hoping to capture the title
of Hong Kong Shopper
of the Year. Teams of two
represent their respective
countries, having won
their national title either
through rounds of beauty
pageant-like competitions

Although Mainland China, South Korea, Taiwan, and
Singapore all have established (and thriving) counterfeit
industries, Hong Kong is the undisputed granddaddy of
the fake.

The city's markets – particularly Stanley Market and
Ladies' Market – are teeming with counterfeit anything
and everything. Fake food, fake drugs, fake electronics
and CDs, and the fakest of fake luxury goods are sold at a
fraction of what you'd pay for an original.

In 1997, the Hong Kong government estimated that
34 percent of all counterfeit seizures were designer
clothes, while watches accounted for seven percent.
Within the luxury goods market there are crude fakes,
ones that purposefully misspell brand names (Calvin
Klein becomes "Gioven Kelvins"; Rolex becomes "Ro-
lux"), invert or blur logos, or feature other obvious signs
of fakery. And then there are the "good fakes," the ones
nearly impossible to detect, that often come complete
with counterfeit certificates of authenticity.

The rise of the label-conscious customer was a boon
to counterfeiters who first started manufacturing fake
luxury goods in the late 1960s. Before that time, brand
names barely registered on the radar of average citi-
zens and logo-laden merchandise was rare. Outside of
society's upper classes, brands weren't about status, but
about quality and price-point.

But once the everyday Joe and Jane had been exposed to designer labels, there was no turning back. They
wanted the status, the caché, and the perceived prestige
that went along with carrying a Gucci handbag or wearing a Polo Ralph Lauren shirt with the pony embroidered
over the left breast, but they didn't necessarily want to
pay the price.

Shifty Hong Kong manufacturers recognized this
bottomless market and got to work, churning out fake
luxury merchandise worth billions each year.

At first, the design houses didn't pay the burgeoning
Hong Kong knock-off business much heed. Poorly manufactured imitations only available at street markets in
Hong Kong were not perceived to be a threat. Some even
considered the Asian fakes as a compliment. But when
the Hong Kong counterfeit business exploded onto the
world market and the quality of the forgeries improved
to a point where they were virtually indistinguishable

from the originals, there was no goodwill to go around.

Expanding past the street stalls of the city, Hong Kong counterfeiters began shipping their goods around the world in the late 1970s, where they were often sold at – surprise, surprise – street market stalls in other countries. In New York City, it's Canal Street, in L.A. it's Santee Street, but the scene is the same and the stock is just as fake as it is in Hong Kong.

Different branches of organized criminals and terrorists, allegedly including the Italian Mafia, Asian Triads, and even Osama Bin Laden's Al Qaeda organization, are believed to be responsible for taking the counterfeit industry global and reaping the financial benefits.

Stories have circulated for years that the 1993 World Trade Center bombing was funded in part by sales of fake designer T-shirts. Such allegations are hard to prove, just as the counterfeiting kingpins are hard to catch. (They've become even more difficult to nab in recent years since many counterfeits are now shipped separately, in bits and pieces, and not assembled until the parts reach their final destination.)

Ladies' Market in Hong Kong.
*Courtesy Hong Kong Tourism Board.*

The Hong Kong government, however, decided to clamp down on the counterfeiting industry shortly after its return to Chinese control in 1997. The city's Intellectual Property Department encouraged legitimate retailers to band together to fight against fakes, and established the Quality Tourism Services sticker program. Retailers that have proven they don't deal in fakes are given a sticker to display, indicating to tourists that only the real deal is sold there.

Tourists, of course, are the key. If there was no demand for counterfeit merchandise, there would be no industry, no market stalls filled with fake Chanel and fake Prada. Hong Kong would never be the same.

– first winning locally, then regionally, and so on – or have simply been picked through a contest held by a newspaper, radio station, or website.

It's the ultimate in competitive shopping, challenging international shoppers to flaunt their skills and prowess on the streets of a city famous for its spectacular shopping.

On July 18, 2002, Daniel and Diane Knowlton of Santa Barbara, California, captured the title, after impressing the five judges with their purchases. The couple, who had won the chance to compete on behalf of the United States by entering the Shoppers Dream Event contest on online travel site *Travelocity.com*, beat out teams from nine other countries: Canada, India, Indonesia, Mainland China, Malaysia, The Philippines, Singapore, Taiwan, and Thailand.

Starting at 11:00 a.m., and armed with a map, a guide listing participating merchants, and a sophisticated cellphone able to transmit live images back to the waiting crowd in front of the Inter-Continental Hotel, the teams were off to spend the HK$4,000 (about US$500) that was burning a hole in their pockets.

The Hong Kong Shopper of the Year competition isn't about the quantity of goods the teams can

# Shopping Mecca: Tokyo

## The rise of a shopper's society

It wasn't always like this. In fact, postwar Tokyo was the antithesis of its current incarnation as the ultimate consumer society. The war years saw both Europe and North America embrace technological advances like refrigerators, televisions, and cars, but Japan emerged a country so far behind the times only 3.2 percent of homes had a washing machine (the wash was commonly done by hand using a washboard) in 1958, and less than one percent of the population owned a car.

How times change – and fast.

Hungry to catch up with the rest of the world, the Japanese government put into motion a plan to raise the wages of its country's workers, and between 1950-1958 the average citizen saw his income double. But having money to spend was one thing, having something to buy was another.

Several factors influenced the rapid rise of Japanese consumerism in the late 1950s through to the early 1960s. As writer Mark Schilling points out in his 1997 book, *The Encyclopedia of Japanese Pop Culture*, the televised marriage of Crown Prince Akihito to Michiko Shoda in April 1959 was the impetus for many Japanese to invest in their first TV. The 1964 Olympic Games in Tokyo also impacted the culture significantly. Tourists came, locals showed off, and the eyes of the world were on Tokyo.

By the mid-1970s, Japan had succeeded, winning its self-imposed game of catch-up with the Western world. Its export business had taken off and Japan was gaining a reputation as a producer of high quality, high-tech goods.

But it wasn't until the economic boom of the 1980s that consumer culture – particularly consumer culture among the country's youth – became globally renowned. The prosperous "bubble economy" encouraged spending, and trend-setting young men and women who hung out in the streets of Tokyo chose to spend their cash on American and European designer goods.

buy in those precious five hours, but rather the quality.

The pairs must purchase one item in four distinct categories: Chinese traditions, consumer electronics, fashion and beauty, and jewelry and watches. The judges then assess the shoppers' finds, basing 30 percent of a team's final score on how well they abided by the rules of the competition, 35 percent on how innovative their purchases were, and 35 percent on the value-for-money factor.

The Knowltons' grand prize-winning loot included a Chinese vase, a DVD player, a pair of hiking boots, and a diamond ring. The hiking boots in particular had the judges swooning, as they also awarded the couple the individual category prize

Western influence could be seen in everything from the names of the most popular brands (such as Ralph Lauren, Calvin Klein, Chanel, Gucci), to the trend in featuring American film stars in print and television ads, to the appropriation of English words to name Japanese products. It wasn't unusual to see misspelled items like "Harbard University" sweatshirts or cookies inappropriately named Snatch (later renamed Snutch).

Prestigious brand-name shops descended upon Tokyo during the buy-buy '80s, often pricing goods 50 percent above the price paid in the company's Paris or New York stores, a practice that continued even when the fabled economic bubble burst in the early 1990s.

Unlike the fall-out of a recession in North America or Western Europe during which designer labels typically suffer as consumers scale back, the Japanese kept on shopping. It may have taken a little longer to save up, but those coveted Hermes bags and pairs of Gucci stilettos were still flying off the shelves.

The economic landscape of modern Japan – and Tokyo in particular – was irrevocably altered as the recession of the 1990s lifted. Job security was no longer guaranteed, couples were having fewer children (just one in many cases), and legions of adult children were choosing to live at home well into their 20s in order to support their highfalutin designer lifestyle.

Image was – and is – the all-important key. Whether it's the music they listen to or the brands of clothes they wear, the youth of Tokyo hold the collective power to make staggering profits for any company or music act deemed worthy.

Japan has the second-largest music industry in the world, after the United States, and powerhouse fashion conglomerates like the LVMH Moet Hennessy Louis Vuitton group generate 15 percent of total world sales from the country. There's a whole lot of money to be made if a company gets that image just right.

While there is no magic formula for determining that exact image, it's a good bet that if it's exclusive it will fly. Japanese youth – both male and female – want what no one else has, and are willing to pay exorbitant prices to get it, especially for clothing. T-shirts from homegrown labels influenced by U.S. skateboard culture sell for upwards of $400 apiece and waiting lists for in fashion and beauty.

For their effort, all contestants receive free return airfare to Hong Kong and a complimentary stay at the swanky Inter-Continental hotel. They also get to keep the items they bought during the competition. The individual winners in each category can keep one of those fancy phones they used racing through the streets of the city, while the grand prize winners receive a two-night extension of their stay, a matching pair of fancy phones, a helicopter tour of Hong Kong, and, of course, a big trophy, so they can prove to the folks back home that they are indeed shopping champions.

sought-after, limited edition items from European and American designers are long.

But the irony of this pursuit of exclusivity is that the most desirable items or complete looks are frequently dictated by Japan's plethora of youth culture fashion magazines. As Jun Takahashi, designer of Tokyo's Under Cover label, told Rebecca Mead of *The New Yorker* in an interview for her story, "Shopping Rebellion" (March 2002), "Japanese people read magazines as their bibles, and when they see images in them they have to have them and will pay anything."

Anything? In Japan, it seems, consumer culture has no limits.

# Shopping Mecca: New York City

*Steals, deals, and Back Room bargains*

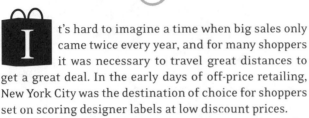

I t's hard to imagine a time when big sales only came twice every year, and for many shoppers it was necessary to travel great distances to get a great deal. In the early days of off-price retailing, New York City was the destination of choice for shoppers set on scoring designer labels at low discount prices.

Off-price retailers were the precursor to the outlet stores that are today scattered throughout the suburbs of every North American city. An off-price retailer strikes deals to buy overruns and samples from designers and manufacturers as well as merchandise that hasn't sold in stores.

The first of the off-price sellers on America's East Coast: Filene's Basement in Boston and New York City's renowned discounter, Loehmann's.

Loehmann's was founded in 1920 by Frieda Loehmann. A former department store buyer, she had impressive inside connections with Seventh Avenue designers and used those connections to launch her business. According to legend, Loehmann would traipse up and down the streets of New York's garment district, bills tucked into her stockings, ready to pay cash on the spot for overstocks of designer clothes.

After starting to resell her finds out of her home in 1920, Loehmann made the leap to legitimate retailer in 1921 when she opened her first store on Bedford Avenue in Brooklyn. Fashion and budget-conscious women made the trek to Loehmann's after hearing of the shop's famous bargains and equally famous Back Room.

The Back Room was where "Mama" Loehmann (as Frieda had become known) kept the most desired items and has been the scene of much bargain-frenzy induced jostling for more than 80 years.

Over those years, however, customers saw Loehmann's change drastically.

When Frieda Loehmann died in 1962 at 89, her store was already a shopping landmark and still a leader in off-price retailing. Her son, Charles, took over the business

## Talking Shop

*What you need to know to get what you want in the world*

Contrary to popular belief, the international language is not one of love, but of shopping. Gestures, body language, and the presentation of cold, hard cash can break down even the most difficult of cultural and language barriers. But that's not to say that shopping overseas isn't at times intimidating.

Stroll into a swanky shop in Paris or Milan and you may well be accosted with a barrage of rapid-fire French or Italian. But instead of hightailing it right out of there, take a deep breath and reach into your brain to find the right thing to say. It's not so bad. After all, there are only three significant things you need to know to say.

When in The Netherlands...

*How much is it?*
Hoeveel is het?

*I'll take it.*
Ik neem het.

*I'm just looking.*
Ik kijk alleen even.

after his mother's death and began to expand beyond the Brooklyn store – that same year he opened a second Loehmann's on Fordham Road in the Bronx. And in 1964, the company went public for the first time.

Loehmann's locations started to pop up across the U.S. and by 1988 there were 82 stores. But the business was troubled. Since its original public offering, the company had been privatized and owned at various times by Associated Dry Goods, May Department Stores Co, and Sefino Ltd. Aggressive competitors in the off-price market – most notably T.J. Maxx stores – surfaced, while designers' lower-priced "bridge" lines like Donna Karan's DKNY, for example, proved to be stiff competition as well. Add to that the fact that more designer labels were opting to open exclusive outlets of their own and the future looked bleak for Loehmann's.

To make matters worse, customers were complaining that there were few big brand pieces on the racks and that even the stock in the store's Back Room was sub-par. Loehmann's luster, it seemed, was gone.

*Newsweek*'s Paula Span quoted Alan G. Millstein, publisher of the *Fashion Network Report*, in her 1988 article, "A Shrine to Bargains," as saying Loehmann's was "the Marlene Dietrich of discounting . . . a great illusionist, but the act is over."

The act may have been suffering, but it was not over. Competition, charges of over-expansion, and an expensive strategy that saw the company snapping up pricey real estate (such as its 60,000-square-foot Manhattan flagship store in the building that once housed swanky department store Barneys New York) in the late 1990s all served to worry investors by severely impacting Loehmanns' bottom line.

At the time of its second public offering in 1996, Loehmann's shares stood at $17. The stock price rose to $30.25 that year, then plummeted to $6.625 in July 1997. The company filed for

Chapter 11 bankruptcy protection two years later.

When it looked like the end for Loehmann's, writers across the United States wrote wistful accounts of their visits to the Back Room in the good old days, waxed on about the myth of the store that was, and the disappointment it had become.

But these retail obituaries were premature. Loehmann's survived. It may not be everything it once was but it still stands, a defiant New York institution that has become a legend.

When in France . . .
*How much is it?*
C'est combien?
*I'll take it.*
Je le prends.
*I'm just looking.*
Je regarde seulement.

When in Germany . . .
*How much is it?*
Wieviel kostet es?
*I'll take it.*
Ich nehme es.
*I'm just looking.*
Ich sehe mich nur ein wenig um.

When in Italy . . .
*How much is it?*
Quanto costa?
*I'll take it.*
Lo prendo.
*I'm just looking.*
Sto solo dando un'occhiata.

When in Japan . . .
*How much is it?*
Kore wa ikura desu ka?
*I'll take it.*
Kore ni shimasu.
*I'm just looking.*
Miteiru dake desu.

When in Portugal . . .
*How much is it?*
Quanto é?
*I'll take it.*
Levo-o.
*I'm just looking.*
Estou só a ver.

When in Spain . . .
*How much is it?*
Cuánto cuesta?
*I'll take it.*
Me lo llevo.
*I'm just looking.*
Sólo estoy mirando.

# From the Crystal Palace to the Crystal Ball

chapter

xiii

# Gazing Into the Future of Shopping

 hen writer Edward Bellamy described a futuristic world where shoppers would see their purchases sped through tubes from the shops to the warehouses to their homes in his 1888 book, *Looking Backward: 2000-1887*, readers were certainly entertained, but few at the time could have predicted how close his work of "science fiction" would come to the truth more than a century later.

Instead of tubes, we have credit and debit cards, can shop virtually cashless, and the tubes he imagined are made up of wireless messages, codes, couriers, and the Internet.

It was a far-fetched idea even 20 years ago, that we could – and would – shop from our homes and offices via computer. Yet this scenario has increasingly become a consumer reality and, if the futurists and marketers are to be believed, will eventually dominate our shopping experience.

Technology is undoubtedly the most influential factor when considering the future of shopping. The time people spend in malls has been in a rapid decline since the 1980s, when shoppers spent an average of 90 minutes per visit; in recent years that time has fallen to less than one hour, according to the financial magazine, *Forbes*.

In his best-selling 1984 book, *Megatrends*, John Naisbitt wrote: "The more technology we introduce into society, the more people will aggregate, will want to be with other people: movies, rock concerts, shopping. Shopping malls, for example, are now the third most frequented space in our lives, following home and workplace."

He went on to write that, "The same people who predicted we would all fly helicopters now say that with computers at home we will shop electronically and stores will become extinct. We will eventually do some shopping by computer, but only for staple items of which we have a very clear sense and experience."

Naisbitt, we know now, was both right and wrong.

Not every product is well-suited to Internet sales. Clothing, for instance, has been a problem, with high return rates due most often to fitting problems, an issue identified by futurist Faith Popcorn in the 1992 edition of her book, *The Popcorn Report*. While she made sweeping comments regarding the demise of elaborate packaging when we've actually witnessed a steady rise in branding, and therefore, packaging, she also assumed that we would one day be able to "try" clothing on onscreen, a prediction that is indeed becoming a reality, thanks to innovative web retailers like American Eagle, Kenneth Cole, and Lands' End, who use the software of a Montreal company called My Virtual Model. She labeled the shopping center a "dinosaur" and wrote that "the home cocoon will be the site of the future shopping center."

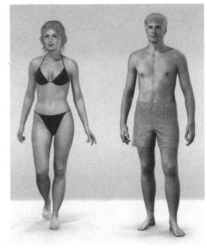

Virtual models created at *MyVirtualModel.com*.

In the last decade, others – from *Time* magazine to *FutureConsumer.com* writer Frank Feather – have fallen in line with such thinking. In his 2000 book, Feather wrote: "By 2010, one-to-one online shopping will have made mass marketing obsolete and driven many retailers to the wall."

Note that Feather and many of his contemporaries are careful to say *many* and not all.

Shopping as we know it may soon disappear into the annals of consumer history, joining Sears' short-lived run selling houses by catalog and downtown department store shopping, but rare is the futurist who predicts the end of in-person shopping entirely. In fact, many believe there will be a place for the tactile shopping of the future, places with a fabricated, folksy feel, and others built on a grand scale, to entertain and amuse.

Both places are about a shopping experience, rather than that of the hum-drum, gotta-pick-up-some-toilet-paper-on-the-way-home variety.

While Faith Popcorn says in her 2000 book, *EVEolution*, that she believes "90 percent of all purchases will be direct-to-customer by 2010," that leaves 10 percent of shopping to be done in a traditional, face-to-face way. What may not be so traditional, however, is where and how consumers do it.

The novelty of a big, generic mall wore off long ago. This is not where we want to shop, the experts concur. A trend has been building toward a kinder, gentler shopping experience, one that emulates the old-fashioned neighborhood stores, the specialty boutiques that had been swallowed (or driven out of town) by giant retailers before many of us were old enough to have money of our own.

The new retail experience is a simulation of sorts, no more real than the modern suburban housing developments designed to look and feel like a small town. And in that prefabricated "small town" suburb, there is a Main Street, complete with quaint little shops and impressive customer service. Never mind that in the future these stores may very likely be owned and operated by retail powerhouses simply offering a scaled-down version of their sprawling stores. It's an aesthetic, a pose, a new wave of retail marketing.

But before you are overcome with intense feelings of warmth and coziness, and visions of a shopping world where staff is genuinely friendly, and where they remember your name and your preferences every time you walk through the door, consider the other part of the future shopping equation.

We don't need big malls, many developers and retailers believe; we need *enormous* malls disguised as *entertainment centers*. Catch a movie, rappel down a climbing wall, shoot some hoops – oh, and do your shopping too. It's shopping as entertainment – shoppertainment, as it's been christened – and it's coming to a city near you.

As a culture we like to shop (for fun things), to socialize, to play, and to travel. Outlet malls may have been the "destination shopping" of the 1990s, but these all-in-one mega-complexes are likely the next step. Developments like The Camp in Costa Mesa, California and the Sony Metreon in San Francisco are among the first to give shoppers a controlled environment to enjoy so

The Sony Metreon in San Francisco.

many of their favorite things, and to further the future of shopping as sport.

The gateway to Sony Metreon in San Francisco.

As we spend more time clicking our way to our next purchase, a certain level of boredom is bound to set in. After all, for many consumers, shopping is a social activity, a real experience, and at times, a competition. We compete with ourselves to find the best bargains, the best stuff; we compete with our friends and family in much the same way. We like to tell war stories after a day in the shops, detailing encounters with snarly sales clerks, describing the process that led us to buy that particular pair of shoes.

Shopping online, however convenient or vast the selection at our ready fingertips, lacks social, experiential, and competitive elements. And it is those factors that will keep in-person shopping alive for as long into the future as shoppers desire, because, ultimately, in the sport of shopping, the consumer always wins.

# It's in the Stars

*What your astrological sign says about your shopping style*

---

**P**erhaps you're a self-confessed shopaholic. Maybe for you it's thrift shops or nothing. Or maybe you'd rather have your eyes cut out with a rusty knife then set foot in mall. Whatever the case, your birth date may reveal your innate shopping style.

## ARIES (MARCH 21 – APRIL 19)

Always on the hunt for the latest, greatest new thing, Aries love nothing more than poking around trendy boutiques before they're trendy, looking for undiscovered brands about to hit big. Often acting on impulse, Aries can get caught up in the shopping moment and have a tendency to spend, spend, spend until the accounts are empty and the credit cards are maxed-out. The Ram's impulsive, trend-seeking nature also puts those born under the sign at risk of becoming fashion victims. A note of caution: just because it's new and daring doesn't mean it looks good.

## TAURUS (APRIL 20 – MAY 20)

It's all about designer labels and big brands for Taurus. The Bull is most likely to be spotted trolling the racks and walking the aisles at well-known upscale stores plotting their next purchase. Always ones to think before they buy, notoriously stubborn Taurus searches high and low for that perfect whatchamacallit before putting down a single penny. A lover of touch and textiles, Taurus is keen on investing in the best of the best for his home and will save for ages if that's what it takes.

## GEMINI (MAY 21 – JUNE 20)

Oh, those crazy indecisive Twins. One minute devout shopper Gemini is considering a new watch, the next it's colorful modern art for her walls. After that, she's onto a kooky-looking vintage doll or perhaps an all-inclusive vacation at a Mexican resort. You never know what to expect when shopping with Gemini, but whatever the gal ends up carting home with her, you can bet it will have been a fun, whirlwind experience. And considering Gemini's gift for gab, you can also be sure that's she's landed the best deal possible – she loves to haggle.

## CANCER (JUNE 21 – JULY 22)

With all that cash hoarded away in bank accounts, term deposits, and mutual funds, you'd think Cancer would be up for some serious spending. But, no. The ever-practical Crab is a homebody who would much rather snuggle up on the couch with a good movie than trek through the mall. When Cancer does shop, however, he relies on his uncanny intuition and gets the job done as quickly and painlessly as possible.

## LEO (JULY 23 – AUGUST 22)

Attention-loving Leo is a splashy status shopper and frequent brand-name dropper. The Lion likes to splurge on showy purchases and then regales his pals with the play-by-play tales of his latest shopping excursion. A Leo shopping spree is always a production. Voted Most Likely to Have a Personal Shopper or Stylist, Leo doesn't do anything halfway. If he buys a car, it's a limited edition European convertible in cherry red. If it's a suit, it's hand-tailored and crafted in Milan.

## VIRGO (AUGUST 23 – SEPTEMBER 22)

Rifling through the racks at high-end outlets is where you'll find Virgo. She's set on finding the best quality at a practical price. She pooh-poohs the latest trends in favor of classic choices and will forever put quality over price. A good designer deal is the ultimate shopping high for The Virgin, however, and she'll be feeling smug for days after a big score. Virgo is also the most organized of shoppers and will map out the most efficient plan of attack before even setting foot in the mall.

## Libra (September 23 – October 22)

Libra was literally born to shop. Armed with great taste and a sixth sense for what's right, right now, she is often called upon by her less gifted friends to offer shopping assistance. A big fan of all things custom-made, Libra eschews cheap and chintzy, preferring to shell out the extra bucks to have the ideal image in her balanced little head become reality. Whether it's a suit or a sofa, Libra will patiently comb through countless shops until she finds the purchase that's just right.

## Scorpio (October 23 – November 21)

The Scorpion is known for being lethally smart and equally sexy, but when it comes to shopping, Scorpio's motives are more mysterious than anything. Never a frivolous spender, you can rest assured there's a strategy behind each and every purchase. Pricey book of ancient Egyptian text? Designer smoking jacket? Wicker file boxes for the office? Whatever Scorpio does buy, it likely has more than a little something to do with getting ahead. And if one little purchase can help him inch ahead of the pack either professionally or personally, Scorpio has no trouble enduring even the most excruciating shopping experience.

## Sagittarius (November 22 – December 21)

Strangely, the sign with luck in his stars and too many gambling wins on his side doesn't do shopping. Sagittarius prefers to stick close to home and only shops when the odd impulse hits. And those quick bursts of shopping activity would leave even the most seasoned shoppers dazed. No extravagance is too great, no price tag too large and, if you happen to accompany big-spending Sag on a rare shopping jaunt, don't be surprised to find your pal treating you to a pricey dinner or a fancy gift at the end of the day.

## Capricorn (December 22 – January 20)

The Goat is the bona fide bargain hunter of the Zodiac. Sure, everyone loves a good deal, but Capricorn relishes saving a penny more than most, and he's been accused of being cheap on more than one occasion. Practical, pragmatic, and sometimes pessimistic, Capricorn views shopping as a necessary, but not particularly enjoyable, part of life. He figures if he's got to shop, he may as well get the best deal, even though he never gets his hopes up too high when embarking on a shopping spree.

## Aquarius (January 21 – February 19)

If there is one thing social Aquarius is not, it's a solo shopper. Not terribly keen on the shops in the first place, when the Water Bearer does venture into a sea of stores, it's with a gaggle of pals to hunt for good quality, must-have items. Good quality to Aquarius, however, does not usually mean top-dog designer looks. Instead, it's eclectic brands or next-to-new consignment or thrift shop finds. Aquarius's legendary social conscience also plays a significant role in the sign's shopping style: he goes out of his way to support companies with clean environmental and labor records as well as charity sales and shops.

## Pisces (February 20 – March 20)

A creative and gifted shopper, Pisces is able to see past labels and price-tags, zeroing in on the potential of a purchase. The Fish loves scurrying about town, visiting vintage stores, flea markets, and thrift shops, and rummaging through bins until she's unearthed another great prize. Pisces especially enjoys shopping for her home and is forever rescuing retro lamps and couches to reno, recover, and revamp into a completely stylish and unique piece.

# Bibliography

## BOOKS

Abelson, Elaine S. *When Ladies Go A-Thieving: Middle Class Shoplifters in the Victorian Department Store.* New York: Oxford University Press, 1989.

Adburgham, Alison. *Shops and Shopping: 1800-1914.* London: George Allen and Unwin Ltd, 1964.

Andrews, Robert et al. *The Columbia World of Quotations.* New York: Columbia University Press, 1996.

Banner, Lois W. *Elizabeth Cady Stanton: A Radical for Women's Rights.* Boston: Little, Brown & Co, 1980.

Barnard, R., Cosgrave, D., and Welsh, J. *Chips and Pop: Decoding the Nexus Generation.* Toronto: Malcolm Lester Books, 1998.

Berlitz, Charles. *Charles Berlitz's World of Strange Phenomena.* London: Sphere Books, 1989.

Bowlby, Rachel. *Carried Away: The Invention of Modern Shopping.* New York: Columbia University Press, 2001.

Brough, James. *The Woolworths.* New York: McGraw-Hill Book Company, 1982.

Callery, Sean. *Harrod's: The Story of Society's Favourite Store.* London: Ebury Press, 1991.

Chapman, Robert L. *American Slang Second Edition: The Abridged Dictionary of American Slang.* New York: HarperCollins, 1998.

Coleman, Sally and Hull-Mast, Nancy. Ca*n't Buy Me Love: Freedom From Compulsive Shopping and Money Obsession.* Minneapolis: CompCare Publishers, 1992.

Cross, Gary. *Kids' Stuff: Toys and the Changing World of American Childhood.* Cambridge. Mass.: Harvard University Press, 1997.

Dunkling, Leslie. *Dictionary of Curious Phrases.* Glasgow: HarperCollins, 1998.

Ehrenreich, Barbara. *Fear of Falling: The Inner Life of the Middle Class.* New York: Pantheon, 1989.

Ellison, Katherine. *Imelda: Steel Butterfly of the Philippines.* New York: McGraw Hill, 1988.

Epstein, Dan. *Twentieth-century Pop Culture.* London: Carlton Books, 1999.

Feather, Frank. *Future Consumer.com.* Toronto: Warwick Publishing, 2000.

Foot, David K. and Stoffman, Daniel. *Boom, Bust and Echo 2000.* Toronto: Macfarlane Walter & Ross, 1998.

Friedan, Betty. *The Feminine Mystique.* New York: W.W. Norton & Company, 1963.

Galus, Henry. *The Impact of Women.* Connecticut: Monarch Books, 1964.

Hauck, Dennis William. *The National Directory of Haunted Places.* New York: Penguin, 1996.

Kline, Stephen. *Out of the Garden.* Toronto: Garamond Press, 1993.

Lewis, Jon E. and Stempel, Penny. *Cult TV.* London: Pavillion Books, 1993.

Mazarr, Michael J. *Global Trends 2005.* New York: St Martin's Press, 1999.

McDowell, Colin (ed). *The Pimlico Companion to Fashion.* London: Random House, 1998.

McNeal, James U. *The Kids' Market: Myths and Realities.* New York: Paramount Market Publishing, 1999.

Mingo, Jack and Barrett, Erin. *Just Curious, Jeeves.* California: Ask Jeeves, 2000.

Mingo, Jack and Javna, John. *The Whole Pop Catalog.* New York: Avon Books, 1991.

Mulvey, Kate and Richards, Melissa. *Decades of Beauty.* New York: Checkmark Books, 1998.

Naisbitt, John. *Megatrends.* New York: Warner Books, 1984.

Olalquiaga, Celeste. *The Artificial Kingdom.* New York: Random House, 1998.

Parker, Dorothy. *The Portable Dorothy Parker.* New York: Penguin Books, 1976.

Popcorn, Faith and Hanft, Adam. *Dictionary of the Future.* New York: Hyperion, 2001.

Popcorn, Faith. *EVEolution: The Eight Truths of Marketing to Women.* New York: Hyperion, 2000.

_____. *The Popcorn Report.* New York: HarperBusiness, 1992.

Rothchild, John. *Going for Broke.* New York: Simon & Schuster, 1991.

Ryan, Mary Shaw. *Clothing: A Study in Human Behavior.* New York: Holt, Rinehart and Winston, 1966.

Rubin, Gretchen Craft. *Power Money Fame Sex: A User's Guide.* New York: Pocket Books, 2000.

Santink, Joy L. *Timothy Eaton and the Rise of His Department Store.* Toronto: University of Toronto Press, 1990.

Schilling, Mark. *The Encyclopedia of Japanese Pop Culture.* New York: Weatherhill, 1997.

Sherrin, Ned. *Oxford Dictionary of Humourous Quotations.* Oxford: Oxford University Press, 1995.

Shwartz, Ronald R. *Men Are Lunatics, Women Are Nuts.* Philadelphia: Running Press, 1996.

Stern, Jane and Michael. *The Encyclopedia of Bad Taste.* New York: HarperCollins, 1990.

Tingley, Judith C., and Robert, Lee E. *Gender Sell: How to Sell to the Opposite Sex.* New York: Simon & Schuster, 1999.

Tosa, Marco. *Barbie: Four Decades of Fashion, Fantasy and Fun.* New York: Harry N. Abrams, 1998.

Traub, Marvin and Teicholz, Tom. *Like No Other Store: The Bloomingdale's Legend and the Revolution in American Marketing.* New York: Times Books, 1993.

Underhill, Paco. *Why We Buy.* New York: Touchstone, 2000.

Wagner, Stephen C. and Closen, Michael L. *The Shopping Bag: Portable Art.* New York: Crown Publishers, 1986.

Warhol, Andy. *The Philosophy of Andy Warhol (From A to B and Back Again).* New York: Harcourt Brace Jovanovich, 1975.

Wesson, Carolyn. *Women Who Spend Too Much: Overcoming the Urge to Splurge.* New York: St Martin's Press, 1990.

Weil, Christa. *Secondhand Chic.* New York: Pocket Books, 1999.

Zolli, Andrew (ed.). *TechTV's Catalog of the Future.* Indianapolis: Que Publishing, 2003.

## Newspapers & Periodicals

"A History of Land's End." *Associated Press* (May 13, 2002).

"A Look at Kids' Spending and Free Time." *Selling to Kids* (February 21, 2001).

Adler, Jerry. "The eBay Way of Life." *Newsweek* (June 17, 2002): 50–60.

_____. "The 'Thrill' of Theft." *Newsweek* (February 25, 2002): 32.

Spree: A Cultural History of Shopping

Albacan, Artisrita. "Centuries of Tradition Result in Modern Christmas." *University Wire* (December 14, 2001).

Alford, Henry. "Head Over Heels." *Harper's Bazaar* (February 2001): 213-214.

"America Relying More on Coupons" *Arizona Republic* (October 21, 2000): D1.

"Americans Plan Botox, But Not Botox Parties." *US Newswire* (August 6, 2002).

"At the Dawn of Civilization, Money Did Not Talk. It Mooed." *Time International.* (April 4, 1990):37.

Axtman, Kris. "Shoplifting Woes Go Beyond Winona Ryder." *Christian Science Monitor* (December 6, 2002): 3.

Bain, Helen. "Why Men Simply Can't Shop." *The Dominion* (December 22, 1995): 10.

Bancroft, Dave. "Offering Convenience and a Fun Night Out." *London Free Press* (September 25, 2000).

"Bartering's Back: Trade Exchanges Take Advantage of Industry-Wide Surplus Capacity. *Dallas Morning News* (March 9, 1998): D6.

Beck, Rachel. "America Celebrates a century of Shopping: Supermarkets See Big Changes in 100 Years." *Associated Press* (October 10, 1999).

Bellafonte, Gina. "That's Retail-tainment!" *Time* (December 7, 1998): 64.

Bergsman, Steve. "Cultivating a Global Village." *Shopping Center World* (May 1999).

Betts, Kate. "Topping Tupper: Kids' Wear Parties." *The New York Times* (July 28, 2002).

Billhartz, Cynthia. "Shattering the Image of Shoplifters." *St Louis Dispatch* (November 4, 2002): D1.

Boroshok, Jon. "Outlet Industry Update: Recession Proof?" *Shopping Center World* (February 2002).

Brinton, Jessica. "Home Made." *Nylon* (May 2002): 87.

Brooks, Libby. "Buy, Buy, Baby." *The Guardian* (July 9, 2001).

Brown, Adam. "Marcos Briefly Reunited With Shoes." *AP Online* (February 16, 2001).

Burke, Raymond. "Virtual Shopping: Breakthrough in Market Research." *Harvard Business Review* (March 1996): 120.

Buzzard, James. "The Great Exhibition of 1851: A Nation on Display/The Great Exhibition." *Victorian Studies* (July 2001): 620.

Carr, David. "Magazine Imitates a Catalog and Has a Charmed Life, So Far." *The New York Times* (September 16, 2002).

"Celebrity Scents." *Vogue* (September 1989): 352.

Chen, Aric. "Better Than the Boys." *Metropolis* (July 2002): 124-127, 150-155.

Cheung, Priscilla. "Have Yourself a Merry, But Fake, Christmas in Hong Kong." *AP Online* (December 14, 1998).

"Click and Clip Takes Off." *MIN New Media Report* (December 7, 1999).

Cohen, Daniel. "Grand Emporiums Peddle Their Wares in New Market." *Smithsonian* (March 1993): 122.

Cohen, Juliet. "Net Results." *British Vogue* (November 2000): 161-162.

Colman, David. "Reality Check." *Vogue* (May 2001): 160-162.

Comita, Jenny. "Cyber Vintage 101." *Vogue* (October 2001): 248.

_____. "Inconspicuous Consumption." *Vogue* (August 2002): 122-124.

"Coupons Coming Back to Bolster Sagging Sales." *Arizona Republic* (August 20, 2001): D3.

Craig, Amanda. "For Kids, Britain is the 51st State." *New Statesman* (December 25 - January 1, 2000): 43-44.

Creno, Glen. "Your Own Internet Shopper." *Arizona Republic* (October 17, 1999): EV8.

Czuczka, Tony. "Wal-Mart to Close First Two Stores in Germany Since Entering European Continent." *AP Worldstream* (July 10, 2002).

Danziger, Pamela N. "The Lure of Shopping." *American Demographics* (July/August
2002): 44–47.

Davis, Alisha and Noonan, David. "Are You Feeling Lucky?" *Newsweek* (June 12, 2000): 62.

Dee, Jonathan. "The Myth of 18 to 34." *The New York Times* (October 13, 2002).

Del Mar, Alexander. "History of Monetary Systems: Part II." *History of the World* (January 1992).

"Designer in Residence." *Elle* (May 2002): 87.

"Disney Magic Comes to Life." *Business Wire* (November 15, 2000).

Dumenco, Simon. "Crimes of Fashion." *Allure* (April 2002): 162–165.

Dunphy, Catherine. "Feminist Stars Stir Passions as Expo Ends." *Toronto Star* (April 3,
2000).

"Easy on the Eyes." *In Touch: Britney: The 100 Most Important Days of Her Life* (Summer
2002): 52.

El Baghdady, Dina. "Starbucks: Coupons Are Fake." *Washington Post* (July 18, 2002): E1.

Epstein, Reid J. "Who Needs eBay?" *Wall Street Journal* (September 11, 2002).

Ernsberger Jr, Richard. "Wal-Mart World." *Newsweek International* (May 20, 2002): 50.

"Europe's Largest Shop Mall Opens in England." *Reuters* (March 16, 1999).

Faludi, Susan. "Don't Get the Wrong Message." *Newsweek* (January 8, 2001): 56.

"Federated Direct Relaunches Bloomingdales.com." *Business Wire* (July 25, 2001).

Feuer, Alan. "How to Succeed in Prison Without Serving Time." *The New York Times*
(November 23, 2001).

Finn, Margot. "Sex and the City: Metropolitan Modernities in English History." *Victorian Studies* (October 2001): 25.

Flaim, Denise. "You Don't Have to Be a Super Hero to Have a Secret Identity." *Newsday*
(November 7, 2000): C7.

Fowler, Rebecca. "Are Those the Emperor's New Clothes?" *Independent* (July 15, 1996):3.

Fraizer, Ian. "The Mall of America." *The Atlantic Monthly* (July/August 2002): 125–130.

Freeman, Hilary. "Addiction: Shopaholic." *The Mirror* (August 30, 2001): 31.

Gallagher, Paul. "German Stores Renew Attack on Opening Hours." *Reuters* (August 3,
1999).

Geiger, Debbie. "Are There Wrinkles in Botox Parties?" *New York Newsday* (July 15,
2002): D3.

"Germans Order Wal-Mart to Raise Prices." *Dallas Morning News* (September 9, 2000):
F2.

Ginsberg, Merle. "The Actress." *W* (March 2002): 276.

Givhan, Robin. "Buy, Buy, Baby!" *Vogue* (December 2000): 120–132.

"Global Teen Scene: Hong Kong." *Teen People* (September 2002): 60–61.

Goldberger, Paul. "The Store Strikes Back." *The New York Times* (April 6, 1997).

Gorov, Lynda. "Star Shoppers Hit Stores to Buy For Those Who Have Everything." *Minneapolis Star Tribune* (November 21, 1999): E4.

Greenberg, Susan H. "Embracing the Outlets." *Newsweek International* (December 18,
2000): 61.

Greer, Germaine. "Shopping as Seduction?" *Daily Telegraph* (July 18, 2000): 18.

Grose, Thomas K. "Too Big for its Riches: Trying to Duplicate its U.S. Retailing Success
in Europe, Wal-Mart Finds Itself Lost in Translation." *Time International* (March
5, 2001): 49.

Haga, Chuck. "Behind the Glitz: The Secret Sides of Shopping." *Minneapolis Star Tribune* (December 7, 1996): A1.

Halkias, Maria. "Trouble Around the Bend: New Mall Struggling to Lure Shoppers but Stands by Concept." *Dallas Morning News* (April 14, 2002): H1.

Hampshire, Mary. "Champagne and Surgery." *The Mirror* (November 21, 2000): 14-16.

Harlow, Tim. "Museum Stores Grow Into Important Revenue Sources." *Minneapolis Star Tribune* (January 22, 1997): E3.

Heimel, Cynthia. "Fear and Clothing." *Vogue* (March 1989): 538.

Helgadottir, Birna. "Outsider Whose Resentment Lives On." *The European* (September 4, 1997.): 13.

Hodgson, Richard. "It's Still the 'Catalog Age'" *Catalog Age* (June 2001).

"Holiday Season to Have New Look in 1998." *Business Wire* (December 23, 1997).

Horovitz, Bruce. "Sales Windows to Macy's Soul: Displays Sell a Season of Merchandise." *USA Today* (November 27, 1998): B1.

"If We Took a Holiday . . ." *Vogue* (June 2002): 226.

"Just a Poor Widow." *Filipino Express* (May 18, 1997).

Kaszuba, Mike. "Mall of America: 10 Years Later." *Minneapolis Star Tribune* (August 6, 2002): 11A.

"Katie Couric." *People* (May 14, 2001): 186.

Keating, Lauren. "The In Crowd: Retail Rushes to Keep Pace with Generation Y." *Shopping Center World* (May 2000).

Keizer, Gregg. "Web Shopping: Bots and Beyond." *Egypt Today* (February 2001).

Keltner, Jane. "House of Style." *Elle* (July 2002): 68-69.

King, Dave. "The Jury's Still Out on Home Electronic Shopping." *New Zealand Infotech Weekly* (May 15, 1995): 6.

Kingston, Anne. "Bridging the Gap." *National Post* (May 4, 2002): SP1.

Kirschbaum, Erik. "American-style Mall Catalyst for Germany's Change." *Reuters* (September 10, 1996).

Kuczynski, Alex. "A Shoe-in for Shopaholics." *Dallas Morning News* (May 17, 2000): E5.

Landau, Sue. "French Hypermarkets Go Exotic in Customer Quest." *Reuters Business Report* (October 25, 1999).

Larocca, Amy. "Virtually Fabulous." *Vogue* (July 2000): 102.

Levy, Melissa. "A Dying Breed?" *Minneapolis Star Tribune* (March 17, 2002): D1.

"Lourdes: Madonna's Mini Me." *Us Weekly* (July 15, 2002): 16-17.

Love, Alice Ann. "Coupon Clippers Keep Cashing In." *Minneapolis Star Tribune* (April 23, 1997): E1.

Maglitta, Joseph and Booker, Ellis. "Seller Beware." *Computerworld* (October 24, 1994): 79.

Makovsky, Paul. "Iconic Workspaces." *Metropolis* (July 2002): 114-119.

Margolis, Lynne. "Andy Warhol's Possession Obsession." *Christian Science Monitor* (March 29, 2002).

Marks, Kathy. "Imelda Marcos Charged Over 'Secret Accounts'" *Independent* (October 17, 2001): 16.

Martin, Nicole. "Shopping Bulimia Strikes!" *The Telegraph* (September 18, 2002).

McChesney, Andrew. "Shopping Centers Take the Capital By Storm." *Moscow Times* (June 22, 2000).

McGray, Douglas. "Japan's Gross National Cool." *Foreign Policy* (May 2002): 44.

McHugh, David. "German Union Starts Two-Day Strike at Wal-Mart Stores in Germany." *AP Worldstream* (July 26, 2002).

McLaughlin, Patricia. "Shop Until You Drop? . . . No, Leave it to the Professionals." *St Louis Post-Dispatch* (December 24, 1997): 3.

Mead, Rebecca. "Shopping Rebellion." *The New Yorker* (March 18, 2002): 104-111.

"Me Issey Miyake Shop." *I.D.* (August 2002): 106.

Miller, Paul and Del Franco, Mark. "Deal of the Century." *Catalog Age* (June 2002).

Mines, Cynthia. "The Outlet Industry Turns 20." *Shopping Center World* (February 2000).

Mishra, Upendra. "SCW Development" Breaking Out of the Box." *Shopping Center World* (August 1998).

Mitchell, Elvis. "Kelly and Jack Osbourne." *Interview* (June 2002): 58-63.

Mitchell, Emily. "Haute Style." *Time International* (January 22, 1996): 46.

Moore, Janet. "Retailing for Men." *Minneapolis Star Tribune* (June 29, 1997): D1.

Morem, Sue. "Many Companies Are Employing Mystery Shoppers." *Minneapolis Star Tribune* (September 28, 1999): D2.

Morrow, Lance. "The Shoes of Imelda Marcos." *Time* (March 31, 1986): 80.

Neal, M. Elizabeth. "Specialty Shopping Galleries, Smaller Stores Are Alternatives to Malls." *Atlanta Journal and Constitution* (November 20, 2001): J1.

"Neiman Marcus Memories." *Shopping Center World* (May 2002).

"Network Built on Faith and Infomercials." *USA Today* (August 28, 1998): E9.

Oritz, Vikki. "Woman Panhandles on Internet." *Milwaukee Journal Sentinel* (August 13, 2002).

"Palms Casino Resort Opens with Celebrity-Studded Grand Opening Ceremony." *Business Wire* (November 16, 2001).

Pearce, Tralee. "A Day in the Life." *Flare* (April 2001): 104-105.

"Personal Shoppers Aren't Just for the Rich Anymore." *Times Herald-Record* (October 22, 2002).

Poul, Alan. "Masters of the Universe Made Easy." *Egg* (August 1990): 25-30.

Powell, Eileen. "Store Coupons Can Be Worth Millions." *AP Online* (June 22, 2001)

"pqGifts Launches Today as First Virtual Personal Shopper." *Business Wire* (November 29, 2000).

Pressler, Margaret Webb. "Spies in the Aisles." *Washington Post* (June 16, 2002): H5.

Quart, Alissa. "Can't Hardly Wait." *Surface* (March 2002): 122-128.

Rampton, James. "Digital, Cable and Satellite Television: Today's Choices." *The Independent* (December 19, 2001): 13.

Raskin, Andy. "Why Retail Rocks." *Business 2.0* (June 2002): 55-57.

Rattray, Bess. "Blame Canada." *Vogue* (November 2000): 270-272.

Rawsthorn, Alice. "Bravo for Burberry." *British Vogue* (November 2000): 111-116.

Reed, J.D. "Magalogs in the Mailbox." *Time* (September 2, 1985): 73.

Richards, Kristina. "$30,000 in Three Hours." *Harper's Bazaar* (September 2002): 214-218.

Rickey, Melanie. "Gucci? No, Darling, It's Oxfam." *Independent* (February 10, 1999): 8.

Rogers, Patricia Dane. "For These Collectors, It's in the Bag." *Minneapolis Star Tribune* (January 2, 1999): E1.

_____. "Here's What to Look for in Collectible Shopping Bags." *Minneapolis Star Tribune* (January 2, 1999): E3.

"Royal Milkmaid Who Drew Blood." *Birmingham Post* (July 21, 2001): 52.

Rudawsky, Gil. "Good Sports: Gart Family Reinvents Itself After Having Sold a Thriving Empire." (December 12, 2000): G1.

"Rules of Engagement." *W* (June 2002): 66.

Schibsted, Evanteia. "Ab Rockers and Ginsu Knives, E320s." *Business 2.0* (May 2001).

Schoolman, Judith. "Shopping Bags: Old Standards Become Fashion Statement." *Reuters Business Report* (December 3, 1996).

Sedaris, David. "Going, Going, Gone." *Vogue* (October 2002): 236.

Sherwood, James. "Fashion & Style: Gentlemen Prefer Tweed." *Independent* (May 16, 2002): 10-11.

"Shopping.com Unveils Internet's First 125 Percent Satisfaction Guarantee." *Business Wire* (May 5, 1999).

"Shopping Back in Fashion at Siam Square Complexes." *The Nation* (Thailand) (January 12, 2000).

"Shopping Malls a Hit With Blokes." *The Evening Post* (March 20, 2001): 23.

Silverman, Edward R. "Federated, Macy's Merger OK'd Firm to Exit Chapter 11 After Nearly Three Years." *Newsday* (December 9, 1994): A63.

Sischy, Ingrid. "The Rebel in Prada." *Vanity Fair* (February 2002): 110-115.

Slatalia, Michelle. "Good and Bad Fashion Advice on the Net." *Minneapolis Star Tribune* (December 17, 1999): E13.

"Small Beats Mall: U.S. Main Streets Make Comeback." *Washington Times* (April 12, 2002).

"Snapshot: The Ultimate Girls' Night In." *Independent on Sunday* (April 1, 2001): 7.

Soifer, Rosanne. "Focus on the Background." *Sound & Video Contractor* (October 2001).

Span, Paula. "A Shrine to Bargains." *Newsweek* (March 21, 1998): 81.

Spethmann, Betsy. "Can We Talk?" *American Demographics* (March 1999).

Spindler, Amy. "A Self-Styled Hollywood Star." *The New York Times* (June 10, 1997).

Stanley, Bruce. "Britons Flock to Big European Mall." *AP Online* (March 16, 1999).

Steinhauer, Jennifer. "Bargain Hunting? Keep Looking." *The New York Times* (July 30, 1997): D1.

Stipp, David. "Brandnapping: Farewell, My Logo, A Detective Story." *Fortune* (May 13, 1996): 128.

Stoughton, Stephanie. "Loehmann's Files for Bankruptcy Protection." *Washington Post* (May 19, 1999): E3.

Sullivan, Robert. "Miracle on 86th Street." *Vogue* (March 2002): 332-336.

_____. "What it Takes to Sell a Bra." *Vogue* (November 2001): 296-302.

"Super Shopper." *Elle Canada* (July 2002): 121.

Swiencicki, Mark A. "Consuming Brotherhood: Men's Culture, Style and Recreation as Consumer Culture, 1880-1930." *Journal of Social History* (June 22, 1998): 773.

Sykes, Plum. "Party On, Shoppers." *Vogue* (November 2000): 316-318.

Tadjer, Rivka. "A Virtual Shopping Paradise Thrives." *Communications Week* (September 30, 1996): 33.

Tangi, Lucia. "Shops Join Campaign to Stamp Out Fakes." *Hong Kong Standard* (November 11, 1998).

Teasley, Sarah. "(Anti)-Hysteric Glamour: Masquerade, Cross-Dressing, and the Construction of Identity in Japanese Fashion Magazines." *Contemporary Women's Issues Database* (January 1995): 45-52.

"Teen Talk." *Shopping Center World* (May 2000).

Teli, Payal. "Finders Keepers: Kleptomania, Shoplifting Different." *University Wire* (March 1, 2002).

"The New Spendthrifts." *The Economist* (April 20, 2002): 69-70.

Treneman, Ann. "Bluewater: A Shopping Centre That Has Everything." *The Independent* (March 17, 1999): 7.

Tubridy, Michael. "U.S. Mall Openings, 2001-2004: Projected to Decline Through 2004." *CSC Research Quarterly* (Winter 2001-2002).

Tuck, Andrew. "Unisex Sells." *Independent on Sunday* (August 26, 2001).

Tung, Jennifer. "Hollywood's Top Shopaholics." *Us Weekly* (September 23, 2002): 52-58.

Turner, Megan. "Why Models Got So Skinny." *Cosmopolitan* (August 2000): 172.

Tyrnauer, Matt. "Empire By Martha." *Vanity Fair* (September 2001): 364-371.

"U.K. Court Rejects Al Fayed Passport Appeal." *Reuters* (October 21, 1999).

"U.S. Makes Largest Fake Watch Seizure." *Reuters* (June 24, 2001).

Valley, Matt. "The Remalling of America." *National Real Estate Investor* (May 2002): 18.

Veitch, Jennifer. "Clothes Hangers-On." *Daily Record* (August 30, 2001): 34-35.

Verdon, Joan. "'Couponing' is the Coming Craze'" *The Record* (June 10, 2001): F2.

Vincent, Isabel. "Selling Chic to the Sheiks." *National Post* (June 8, 2002): SP1.

"Virtual Personal Shoppers Helps With the Holidays." *Business Wire* (November 22, 1998).

Walker, Leslie. "High-Tech Bartering on the Internet." *Minneapolis Star Tribune* (April 23, 2002): 07E.

Walton, David. "Biography of Money Tells the History of Civilization." *Minneapolis Star Tribune* (March 16, 1997): 16F.

Weil, Anita. "The Dangerously Extravagant Man." *Cosmopolitan* (July 1995): 88.

Weiss, Michael T. "Inconspicuous Consumption." *American Demographics* (April 2002): 31-39.

Wellner, Alison Stein. "The Power of the Purse." *American Demographics* (July/August 2002): S3-S10.

Wells, Melanie. "Teens and Online Shopping Don't Click." *USA Today* (September 7, 1999): 38.

Welner, Chris and Briggs, Douglas. "Customer Conviction." *Albert Venture* (June 2002): 47-48.

"What's Hot This Holiday Season? National Survey Profiles Who Steals What." *Business Wire* (November 11, 1999).

Willmott, Don. "Touching Bases." *Yahoo! Internet Life* (July 2002): 30.

Wilson, Eric. "Space Race." *W* (March 2002): 124.

Wilson, Craig. "'Right Back Atcha' is Mantra For Some Shoppers." *USA Today* (August 6, 1998): D10.

"Women Have Mixed Feelings About Shopping." *United Press International* (August 17, 2001).

Zizzo, David. "Knowing Why You Love to Shop May Explain How You Shop." *Minneapolis Star Tribune* (January 8, 1997): E3.

"Yahoo! Shopping Takes Fans On a Shopping Spree With Britney Spears and Justin Timberlake." *Business Wire* (June 11, 2001).

Yancey, Kitty Bean. "Parties That Get Under Your Skin." *USA Today* (April 2, 2002).

## TRANSCRIPTS

Edwards, Bob. "Interview: Kalle Lasn Discusses Buy Nothing Day." *Morning Edition,* National Public Radio (November 22, 2001).

"One Man's Road to Riches: Penny-Pinching Millionaire Clark Howard." abcnews.com (February 28, 2002).

# WEBSITES

127sale.com

about.com
acrweb.org
adbusters.org
amazon.com
amway.com
askasia.org

bartercard.com.au
bloomingdales.com
bluewater.co.uk

canadianencyclopedia.com
cheapskatemonthly.com
consumerpsychology.com
countryclubplaza.com
ctebarter.com

davemackey.com
discover.com
dsa.org

encyclopedia.com

federated-fds.com
fordham.edu
funsocialstudies.learninghaven.org

gbarter.com

hbc.com
howstuffworks.com
hpvillage.com
hsn.com

icsc.org
imdb.com
information engineer.com
irta.com

kadewe.com

macys.com
marykay.com
mintmark.com

mward.com
mysteryshop.org

neimanmarcus.com
newdream.org

paperonline.org
pbs.org
playnetwork.com
pmalink.org
primeoutlets.com
prisonhelp.com

responsemagazine.com

salon.com
salvationarmy.ca
shopnchek.com
starbucks.com

trendcentral.com
tupperware.com

walksport.com
walmartstores.com
wampumworks.com
westedmontonmall.com
wire.ap.org
word-detective.com

yearbook.com

# Index

Spree: A Cultural History of Shopping

Index

Spree: A Cultural History of Shopping

PAMELA KLAFFKE has worked as a pop culture journalist for the last decade, enjoying
an extensive freelance career in newspapers,
magazines, and radio. She has held editorial
positions at *FFWD Weekly*, *Avenue* magazine, and was the trends columnist for the
*Calgary Herald* for four years. She is currently
the *Herald*'s literary editor and is at work on
her second book.